طيران الخ

COMMERCIAL AIRCRAFT

COMMERCIAL AIRCRAFT

MICHAEL J.TAYLOR

This edition produced exclusively for

WHSMITH

Photographic acknowledgments

Aero Boero SRL 136 top; Aeronautica Agricola Mexicana SA 138; Aérospatiale 165; Agusta SpA 167 top; Air Bridge Carriers 57 bottom, 115 bottom, 116 top; Airbus Industrie 10, 45, 46, 118 bottom, 129 top; Air Canada 24 bottom, 42, 125 bottom; Air Inter 14 bottom, 34; Air New Zealand 26–7, 124; Air Portraits 177 top; Air Tractor Inc. 142, 142–3, 143; Air U.K./Fleet P.R. 58 bottom, 61; All Nippon Airways 69 bottom; Aviogenex 21; Ayres Corporation 139 top, 140 top; Bangladesh Biman 12–13; Beech Aircraft Corporation 104, 105, 110 top, 186 top; Bell Helicopter Textron 158, 170 bottom, 176 top; Peter J. Bish 120 top; Boeing 7, 12, 22, 23, 27, 28, 29, 30 top, 30 bottom, 31, 126 top, 126 bottom, 127, 128, 129 bottom; Boeing Vertol 170 top, 173 bottom; Braathens S.A.F.E. 32; Bristow Helicopters 170–1; British Aerospace 19, 20, 35 top, 35 bottom, 48–9, 60, 75 bottom, 76 top, 76 centre, 117, 130 top, 181; Austin J. Brown 14 top, 54, 76 bottom, 77 top, 121, 122 top, 172, 187 bottom; Antonio Camarasa 37; Canadair 88 bottom, 89, 130 bottom; CASA 98 top; Cessna Aircraft Company 106 top, 106 bottom, 144 top, 144 bottom, 145, 146, 146–7, 178 bottom, 186 bottom; de Havilland Canada 67 top, 67 bottom, 68, 69 top, 84, 86 top, 86 bottom, 87; Dornier 91, 92 top, 92 bottom, 93, 94, 95 top; Philip G. Dunnington 100 bottom; Eagle Aircraft Company 148 top; EMBRAER 78–9, 80, 81, 82–3, 83, 137 top, 137 bottom; The Enstrom Helicopter Corporation 168–9; Fairchild Swearingen Corporation 187 top; Fan Holdings 178 top; Federal Express 131 top; Fokker 33, 62; Martin Fricke 35 centre; Gates Learjet Corporation 179 top, 179 bottom; Government Aircraft Factories 78; J.M.G. Gradidge 155 bottom; Robert S. Grant 84–5; Grumman Aerospace Corporation 112; Gulfstream Aerospace Corporation 113 bottom, 180–1; Hawaiian Airlines 24 top; Hawk Industries 131 bottom; Heavy Lift Air Cargoes 116 bottom; Hiller Aviation 160–1, 161; Hughes Helicopters 162 top, 163, 168; Instone Air Line 115 top; Instytut Lotnictwa 102; Israel Aircraft Industries Ltd 95 bottom, 184 top, 185; Marian Kobrzynski 65; Lockheed 41, 43; Lockheed Georgia 119 bottom; LOT Polish Airlines/Janusz Czerniak 114; LOT Polish Airlines/Andrzej Pawliszewski 20–1; McDonnell Douglas 15, 25, 38–9; Ian MacFarlane 53; MAP 63; Marsh Aviation Company 140 bottom, 141; Harold G. Martin 16 top, 52 top, 52 bottom, 125 top; MBB 166 top, 166 bottom; Mitsubishi Aircraft International 184 centre, 184 bottom; Mount Cook Line 59, 111; NDN Aircraft Ltd 156 bottom, 157 bottom; NDN Aircraft Ltd/Brian Bradbury 157 top; Olympic Airways 70, 71, 110 bottom; Partenavia Costruzioni Aeronautiche 183 top; Photo AMD-BA 180; S. Piercey 58 top; Pilatus Britten-Norman 73 top, 74, 75 top; Pilatus Flugzeugwerke AG 100 top, 156 centre; Piper Aircraft Corporation 107, 108, 108–9, 109, 147, 187 centre; PT Nurtanio 98 bottom; PZL-Mielec 133 top; Saab-Scania 99; Schweizer Aircraft Corporation 148 bottom; Schweizer Aircraft Corporation/Norm Swafford 149; Brian M. Service 36, 47, 97, 122 bottom, 123 top, 176 bottom; Service Presse: GIFAS 119 top, 171; Shorts 72, 73 bottom; Sikorsky Aircraft 169, 173 top; Erik Simonsen 9; Javier Taibo 16 bottom; Texas Helicopter Corporation 162 bottom; Transavia Division, Transfield (NSW) Pty Ltd 152 top, 152 bottom, 153; Volpar 104–5; Weatherly Aviation Company Inc. 150, 151 bottom; Westland 174–5; Gordon S. Williams 18–19, 55, 64–5, 66, 85, 113 top; WSK-PZL Mielec 135; WSK-PZL Warszawa-Okecie 133 bottom, 134 top, 134 bottom.

Cutaway drawings © Pilot Press

Author's note

The highly professional and attractive appearance of this book, and of its companion volume on fighter aircraft, is due in part to the assistance offered by many of the world's aircraft manufacturing companies and aircraft operators. To these and the other photographers whose work appears in the two volumes, I am sincerely grateful. A special acknowledgment has also to be made to Bill Gunston, a fellow author and friend.

**This edition produced exclusively for
W H Smith**

Published by
Deans International Publishing
A division of The Hamlyn Publishing Group Limited
London · New York · Sydney · Toronto
Astronaut House, Feltham, Middlesex, England

Copyright © The Hamlyn Publishing Group Limited 1983
ISBN 0 603 03118 8

Printed in Italy

Contents

Cutaway Drawings

Introduction

Commercial aviation, or the operation of aircraft for hire or reward, originated before the First World War. It was due largely to the efforts of one man that the first air services were begun, a man not readily associated by most people with commercial aviation. Count Ferdinand von Zeppelin's interest in huge dirigibles (or airships that could be steered) began towards the end of the 19th century and in the final decade of that century he applied for a patent for his method of airship construction. In 1900 his first airship, the Zeppelin LZ 1, lifted from Lake Constance. It took many years to perfect an airship with some practical use.

In October 1909 the Count formed the world's first commercial airline as Delag (Die Deutsche Luftschiffahrt Aktienge-sellschaft). In June of the following year Delag began the world's first airline oper-ations with Zeppelin LZ 7 *Deutschland*, flying between Frankfurt, Baden-Baden and Düsseldorf. Other airships joined Delag's fleet and, by the close of operations in late 1913, tens of thousands of passengers had been carried. This was an encouraging beginning for commercial aviation, espe-cially in view of the fact that no passengers had been killed. A similar 100 per cent safety record could not be claimed for the airships themselves, as three had been lost.

On the other side of the Atlantic, the world's first scheduled aeroplane passenger service began on 1 January 1914, when the Benoist Company carried a single passenger from St. Petersburg to Tampa, Florida. With the surplus of military aircraft that could be converted cheaply into makeshift airliners after the First World War, and the pool of ex-military pilots wanting employ-ment, commercial aviation began in earnest in 1919. The gradual acceptance of air travel by civilians, and the year-by-year reduction in route charges, gave birth to a new industry for the manufacture of air-liners.

Even during the so-called 'interwar' period, the airship had not been forgotten. Great success was attained by these giants of the sky (mostly German and British) until the tragic loss of the German passenger-carrying airship *Hindenburg* in the United States of America in 1937, as it ended a transatlantic journey from Frankfurt. But, by now, the airship had a rival for long ocean routes in the form of long-range flying-boats. Neither type, however, sur-vived to any extent the post-Second World War changes in commercial aviation.

Nonetheless, it was an airship that opened the Farnborough Air Show of 1982, and indeed interest is again being shown in modern airships for commercial and mili-tary roles. However, few consider a major revival of passenger-carrying airships likely, although there could be a future for those employed as cargo carriers. Unfortunately the 1980s are not proving to be the happiest for many aircraft manufacturers or airline operators, making major investment in new forms of aircraft less likely. In 1981 IATA (International Air Transport Association) announced that airlines had lost a stagger-ing $1,660 million on scheduled services and this figure increased in 1982. Several of the world's better known airlines have actually stopped trading and others are in serious financial trouble.

It is not all gloom. Airlines made profits in the years prior to the current world recession and they will do so again. Manu-facturers, who have been hit by the cutback in the numbers of new aircraft ordered by airlines, have produced a new range of more economical airliners, powered by less-thirsty high-technology engines. Incred-ibly, some of the manufacturers of small commuter-type airliners are experiencing growing markets and are working flat-out to meet bulging order books.

This book details the world's airliners in use today, from the largest high-capacity aircraft to the small commuter types. Those aircraft used for carrying freight have their own chapter, as do helicopters and business types, and agricultural aircraft. The latter are of particular interest as they represent an aspect of aviation all too often over-looked. These aircraft, operated extensively in the Soviet Union, the U.S.A. and else-where in the world, offer a fast and easy way of spraying crops against disease and pests, and can also dust, top dress and seed. The chapter on agricultural aircraft is the only one in the book that covers aircraft ranging from jets to specially adapted microlights.

1 How Airliners Work

Even people uninterested in aircraft know how airliners rather suddenly changed in the mid-1930s from fabric-skinned biplanes to streamlined all-metal monoplanes. By the mid-1950s they had grown sharply sweptback wings with engines pylon-mounted below the wings in pods. The Model 747 and others are still built that way, but the latest airliners have much less sweep and the engines can be anywhere. Behind these obvious visible changes in shape lie many other differences, all aimed at carrying people in greater safety and with increased reliability, whilst burning less fuel and making less environmental disturbance.

The fundamental part of an aeroplane is its wing. In early jetliners the wing was made quite thin, swept back at 35 degrees to enable the aircraft to cruise at more than 885 km/h (550 mph). This complicated the flight control problems, but gradually the unpleasant qualities were eliminated and since 1970 the so-called 'supercritical' wing has revolutionized efficiency. Instead of having a very cambered (curved) upper surface and less-curved underside, the new wing has a bulged underside and flatter top – almost like an old wing upside down! This can be made to generate lift over almost the whole upper surface, instead of in an intense strip along the upper front of the wing. For any given high cruising speed the super-critical wing can be made deeper and less swept, and this makes the wings much lighter, eliminates handling problems and greatly reduces fuel consumption. In long-range aircraft it has a further advantage in that there is more room in the wing for fuel. Examples of the new wings can be seen on the Airbus A310, Boeing Model 757 and BAe 146.

Invariably the wing is sized and shaped for the highest efficiency in cruising flight, which in most jets is at a height of 6 100 to 12 200 metres (20,000 to 40,000 feet). For

The Boeing 757 is one aircraft fitted with wings incorporating the latest technology.

flight at low speeds, and especially for take-off and landing, the wing needs to be much larger and more strongly cambered (curved, when viewed from the end). The most powerful way of accomplishing both objectives is to fit large flaps under the trailing edge. When the pilot selects 'take-off flap' these are extended by hydraulic motors or rams so that they slide out from the wing to increase its area and increase the camber slightly, thus giving much more lift. As the aircraft reaches the top of its initial climb and 'cleans up' for cruising flight, the flaps are retracted back inside the profile of the wing. For landing the pilot selects 'landing flap' which, usually in easy stages, brings the flaps much further out and down so that they make a large angle with the airflow, typically 35 to 50 degrees. In this condition they increase not only lift but also drag, slowing the approach to the airport and assisting the wheelbrakes to pull the aircraft up after landing.

There are many kinds of flap, with significant differences. Old DC-3s and some modern aircraft have simple split flaps in which the lower part of the trailing edge is hinged. Slotted flaps open to leave a thin slit between the depressed flap and wing, and the air rushing through this gap helps to keep the flow running smoothly back and down over the flap's upper surface. Double-slotted flaps have an extra thin curved strip, like a very thin wing, fixed ahead of the flap, thus leaving two slots (gaps) for even more powerful high-lift effects. The Fowler flap runs out to the rear on tracks, greatly increasing wing area. The tabbed Fowler rolls out on tracks and in the high-drag (landing) position opens a hinged tab along its trailing edge to give still more drag.

Movable surfaces can also be added at the leading edge. The most common is the slat, which is like a very thin curved extra wing normally carried snugly against the main wing's leading edge from root to tip. In some aircraft the slats are freely carried on pivoted arms or tracks; when the aircraft flies very slowly the extra lift sucks the slats away from the main wing and the air rushing through the slot between the slat and the main surface keeps the air flowing back smoothly across the wing, preventing the sudden breakdown of flow (and loss of lift) called the stall. In modern airliners the slats are usually pushed out by hydraulic power. An alternative leading-edge device is the Krueger flap, which is a more or less flat plate which normally forms part of the undersurface just behind the leading edge; for take-off or landing it is opened hydraulically and rotated round to form a kind of diagonal wall ahead of and below the leading edge to guide the air up and over the wing at high angles. Yet another alternative is the hinged leading edge, or leading-edge flap, commonly called the 'droop-snoot': the entire leading edge can be hinged downwards for take-off and landing which again makes it easier for the air to flow up and over the wing when the latter is meeting the air at a large angle.

Lateral control used to be provided by ailerons hinged near the wingtips. To avoid problems due to wing flexure, and other real or potential difficulties, some early jetliners also had small inboard ailerons fitted, and locked the outboard ailerons except at low speeds. Today spoilers are hinged along the upper surface of the wing, usually ahead of the flaps, and arranged to open differentially to provide trouble-free roll control. On the Airbus A300B such spoilers were provided to allow the conventional ailerons to be made small and thus allow most of the trailing edge to be occupied by flaps. The latest A300Bs have no outboard aileron, the wing being simplified and, if necessary, the flaps can extend to the tips. In many aircraft the spoilers can be extended symmetrically for rapid letdown without excessive airspeed, and after landing they can be fully opened as lift-dumpers, to destroy as much lift as possible and thus make the wheelbrakes more effective.

All airliners rely heavily on wheelbrakes, which are normally designed to absorb the colossal kinetic energy of a maximum weight take-off abandoned at the last possible moment (so-called decision speed – for Concorde this can be near 322 km/h; 200 mph). Metal brakes would glow almost white-hot after such a test, but carbon brakes stay relatively cool. Reverse thrust is a powerful aid to stopping on wet or icy runways, but building reversers for large modern turbofan engines can add greatly to weight and complexity. This is because to reduce the average jet velocity and thus cut noise and fuel consumption, the modern airline engine handles an enormous airflow. Engines for wide-body transports have a fan of 2.1 to 2.4 metres (7 to 8 feet) in diameter, through which passes about 680 kg (1,500 lb) of air each second on take-off. In such an engine the giant fan generates almost all the

The large diameter of the engine fan on this Lockheed L-1011-500 TriStar is clearly visible.

thrust, the primary (core) flow of hot gas having as much energy as possible extracted by the turbines before it escapes through the jetpipe. Thus this engine closely resembles a turboprop, which also handles a large airflow and is very fuel-efficient. The main difference is that the turbofan has fixed-pitch blades, spinning at higher speed, and the surrounding duct reduces external noise.

Most turboprops are arranged to twist the propeller blades to blow the air forward and thus give reverse thrust, and this quick-acting control can simplify the pilot's task in manoeuvring in confined spaces. Unlike a car, the airliner can, with reverse thrust, pivot round through 180 degrees while neither moving forwards or backwards. Nose units of the undercarriage are steerable, and in small aircraft it is possible to steer by differential braking of the main wheels. Other aids to slowing after landing include lift-dumping/spoilers, flaps and special airbrakes.

Virtually all long-range airliners are pressurized. While all passenger airliners have air-conditioning systems to heat or cool the interior in extremes of climate, pressurization prevents the internal pressure from

falling to match that outside as the aircraft climbs up to high altitude. Up to heights of about 2 440 metres (8,000 feet) it may be possible to keep the interior at the same pressure as at the departure airport, giving perfect passenger comfort. Climbing above this level the pressure is allowed to fall gradually, but it is regulated to remain above that in the rarefied atmosphere outside. This dictates a basically circular fuselage cross-section, though when there are large pressurized baggage/cargo holds under the floor the best section turns out to be a pear shape, often formed by a large circle above merging into a smaller circle below. Great care is needed to make the doors, windows and other apertures absolutely foolproof and able to withstand thousands of 'reversals' (being pumped up and then let down). Where journeys are short, the cruising height is made lower and the great cost in weight, complexity and pressurization is not worthwhile. The cabin can then be a more suitable box-shape, with seats near the windows (which can be much larger) and vertical outer walls. The Shorts 330 and 360 are best-selling examples of unpressurized short-haulers.

The pressurized fuselage of a European Airbus has a circular cross-section. Here final assembly of A300s from sections manufactured in other factories is being undertaken.

2 In the Path of the Comet

In 1952 a new chapter in commercial aviation's short but exciting history was opened with the introduction of the first turbojet-powered airliner. This was Britain's pioneering de Havilland Comet which, in the livery of BOAC, inaugurated jet travel for passengers with a service between London and Johannesburg. Other routes followed and flying times were slashed, on the longest journeys by as much as 60 per cent.

The Comet's acceptance seemed assured until tragedy struck. In May 1953 a BOAC Comet 1 crashed while taking-off at Calcutta, followed in 1954 by two further accidents to Comets. The Comets in service were withdrawn from use while the cause of these accidents was established. When eventually the Comet was re-introduced, in modified and higher-capacity Comet 4 form, to begin a long period of successful service with BOAC and other airlines, it had new rivals in the forms of the U.S. Boeing Model 707, the Soviet Tupolev Tu-104 and the French SE 210 Caravelle. The final Comets passed out of service fairly recently, as did the last Tu-104s, but the Model 707 and Caravelle remain in use today, the former in worldwide operation.

Arguably the most important jet airliner ever built is the Boeing Model 707. Although not the first jet airliner, as already stated, and not the jet airliner built in the greatest number, it was responsible, nevertheless, for introducing jet travel to the masses. The facts support this statement. A total of 112 Comet airliners was built and production of the Tu-104 is believed to have been about twice this number, but when the final commercial Model 707 was delivered in 1982, to the Moroccan government, the total number of Model 707s (and related 720s) built exceeded 900. The Model 707 is also important for introducing both a long range and a seating capacity roughly equal to those of the Comet 4 and Tu-104 combined, making it the first 'jumbo jet'.

The Model 707 was not Boeing's first turbojet-powered aircraft by a long shot – Boeing had already produced the B-47 Stratojet and the B-52 Stratofortress jet bombers. The prototype of the Model 707 was company-designated Model 367-80 but this prototype had a dual purpose. Initially it was with military orders in mind that Boeing produced the Model 367-80 as a private venture, designed as a modern and high-speed replacement (in production form) for the U.S.A.F.'s fleet of piston-engined C-97 Stratofreighter tanker-transports. The Model 367-80 first flew in July 1954. A year later Boeing was given permission by the military to produce commercial airliners based on the Model 367-80 and to construct them simultaneously with U.S.A.F. production KC-135A Stratotankers.

With the Model 367-80 forming the basis of military and commercial aircraft to be built in high volume, it ranks as one of the most successful gambles in aviation history. Interestingly, Boeing awarded its jet airliner the company designation Model 707, and the military tanker-transport the designation Model 717.

Production of the airliner began with the Model 707-120, powered by four 6 123-kg (13,500-lb)st Pratt & Whitney JT3C-6 turbojet engines installed in pods below the swept wings. Compared to the prototype, the Model 707-120 was given a longer and wider fuselage, allowing accommodation for a then-staggering 181 passengers. The first Model 707-120 (actually 707-121) was delivered to Pan American World Airways, which inaugurated 707 services on 26 October 1958. Although this version was intended for domestic operations, Pan American used it initially on its New York–Paris transatlantic route.

In late 1959 Boeing flew the first Model 720. This, despite its model number, was very much a member of the 707 family; its differences mainly consisted of a shorter fuselage, modified wings, slightly less powerful JT3C-7 or JT3C-12 turbojet engines and a considerably reduced maximum take-off weight. As a result of these changes, this model proved to have higher performance than the 707-120, although typical accommodation was just 38 first-class and 74 second-class passengers. The Model 720B that followed in 1960 was provided with four 8165-kg (18,000-lb)st JT3D-3 turbofan engines or less powerful JT3D-1s. This became one of the fastest versions of the 707/720 family, with a cruising speed of 983 km/h (611 mph).

Some months before the Model 720B flew, Boeing had produced a turbofan-engined version of its Model 707-120, known as the 707-120B. Wing improvements were also a feature of this model, which demonstrated better take-off performance and a cruising speed of 995 km/h (618 mph) at an altitude of 7620 metres (25,000 feet). The first Model 707-120B made its maiden flight in June 1960. In the early 1980s, six major airlines continue to fly examples of these early Model 707s and more than 20 fly versions of the 720 and 720B.

True intercontinental performance was introduced into the Model 707 family with the 707-320. This model had been developed very early in the 707 programme and indeed the sixteenth aircraft of the 707 family was the first 707-320. The first flight of a 707-320 took place in 1959. Compared to the 707-120 models, the 707-320 was given a longer fuselage to accommodate up

The very last Boeing Model 707 to be built in commercial form.

to 189 passengers, a greater wing span with four Pratt & Whitney JT4A turbojet engines pylon-mounted beneath, and increased fuel capacity for its over-ocean routes. A version of the Intercontinental with 7 938-kg (17,500-lb)st Rolls-Royce Conway Mk 508 turbofan engines became the 707-420. Only a handful of major airlines fly the 707-320 and 707-420, but a very large number still operate the 707-320B and 707-320C.

The Model 707-320B first flew in 1962 as a version of the 707-320 with Pratt & Whitney JT3D-3B turbofan engines and double thrust reversers. Each engine is rated at 8 165-kg (18,000-lb)st. Other changes introduced included new leading and trailing edge flaps and low-drag wingtips. The 707-320C was built in two versions, as the Convertible and the Freighter. It was a

707-320C that became the very last commercial Model 707 built, delivered to the Moroccan government in March 1982. In Convertible form the 707-320C can accommodate up to 219 passengers or the equivalent weight in cargo, or a mixture of passengers and cargo. An executive configuration was also made available. Power is provided by four 8 618-kg (19,000-lb)st Pratt & Whitney JT3D-7 turbofan engines with double thrust reversers. Some 707-320Bs also use this engine type. Pan American introduced the Convertible into service in 1963. Further details of the Model 707-320C can be found in Chapter Five. About 400 Model 707/720s remain in use.

France entered the turbojet airliner business in the early 1950s, as a result of the call for a medium-range aircraft of this type from the Secrétariat Général à l'Aviation

Bangladesh Biman, the national carrier of Bangladesh, operates five Boeing 707-320s.

turbojet-powered models remain so. These include the Series III with Rolls-Royce Avon 527 turbojets, the Series VI-N with Avon 531s and the Series VI-R. The latter is powered by two 5 715-kg (12,600-lb)st Avon 533R turbojet engines with thrust reversers and can accommodate 99 passengers. Its maximum cruising speed is 845 km/h (525 mph) and its typical range is 2 300 km (1,429 miles).

Other current versions of the Caravelle are the Series 10-R with Pratt & Whitney JT8D-7 turbofan engines, the similar Series 11-R with a lengthened fuselage and a new freight door, the Super B (or Series 10-B) with a longer fuselage than the Series 10 model (upon which it was based), and the Series 12. The Caravelle 12 was the final production version and is the longest and most powerful. Accommodating up to 139 passengers, it has a length of 36.24 metres (118 feet 10 inches), compared to the Caravelle VI-R's 32 metres (105 feet), and is powered by two 6 575-kg (14,500-lb)st Pratt & Whitney JT8D-9 turbofan engines. Air Inter (France) and Sterling Airways (Denmark) became the operators of the Caravelle 12. The maximum cruising speed of this final version is 825 km/h (512 mph) and the range is 3 465 km (2,150 miles).

Hot on the heels of the Boeing 707 came a similar four-turbojet airliner from Douglas, known as the DC-8. A prototype first flew in May 1958 to become the second type of American jet airliner. Services with the DC-8-10, a 176-passenger airliner for domestic routes, began in September 1959. Series 10s were followed by DC-8-20s with more powerful Pratt & Whitney engines. Of these early versions of the DC-8, some were modified later into Series 50s. The only examples still in use today are operated as DC-8-20F freighters.

The initial intercontinental version of the DC-8 appeared as the Series 30, powered by 7 620-kg (16,800-lb)st Pratt & Whitney JT4A-9 or 7 938-kg (17,500-lb)st JT4A-11 turbojet engines. Virtually all of the Series 30s still operated are employed as freighters, but Air Zaïre counts the passenger version in its fleet of airliners. A similar story relates to the Series 40 with Rolls-Royce Conway 509 turbojet engines, leaving the DC-8-50 as the only early version of the airliner still to be found in passenger service with several airlines (as well as in freighter use).

DC-8-50s were built as new aircraft and were produced also by modification of

Civile et Commerciale. The Caravelle was viewed originally for operations between France and North Africa and the first of the prototypes flew for the first time in May 1955, making it the third type of jet airliner in the world. It also has the distinction of being the world's first jet airliner with rear-mounted engines, comprising originally two turbojets positioned one each side of the rear fuselage.

Best known as an Aérospatiale type (despite this company being formed only in 1970 following the merger of Nord-Aviation, Sud-Aviation and SEREB), the Caravelle can still boast nearly 100 in commercial use. This figure represents a reasonable proportion of the 282 Caravelles produced by the close of production in 1972. The initial production Caravelle Is and IAs are no longer in use but several other

The first McDonnell Douglas DC-8 Super 71, one of thirty built for United Air Lines.

earlier DC-8s. The DC-8-50 was the first version to use turbofan engines. These comprise either four 7 718-kg (17,000-lb)st Pratt & Whitney JT3D-1s, 8 172-kg (18,000-lb)st JT3D-3s or JT3D-3Bs. With the latter fitted, the aircraft became known as the DC-8-50 Model 55. Accommodating up to 179 passengers, the Series 50 has a cruising speed of 933 km/h (580 mph) and a range of 9 200 km (5,720 miles) with a full load.

Currently by far the most important DC-8s in service as passenger and freight transports are the versions of the Super Sixty Series. With this series Douglas offered increased capacity and aerodynamic refinements, with the fuselage 'stretched' to allow accommodation for a greater number of passengers. The Super Sixty Series was announced in the mid-1960s and the first Super 61 flew for the first time in March 1966. This airliner had obvious external changes to the previous DC-8-50, with a length of 57.12 metres (187 feet 5 inches) compared to the Series 50's 45.87 metres (150 feet 6 inches). This allowed the accommodation of 259 passengers. In August 1966 and April 1967 respectively, the first Super 62 and Super 63 appeared. The Super 62 offered airlines the ability to carry 189 passengers over even longer ranges, and as such was produced with a fuselage only 2.03 metres (6 feet 8 inches) longer than that of the Series 50 but with a wing span increased from 43.41 metres (142 feet 5 inches) to 45.23 metres (148 feet 5 inches). The Super 63 combined the fuselage and passenger-carrying capacity of the Super 61 with the wing refinements of the Super 62.

Powered by four 8 618-kg (19,000-lb)st Pratt & Whitney JT3D-7 turbofan engines, carried in refined pods on low-drag pylons, the Super 63 can cruise at 965 km/h (600 mph) and has a range with maximum payload of 7 242 km (4,500 miles). Not including freighter versions, also called Jet Traders, the operators of the largest numbers of Super Sixty Series airliners are United Air Lines, KLM and Japan Air Lines. Of more than 550 DC-8s of all versions built by the close of production in 1972, 262 were of the Super Sixty Series.

The close of production does not end the DC-8 story. Apart from freighters, McDonnell Douglas (a company formed in 1967 after the merger of the Douglas Aircraft Company and the McDonnell Company) is now offering its Super Seventy Series. Unlike the Super Sixty Series, this does not encompass newly built aircraft but represents re-engined Super Sixties. With 10 886-kg (24,000-lb)st General Electric/ SNECMA CFM56-2-1C turbofan engines installed, the Super 61, Super 62 and Super 63 become the Super 71, Super 72 and Super 73 respectively. These engines are extremely advanced, offering a major reduction in noise level and yet improved efficiency. The cruising speed of the Super Seventy Series is 854 km/h (531 mph), and the range with the maximum number of passengers is between 7 485 and 11 620 km (4,650 and 7,220 miles). The first Super Seventy to fly was a Super 71 in August 1981. United Air Lines and Delta Air Lines became the first customers, receiving airliners of this series from the spring of 1982.

Right: Inair, a Panamanian airline, operates one Convair CV-880-22 within its fleet.

Spantax Convair 990A Coronado.

Several other airlines have placed orders for Super Seventies.

Like Boeing and Douglas, Convair had been busy after the end of the Second World War constructing new piston-engined airliners for airline service. It had attained very great success with its CV-240, primarily seen as a DC-3 replacement, and had followed this with its CV-340 and CV-440 Metropolitan. Examples of these early airliners remain in service today and are detailed in the following chapter. The company's first venture into jet airliners produced the CV-880, a medium-range aircraft that first flew as a prototype in January 1959. Two versions were built: the 110-passenger CV-880 Model 22 for U.S. domestic operation and the Model 22-M. The former was produced with four 5 080-kg (11,200-lb)st General Electric CJ805-3 turbojets and entered service from 1960. The Model 22-M was given slightly more powerful CJ805-3Bs, more fuel and a higher all-up weight, and incorporated refinements suited for operations from shorter-length runways. Sixty-five Convair 880s were built, most of which had been super-

seded by other airliners with their original operators by the early 1970s. However, in the early 1980s 11 were still is use (including freighters).

A year after the first flight of a CV-880, Convair flew its CV-990 Coronado. This was basically an intercontinental version of the CV-880, with a longer fuselage, various airframe refinements and powered by four 7 280-kg (16,050-lb)st General Electric CJ805-23B turbofan engines. This aircraft was developed specifically for American Airlines, which began CV-990 services in March 1962. However, wing and engine-pod refinements brought about a change of designation to CV-990A and all Coronados were so modified or built as such. Less successful than the CV-880 in terms of numbers ordered for service, the CV-990A nevertheless offered accommodation for up to 106 passengers, a high cruising speed of 1 005 km/h (625 mph) and a range of 6 115 km (3,800 miles). In the early 1980s only Spantax operates CV-990As. Spantax is a Spanish airline which operates scheduled passenger services, charter and inclusive tour flights.

The next generation

In 1963 several well-known British aircraft manufacturing companies merged into Hawker Siddeley Aviation Limited, itself becoming part of British Aerospace with nationalization in the latter 1970s. Prior to 1963 the de Havilland Aircraft Company, one of the companies that later formed part of Hawker Siddeley Aviation, had been working on a new airliner to meet the requirements of British European Airways (BEA) for a short-range jet airliner with a cruising speed of about 965 km/h (600 mph). Actual construction of a D.H.121 began in 1959, having been selected at design stage against competing proposals from Avro and Bristol. Interestingly, Avro also later became part of Hawker Siddeley Aviation but Bristol merged into the newly formed British Aircraft Corporation (BAC) in 1960. The first D.H.121 Trident, the initial aircraft of this type for BEA service, made its maiden flight in January 1962.

Like the other new British airliner of 1962, the Vickers VC10, the Trident had rear-mounted engines, in this case on either side of the rear fuselage and one inside the rear fuselage. Twenty-four 103-passenger Trident 1s were built, none of which remains in use today. A high-density version of the Trident 1 appeared thereafter as the Trident 1E and 15 were completed. Apart from accommodating 115 passengers, this version was given an increased wing span and more powerful Rolls-Royce RB 163-25 Spey Mk 511-5 turbofans, each rated at 5 171-kg (11,400-lb)st. A very small number of Trident 1Es remain in service with British Airways.

Further changes produced the Trident 2E, which first appeared in 1967. This version introduced a further increase in wing span and 5 425-kg (11,960-lb)st Spey Mk 512-5W turbofan engines, offering longer range and higher operating weights. Seating was provided for 115 to 132 passengers. Its cruising speed can be as high as 972 km/h (605 mph) and its range 3 965 km (2,464 miles) with a payload of 9 679 kg (21,378 lb), the latter of which is 2 459 kg (5,422 lb) under its maximum payload. Trident 2Es remain in use today with British Airways and CAAC (Civil Aviation Administration of China). Of the 50 Trident 2Es built, China purchased no fewer than 33, of which 29 remain flying in the early 1980s. But more than half of these had been handed over to the Air Force of the People's Liberation Army.

In 1969 Hawker Siddeley produced its ultimate version of the Trident, as the Trident 3B. This is basically a development of the Trident 1E, with a lengthened fuselage to accommodate 128 to 180 passengers and the wing span of the Trident 2E but incorporating modifications to the wings themselves. Power is provided by Spey Mk 512-5W turbofan engines, and a 2 381-kg (5,250-lb)st Rolls-Royce RB 162-86 turbojet is installed below the tail unit to improve take-off performance. Of 26 built, all but one remained in service with British Airways in the early 1980s. In the mid-1970s CAAC received two Super Trident 3Bs, basically similar to Trident 3Bs but with increased fuel capacity to allow longer range, an increase in the maximum take-off weight of 3 629 kg (8,000 lb), and accommodation for 152 passengers. The maximum cruising speed and the range of the Trident 3B are 967 km/h (601 mph) and 1 761 km (1,094 miles) respectively. Production of the Trident ended in 1978, with the delivery of the final Trident 2E to CAAC.

The period between 1963 and 1964 witnessed a influx of new airliners, including two important jets from the Soviet Union. For Britain it was the launch of the BAC One-Eleven, a fairly small short-range twin-engined airliner. Its design was based on an earlier airliner that had been the brainchild of Hunting Aircraft Limited before BAC acquired a controlling interest in the company, followed by a complete take-over. Details of the One-Eleven were first given in 1961, together with the news that BUA (British United Airways) had ordered a total of 10. This order was significant in two respects. Firstly, it allowed the launch of the airliner and secondly it brought public attention to BUA (formed in 1960) and its Managing Director, Freddie Laker (later of Skytrain fame).

The initial production version of the One-Eleven was the Series 200, an 89-passenger short-range airliner powered by two 4 686-kg (10,330-lb)st Rolls-Royce Spey Mk 506 turbofan engines, one carried on each side of the rear fuselage. BUA began One-Eleven services in April 1965. Among other customers for the 56 Series 200s built was Aer Lingus, which remains a user in the early 1980s. Three months after One-Eleven services began, BAC produced a

CAAC Hawker Siddeley Trident 2E at Guangzhou in China.

prototype of the Series 300 and 400. These versions are basically the same, with 5 171-kg (11,400-lb)st Rolls-Royce Spey Mk 511 turbofans and increased fuel capacity for extended range, but the latter has various modifications to commend it to the North American market. Indeed, 69 of the 78 Series 300/400s produced were Series 400s. The British operator, Dan-Air, flies the Series 300, and among several users of the Series 400 can be counted British Airways and Tarom, the Romanian airline.

In mid-1967 the prototype of the One-Eleven Series 500 flew for the first time. With a lengthened fuselage to accommodate 97 to 119 passengers, increased wing span, a heavier take-off weight and associated strengthened undercarriage, and

powered by two 5 692-kg (12,550-lb)st Rolls-Royce Spey Mk 512 DW turbofan engines, production examples first went to BEA (which merged with BOAC to form British Airways in 1972). British production of the Series 500 continued into the 1980s, when 87 had been built. Maximum cruising speed of the Series 500 is 870 km/h (541 mph); typical range 2 726 km (1,694 miles).

The final British-built version of the One-Eleven was the Series 475. This combines the fuselage and accommodation of the Series 400 with the engines and wings of the Series 500. Modifications to the undercarriage also allow its operation from less sophisticated runways. The Peruvian airline Compania de Aviacion Faucett received the first Series 475 in 1971.

ponents, leading to the production of airliners from locally built components in the latter 1980s.

In roughly the same class as the One-Eleven is the Soviet Tupolev Tu-134. This has been given the reporting name *Crusty* by NATO. It is a short- to medium-range airliner, powered by two rear fuselage-mounted 6 800-kg (14,991-lb)st Soloviev D-30 Series II turbofan engines (with thrust reversers on the Tu-134A). Although based on Tupolev's first successes, the Tu-104 and similar Tu-124, it has several major differences in configuration apart from an increase in overall dimensions. As already mentioned, the engines are rear mounted, but other changes include a T-tail. The initial production version, known simply as the Tu-134, entered service on domestic routes within the U.S.S.R. in 1967, in the livery of Aeroflot. In September of the same year international services with the airliner began, with Aeroflot using the type on its Moscow-Stockholm European route. Today six airlines fly 64/72-passenger Tu-134s: Aeroflot, Yugoslavia's Aviogenex, Bulgaria's Balkan Bulgarian Airlines, East Germany's Interflug, Poland's LOT and Hungary's Malev.

From the Tu-134 was developed the Tu-134A, a lengthened version accommodating up to 84 passengers. Maximum cruising speed of this version is 885 km/h (550 mph) and its range is 1 890 km (1,174 miles) with a full passenger load. Tu-134As are operated by the previously mentioned airlines plus CSA of Czechoslovakia and Hang Khong Viet-Nam. The number of Tu-134/134As built is not known and the

One of Faucett's One-Eleven Series 475s, equipped with a low tyre pressure system to allow operation from unpaved and gravel runways.

Production of the One-Eleven Series 475 and 500 continues today, but in the form of the Romanian-produced Series 495 and 560. An agreement between Britain and Romania for the licenced production of the One-Eleven was concluded in 1979, each airliner being powered by two 5 697-kg (12,550-lb)st Spey Mk 512-14 DW turbofan engines. IAv Bucuresti is in charge of Romanian production and the aircraft are known as Rombac 1-11s. Three British-produced aircraft of Romanian type were delivered to Romania during 1981–82 to help establish manufacturing techniques, and the first 1-11 to be assembled in Romania from British components flew in September 1982. The first 22 Rombac 1-11s will incorporate British-manufactured com-

estimates vary greatly, but it runs into hundreds, most of which fly with Aeroflot. Development continues with the recent appearance of the 90-passenger Tu-134B, which incorporates many refinements including an FFCC (forward-facing crew cockpit) flight deck. With the FFCC, the instruments and controls formerly positioned on a side panel in the cockpit are transferred to the front panel, allowing the two pilots to monitor the instruments and perform control functions. Whereas on aircraft like the European Airbus A300 the FFCC concept allows for a flight crew of two, the Tu-134B also carries a flight engineer but no navigator. Other versions of the Tu-134 developed, or under development, include the 96-passenger Tu-134A3, with D-30 Series III turbofan engines, and a convertible passenger/cargo version.

The Ilyushin Il-62 is the Soviet equivalent of the British VC10, the latter which is no longer in commercial service. Like the VC10, the Il-62 has four turbofan engines carried in pairs on the rear fuselage and a T-tail, the former comprising 10 500-kg (23,149-lb)stKuznetsov NK-8-4 turbofans. It was designed to operate over distances equivalent to that from Moscow to New York carrying 150 passengers. The prototype made its maiden flight in January 1963, thus beating the previously mentioned Tu-134 into the air but following the British VC10. Aeroflot introduced the Il-62 into international service in September 1967, superseding the turboprop-powered

BAe One-Eleven Series 525 in the livery of Tarom of Romania.

Right: LOT Ilyushin Il-62M.

Tupolev Tu-114 on its route from Moscow to Montreal.

Aviogenex Tupolev Tu-134A.

It is likely that more than 200 Il-62s have been built, including the 11 000-kg (24,251-lb)st Soloviev D-30KU turbofan-engined Il-62M and the similar but higher-weight and strengthened Il-62MK. Accommodation in these later versions is 174 and 195 passengers respectively. Seven airlines fly versions of the Il-62, Aeroflot operating by far the largest number. The standard version of the Il-62 has a cruising speed of 900 km/h (560 mph) and a range of 8 000 km (4,970 miles) with a full load. Of the foreign users, CSA's seven probably comprise the greatest number.

The final aircraft of 1963–64 first appearance to be detailed in this chapter is the world's best-selling jet airliner, the remarkable Boeing 727. Another rear-engined airliner, it was developed by Boeing to supplement its already successful Model 707

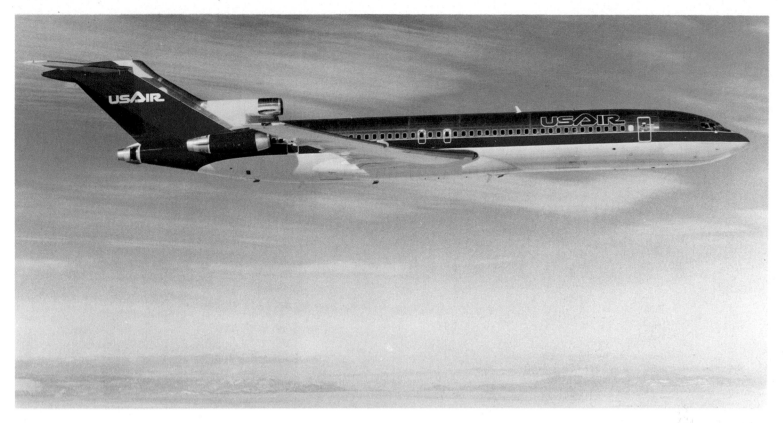

and 720 range, and to gain a section of the short- to medium-range market. Not even Boeing could have anticipated the aircraft's impact over the next two decades. First flown in February 1963, the Model 727 was designed to use some component parts of the Model 707, including the same upper fuselage, but in general configuration it is very different. The most obvious external changes are the Model 727's three rear-mounted engines and the T-tail.

The initial production version of the Model 727 was the Model 727-100, powered by three 6 350-kg (14,000-lb)st Pratt & Whitney JT8D-7 or 6 577-kg (14,500-lb)st JT8D-9 turbofan engines. Accommodating 131 passengers, 727-100 services were inaugurated in February 1964 by Eastern Air Lines and United Air Lines. Other versions of the 727-100 series produced before the end of production included the Model 727-100C convertible airliner, accommodating passengers only, up to 17 236 kg (38,000 lb) of freight only, or a mixture of passengers and freight; the Model 727-100QC version of the 727-100C, allowing changeover from all passenger to all freight interior in under 30 minutes using a palletized seating arrangement; and the Business Jet with a luxury interior.

The -100 series of the Model 727 is no longer in production. In 1967 Boeing introduced a longer version known as the Model 727-200, with the length increased from

40.59 metres (133 feet 2 inches) to 46.69 metres (153 feet 2 inches). Accommodation is provided for up to 189 passengers and power is provided by three JT8D-7, JT8D-9 or 6 800-kg (15,000-lb)st JT8D-11 turbofan engines. This initial version of the 727-200 series is no longer available. Neither is the convertible derivative known as the Model 727-200C. However, production of the 727-200 series continues with the Advanced 727-200 and 727-200F, the latter as a freighter.

The Advanced 727-200 entered service in 1972 and accommodates up to 189 passengers. In order to give passengers the feeling of space, this aircraft uses the so-called 'Superjet-look' interior, in which, by the careful use of lighting and with some interior redesign, an effect of increased width is achieved. Several variants of the JT8D engine can be used on this airliner, from the 6 577-kg (14,500-lb)st JT8D-9A to the 7 893-kg (17,400-lb)st JT8D-17R, raising the maximum take-off weight to a possible 95 027 kg (209,500 lb). Maximum cruising speed of the Advanced 727-200 is 964 km/h (599 mph) and its range is 4 003 km (2,487 miles). Well over 1,800 Model 727s of all versions have been sold to about 100 customers, the only airliner to have exceeded 1,500 sales. The majority are of the 727-200 series, and one delivered in 1981 became Boeing's 4,000th jet airliner. However, although still available for purchase, Boeing's latest airliners, the Models 757 and 767, will

Boeing Advanced 727-200, one of five flown by USAir.

Facing page: Newly built Advanced 727-200s for Western Airlines stand alongside other Boeing military and commercial aircraft.

Hawaiian Air McDonnell
Douglas DC-9-50.

Air Canada DC-9-30.

undoubtedly attract orders away from the
Model 727.

Having ventured successfully into jet airliners with its DC-8, Douglas (later McDonnell Douglas) became interested in the twin-
jet short- to medium-range airliner market.
The resulting aircraft is not unlike Britain's
One-Eleven but has achieved a far higher
sales figure, in fact more than four times
greater. The prototype DC-9 twin-jet flew
for the first time in February 1965 and
production began with the DC-9 Series 10.
Two versions of the Series 10 were built, the

first with 5 557-kg (12,250-lb)st Pratt &
Whitney JT8D-5 turbofan engines as the
Model 11 and the second with 6 350-kg
(14,000-lb)st JT8D-1s as the Model 15.
Both accommodate 80 to 90 passengers.
Several major airlines still operate Series
10s, including Aeromexico, Avensa of
Venezuela and Finnair of Finland. Actual
production of the Series 10 totalled 142
aircraft.

Many versions of the DC-9 have followed
the Series 10. The first of these was the Series
30, a 'stretched' version with accommo-

dation for 105 to 119 passengers. This has wings of greater span incorporating new high-lift devices, and engine options from the initial 6 350-kg (14,000-lb)st JT8D-7 to the 7 257-kg (16,000-lb)st JT8D-17. First flown in August 1966, it was inaugurated into service by Eastern Air Lines in early 1967 and has proved the most important version in terms of numbers sold. The next version to fly was the Series 40, offering an even longer fuselage to accommodate up to 132 passengers, increased fuel capacity and a choice of engine models. SAS, the national airline of Denmark, Norway and Sweden, introduced this version into commercial service in early 1968.

The least successful model of the DC-9, in terms of the number built, has been the Series 20, of which only 10 were produced. The first of SAS's Series 20s entered service at the beginning of 1969 and seven are still in the airline's fleet of 58 DC-9s. Each Series 20 can accommodate up to 90 passengers in the short-length fuselage, fitted with Series 30-type wings and powered by two 6 577-kg (14,500-lb)st JT8D-9 turbofan engines. These features make the Series 20 ideal for operation in hot climates or from high-altitude runways.

The DC-9 Series 50 can be regarded as the ultimate 'stretch' of the original DC-9s, with a length of 40.72 metres (133 feet $7\frac{1}{4}$ inches) compared to the Series 10's 31.82 metres (104 feet $4\frac{3}{4}$ inches). Powered by JT8D-15 or JT8D-17 turbofans, it can accommodate up to 139 passengers in a restyled interior. Ordered initially by Swissair, it entered commercial service in August 1975. Its maximum cruising speed is 898 km/h (558 mph) and its range with 97 passengers is 3 326 km (2,067 miles).

With the prospect of producing a 172-passenger DC-9 for short- to medium-range routes, McDonnell Douglas began development of its Super 80 series. The initial version is the Super 81, first flown in October 1979. It has a wing span of 32.87 metres (107 feet 10 inches), compared to a span of 28.47 metres (93 feet 5 inches) for the Series 30/40/50, and a length of 45.06 metres (147 feet 10 inches). Power is provided by two 8 391-kg (18,500-lb)st JT8D-209 turbofan engines. Swissair, the first customer, ordered 15 and used the first of these on its Zurich-London route in late 1980.

A proportion of the Super 80s so far ordered, included in the overall total of well over 100, are of the Super 82 type. Basically similar to the Super 81, this model is

Austrian Airlines DC-9-81 prior to delivery.

Right: The Boeing 737 has freight holds under the floor, forward and to the rear of the wings. Here an Air New Zealand 737-200 is having freight loaded.

powered by two 9 072-kg (20,000-lb)st JT8D-217 engines, making it ideal for operation from high-altitude runways or in hot climates or for carrying an increased payload. The maximum take-off weight of this version is 3 175 kg (7,000 lb) greater than that of the Super 81. The maximum cruising speed of both Super 80 versions is Mach 0.8 and the range for the Super 81 is up to 4 925 km (3,060 miles). The total number of DC-9s built of all versions, not including those for military service but including convertible passenger/freight, mixed and freighter versions, exceeds 1,000.

Plugging the gaps

The success of jet airliners over short, medium and long ranges left aircraft manufacturers in little doubt that there would be a continuing market for new airliners and intense competition for orders. The advantages of jet airliners over long ranges in terms of flying time and passenger comfort were obvious from an early point, but a more cautious advance into short-haul operations was made. Nevertheless, by the 1960s it was clear that major airlines would accept jets on all routes longer than commuter length and that future aircraft sales would depend on producing the right airliner for a specific task. While existing airliners were modified to fulfil expanding requirements, work on a new range of airliners had begun or was starting. This is not to say that the newer types were to oust existing airliners, for, as already stated, several early types remained in production into the 1970s and beyond and those of 1963–64 origin continue to be developed. It is truer to say that subsequent airliners have plugged gaps, by offering exactly the accommodation required for specific uses, by offering improved operating economy, or by vastly increasing the number of passengers that can be carried by a single aircraft. The latter also had important ramifications for busy airports, allowing an increased number of passengers to depart or arrive without an overwhelming increase in air traffic.

Soon after getting its Model 727 into commercial service, Boeing began work on a new airliner specifically for short-haul routes. Using some component parts already available for the Model 727, and marrying these to newly prepared components, the Model 737 was born. The first

Facing page, bottom: Primeras Lineas Uruguayas de Navegacion Aerea, better known simply as Pluna, is one operator of the Advanced 737-200.

flight was achieved in April 1967. Announcement of the new airliner, back in 1965, had been timed to coincide with an order for 21 aircraft placed by the German airline Lufthansa. The initial production version was the Model 737-100, a 103-passenger airliner powered by two Pratt & Whitney JT8D-9 turbofan engines carried under the wings in pods. Convertible and QC (Quick Change) convertible versions were also made available, but major success came with the launch of the Model 737-200.

The first Model 737-200 made its maiden flight in August 1967. From the close relation of first flight dates for the 737-100 and 737-200, it is clear that the Model 737-200 was expected to supplement the range. However, with the later version offering seating for 115 or 130 passengers by virtue of a slightly longer fuselage, demand for the

26

737-100 curtailed and only 30 were built.

Engine options for the 737-200, which remains the standard version today in Advanced form, include the 6 575-kg (14,500-lb)st JT8D-9A, 7 030-kg (15,500-lb)st JT8D-15, 7 257-kg (16,000-lb)st JT8D-17 or 7 710-kg (17,000-lb)st JT8D-17R turbofan. These allow a maximum cruising speed of 856 km/h (532 mph) and a range of 4 179 km (2,596 miles) with a full passenger load. Other variants of the Model 737-200 are the 737-200C convertible, the 737-200QC quick-change convertible, the 737-200 Executive Jet for business and executive use, and the Advanced 737-200 High Gross Weight Structure variants with greater fuel capacity for longer range.

Included in the total of more than 1,000 Model 737s ordered are 25 examples of the latest Model 737-300, ordered by Orion

Airways (a British operator already flying 737-200s), Southwest Airlines and USAir. The 737-300 is an enlarged version of the 737, with a slightly increased wing span of 28.91 metres (94 feet 10 inches) and a length of 33.40 metres (109 feet 7 inches), compared to the previous standard length of 30.53 metres (100 feet 2 inches). Accommodation is for 122 to 149 passengers and power is provided by two 9 071-kg (20,000-lb)st CFM International CFM56-3 turbofan engines. These engines offer greater fuel economy and reduced noise levels. The first Model 737-300 appeared in early 1984. This version is expected to supplement the Model 737-200 but only time will tell if it has the same impact on the 737-200 as that version had on the Model 737-100.

Although the Model 737 broke new ground for Boeing, no airliner since the Comet and Model 707 has had greater impact on commercial air travel than Boeing's mighty Model 747. Some might argue that the supersonic Concorde has had greater impact, giving civilians their first opportunity to fly at twice the speed of sound, but this is not so. There can be no doubt that technically Concorde surpasses all other airliners, but the small number built and operated means that its impact on the travelling public has been limited. It has been calculated that, in each month, all the Model 747's in service around the world carry about 4,700,000 passengers.

News of the Model 747 was released by Boeing in 1966, together with the customary first order. The order came from Pan American, for no fewer than 25. To some of the world's press, the thought of a gargantuan airliner capable of carrying 500 passengers at a time led to a reaction of enthusiastic astonishment tempered by doubts of its worth and the horrific vision of an accident involving so many people. It was also the press that first mooted the nickname 'Jumbo Jet', an appropriate name for such a huge aircraft and the world's first wide-bodied jet. Concern about the Model 747's worth and safety proved unnecessary, for it has shown itself to be a winner in all respects, not only as a passenger carrier but as a high-capacity freighter.

Although the term seems inappropriate, the Model 747 is technically conventional. One of its unusual design features is its upper deck cabin. Intended as a lounge for first-class passengers (in this respect reminiscent of bygone airliners like the Stratocruiser with its stateroom) it is often employed to increase the number of passengers carried. Indeed, use of the 32-passenger accommodation option available for the upper deck cabin has led Boeing to offer the further option on some models covering an extended upper deck to accommodate 69 economy-class passengers. In addition, a version of the airliner with the extended upper deck as standard is now available as the Model 747-300. Interestingly, the Model 747 is also one of the few aircraft actually to offer a reduced-length version as a variant of the standard model.

Air Gabon's single Boeing 747-200B Combi.

The first Boeing Model 747 made its maiden flight in February 1969 and the first of Pan Am's aircraft was delivered in December of that year. This airline inaugurated 747 services in January 1970, using the type on its important New York–London service. Overnight the number of passengers that could be carried by a single aircraft had more than doubled. This aircraft was a Model 747-100, of which a total of 167 was produced. Each 747-100 has four 21 296-kg (46,950-lb)st Pratt & Whitney JT9D-7A turbofan engines or more powerful JT9D-7AWs, JT9D-7Fs or JT9D-7FWs, carried in pods under the 59.64 metre (195 feet 8 inch)-span wings.

Although the original Model 747-100 is no longer built, there are eight versions of the 747 available for purchase, including the 747-300 already mentioned. The current basic model is the 747-100B, a strengthened version with the maximum take-off weight raised from 334 751 kg

(738,000 lb) to a possible 340 195 kg (750,000 lb). Engine options include the JT9D-7, General Electric CF6 and Rolls-Royce RB.211-524. Delivery of this version started in 1979 (to Iran Air), but production has been only a fraction of the overall total of nearly 600 747s ordered at the time of writing.

The main passenger version of the Model 747 is the 747-200B. This has a higher take-off weight, a greater engine choice and increased fuel capacity. Its maximum level speed with CF6-50E engines is 969 km/h (602 mph), and the range is 10 562 km (6,563 miles) at a maximum take-off weight of 377 840 kg (833,000 lb) while carrying 452 passengers. The first Model 747-200Bs entered service in 1971 and more than 200 examples of this model have been ordered by customers. Furthermore, 63 Combi versions of the Model 747-200B have also been built, each with a large cargo door in the port side of the fuselage and a cabin bulk-

Boeing holds a ceremony to mark the completion of the first 747-300 for Swissair.

Plate I

Boeing 757-200

cutaway drawing key

1 Radome
2 Weather radar scanner
3 VOR localiser aerial
4 ILS glideslope aerials
5 Front pressure bulkhead
6 Rudder pedals
7 Windscreen wipers
8 Instrument panel shroud
9 Windscreen panels
10 Cockpit roof systems control panels
11 First officer's seat
12 Centre console
13 Captain's seat
14 Cockpit floor level
15 Crew baggage locker
16 Observer's seat
17 Optional second observer's seat
18 Coat locker
19 Forward galley
20 Cockpit door
21 Wash basin
22 Forward toilet compartment
23 Nose undercarriage wheel bay
24 Nosewheel leg doors
25 Steering jacks
26 Spray deflector
27 Twin nosewheels
28 Taxying and runway turn-off lamps
29 Forward entry door
30 Cabin attendant's folding seats
31 Closets, port and starboard
32 Overhead stowage bins
33 DABS aerials
34 First-class cabin four-abreast seating, 16 seats
35 Cabin window panels
36 Fuselage frame and stringer construction
37 Underfloor radio and electronics compartment
38 Negative pressure relief valves

39 Electronics cooling air ducting
40 Radio racks
41 Forward freight door
42 Curtained cabin divider
43 Tourist-class six-abreast seating, 162-seats
44 Ventral VHF aerial
45 Underfloor freight hold
46 Passenger entry door, port and starboard
47 Door mounted escape chutes
48 Upper VHF aerial
49 Overhead air conditioning distribution ducting
50 LD-W cargo container (seven in forward hold)
51 Graphite composite wing root fillet
52 Landing lamp
53 Air system recirculating fan
54 Air distribution manifold
55 Conditioned air risers
56 Wing spar centre-section carry-through
57 Front spar/fuselage main frame
58 Ventral air conditioning plant, port and starboard
59 Centre section fuel tank
60 Floor beam construction
61 Centre fuselage construction
62 Starboard wing integral fuel tank; total system capacity 10,880 US gal (41 185 l)

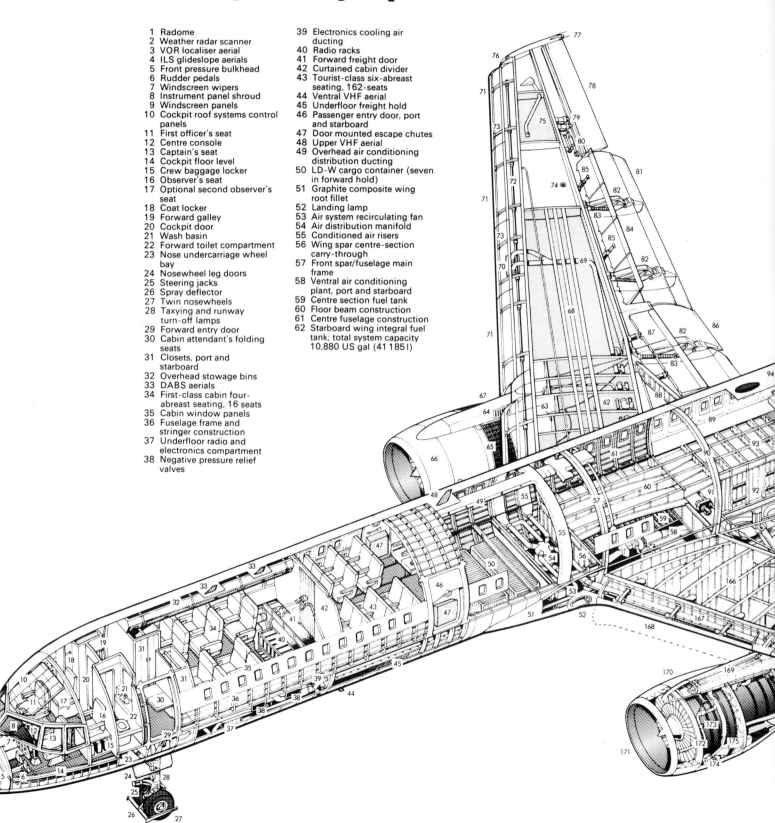

63 Dry bay
64 Bleed air system pre-cooler
65 Thrust reverser cascade doors, open
66 Starboard engine nacelle
67 Nacelle pylon
68 Fuel venting channels
69 Fuel system piping
70 Pressure refuelling connections
71 Leading edge slat segments, open
72 Slat drive shaft
73 Guide rails
74 Overwing fuel filler cap
75 Vent surge tank
76 Starboard navigation light (green) and strobe light (white)
77 Tail navigation strobe light (white)
78 Starboard aileron
79 Aileron hydraulic jacks
80 Spoiler sequencing control mechanism
81 Outboard double-slotted flaps, down
82 Flap guide rails
83 Screw jacks
84 Outboard spoilers, open
85 Spoiler hydraulic jacks
86 Inboard flap outer single-slotted segment
87 Inboard spoilers
88 Starboard main undercarriage mounting beam
89 Cabin wall trim panels
90 Rear spar/fuselage main frame

91 Flap-drive hydraulic motor (electric motor back-up)
92 Port mainwheel bay
93 Pressure floor above wheel bay
94 DF loop aerials
95 Cabin roof lighting panels
96 Port overhead stowage bins, passenger service units beneath
97 Mid-section toilet compartments (two port, one starboard)
98 Emergency exit doors, port and starboard
99 Rear freight door
100 APU battery and controls
101 Rear cabin seating
102 Overhead stowage bins
103 Starboard rear galley unit
104 Fin root fillet
105 Fin construction
106 Fin "logo" spotlight
107 Starboard tailplane
108 Starboard elevator
109 HF aerial couplers
110 Leading edge HF aerial
111 Fin tip aerial fairing
112 Tail VOR aerials
113 Static dischargers
114 Rudder
115 Rudder hydraulic jacks
116 Honeycomb rudder panel construction
117 APU intake plenum
118 Tailcone
119 APU exhaust
120 AiResearch GTCP 331-200 auxiliary power plant (APU)
121 Port elevator

122 Elevator hydraulic jacks
123 Honeycomb panel construction
124 Static dischargers
125 Tailplane construction
126 Fin "logo" light
127 Tailplane sealing plate
128 Fin support frame
129 Tailplane centre-section
130 Tailplane trim control jack
131 Rear pressure bulkhead
132 Aft galley
133 Rear entry door, port and starboard
134 Underfloor freight hold
135 LD-W cargo containers (six in rear hold)

136 Ventral VHF aerial
137 Roller tray cargo handling floor
138 Graphite composite wing root fillet
139 Port inboard double slotted flap
140 Main undercarriage mounting beam
141 Undercarriage leg side strut
142 Hydraulic retraction jack
143 Inboard spoilers
144 Flap hinge linkage
145 Inboard flap single slotted outer segment
146 Flaps down position
147 Flap track fairings
148 Outboard double slotted flap
149 Outboard spoilers
150 Aileron hydraulic jacks
151 Port aileron honeycomb construction

152 Tail navigation strobe light (white)
153 Port navigation light (red) and strobe light (white)
154 Vent surge tank
155 Port leading edge slat segments
156 Slat guide rails
157 Drive shaft
158 Port wing dry bay
159 Ventral access panels
160 Port wing integral fuel tank
161 Wing rib construction
162 Wing stringers
163 Wing-skin plating
164 Four-wheel main undercarriage bogie
165 Main undercarriage leg strut
166 Inboard wing ribs
167 Bleed air ducting
168 Inboard leading edge slat
169 Engine mounting pylon
170 Detachable engine cowlings
171 Port engine intake
172 Intake de-icing air duct
173 Rolls-Royce RB.211-535C turbofan engine (General-Electric CF6-32 optional fit)
174 Engine accessory gearbox
175 Oil cooler
176 Fan air exhaust duct
177 Hot stream exhaust nozzle

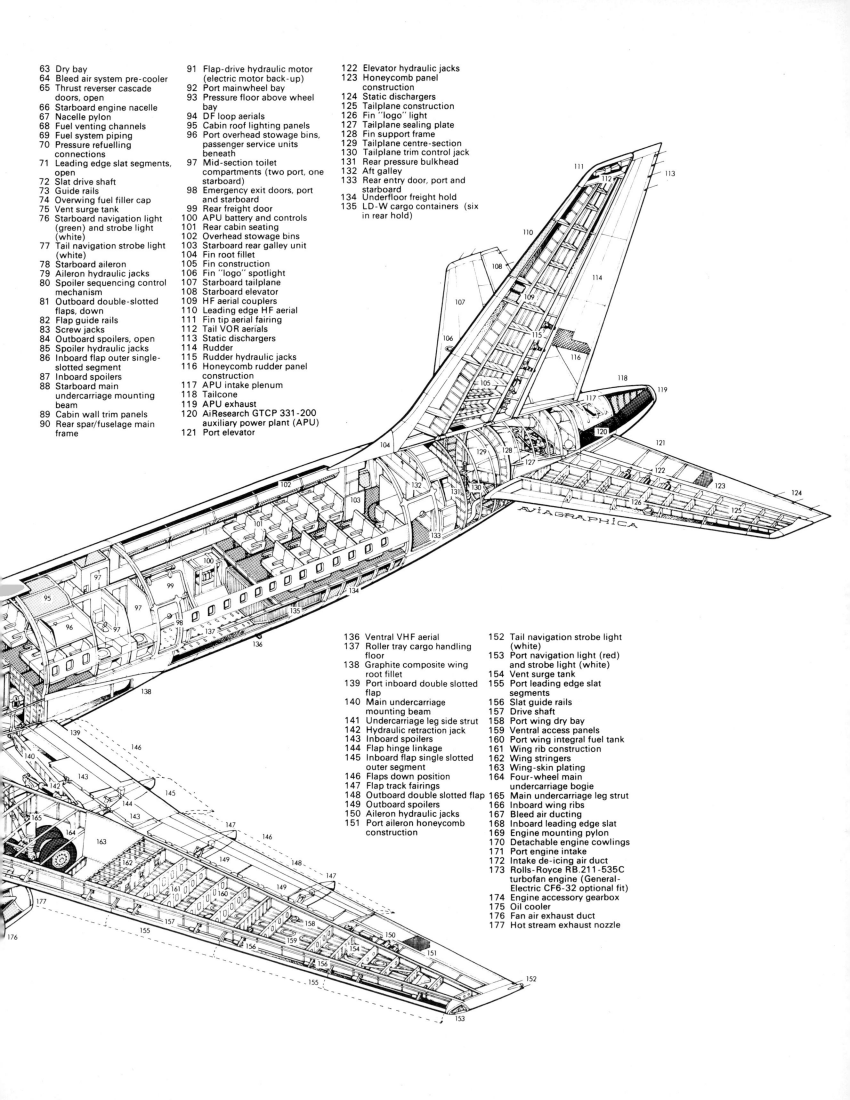

Right: Boeing 747SP operated by Qantas of Australia.

Boeing 757-200 in the insignia of Eastern Air Lines, flying over the snow-covered western Washington mountains.

head that can be removed when required. This allows an all-passenger layout or a mixture of passengers and cargo. The first Combi went to Air Canada in early 1975. Previously, a version that can be employed in all-passenger, all-cargo or combi forms became available as the Model 747-200C Convertible. The first Convertible was delivered to World Airways in 1973 but this version has not been a high seller, probably because the Combi fulfils mixed transport roles and the Model 747-200F Freighter covers all-cargo transport.

Two special versions of the Model 747 have been produced by Boeing. The first of these to appear was the Model 747SR (the letters standing for Short Range). Based on the 747-100B, it is intended to be used by airlines that operate short-haul routes over which passenger traffic is high. The first Model 747SR was one of several for Japan Air Lines and was delivered in 1973.

The other special version of the Model 747 is the 747SP or Special Performance. First flown in 1975, it has the standard 747 fuselage shortened by 14.35 metres (47 feet 1 inch), to give an overall aircraft length of 56.31 metres (184 feet 9 inches) compared to the standard 747 length of 70.66 metres (231 feet 10 inches). Maximum accommodation is therefore reduced to 440 passengers. A layout for 331 passengers provides for 28 first-class passengers and 303 other passengers on the main deck and in the upper cabin. The range has been increased, typically to 10 841 km (6,736 miles) with 331 passengers on board. The maximum take-off weight of this version is 317 515 kg (700,000 lb). Pan Am received the first Model 747SPs, inaugurating services in 1976. More than 40 have been delivered to various airlines, the 10 to Pan Am proving the largest number, followed by the six for South African Airways.

The first of two new Boeing airliners made its maiden flight in September 1981 as the Model 767. This is a twin-turbofan, wide-bodied, medium-range airliner, very much in the style of the European Airbus. Initially offered with 21 682-kg (47,800-lb)st Pratt & Whitney JT9D-7R4D or slightly more powerful General Electric CF6-80A turbofans, it has accommodation for 211 to 289 passengers and a cruising speed and maximum range with 211 passengers of Mach 0.80 and 6 013 km (3,736 miles) respectively.

United Air Lines, an operator that worked with Boeing on the overall design of the aircraft, received the first of its 39 Model 767s in August 1982. At the time of writing orders for this airliner stood at more than 170, including 30 for American Airlines, 25 for All Nippon Airways of Japan and 20 for Delta Air Lines. The United aircraft have Pratt & Whitney engines but the others mentioned have CF6s. The Model 767 incorporates some components produced in Italy and Japan.

The second of Boeing's new airliners, the Model 757, also has two turbofan engines carried in pods under the wings but this is where the similarity ends. Unlike the Model 767, the Model 757 is seen as a Model 727 replacement and is therefore not a wide-bodied aircraft. It has new high-technology wings, with less sweepback than on the Model 727's wings or on the 767's high-technology wings. Initial production aircraft, known as Model 757-200s and first delivered to Eastern Air Lines and British Airways, are each powered by two 16 964-kg (37,400-lb)st Rolls-Royce RB.211-535C turbofans, offering great savings in the fuel

used compared to existing medium-range airliners. The choice of Rolls-Royce engines by Eastern had two important ramifications. The first was that the U.S. engine manufacturer Pratt & Whitney had to wait for subsequent production aircraft before its PW2037 engine powered any commercially operated Model 757s, and the second was that this airliner became the first Boeing transport with non-American engines fitted at launch. The intense competition for 757 engine orders had already seen the withdrawal of General Electric during the development stages, leaving Pratt & Whitney and Rolls-Royce as rivals. Both types of engine are, of course, extremely fuel-efficient. Rolls-Royce is also offering a more advanced version of its RB.211-535 turbofan, known as the RB.211-535E4. This has a higher rating than the RB.211-535C and the PW2037, at 18 189-kg (40,100-lb)st. Eastern Air Lines' Model 757-200s will all eventually have the RB.211-535E4 installed, although the RB.211-535C has been fitted initially.

First flown in February 1982, the Model 757 accommodates between 178 and 224 passengers in eight basic seating layouts. Intended for use over short and medium routes, it has a cruising speed similar to that

Boeing 767-200s in the insignias of Delta Air Lines and United Air Lines stand alongside the first 767. An All Nippon Airways 747SR is in the background.

Facing page: NLM City
Hopper F28 Mk 4000
Fellowship. NLM is a
subsidiary of KLM.

of the Model 767 and a range with 186 passengers of up to 4 281 km (2,660 miles) on the power of RB.211-535E4 turbofan engines. The total number of Model 757s ordered is more than 120, which includes a staggering 60 powered by Pratt & Whitney enginesfor Delta Air Lines. It appears that, with either type of engine fitted, the Model 757 is destined to be every bit as successful as the Model 727 it supersedes.

In May 1967 the first flight took place of the F28 Fellowship, a short-range airliner with a configuration not dissimilar to that of a smaller McDonnell Douglas DC-9. Produced by Fokker of the Netherlands, the initial production version was the F28 Mk 1000, powered by two 4 468-kg (9,850-lb)st Rolls-Royce RB.183-2 Spey Mk 555-15 turbofan engines carried in pods on the rear fuselage. The airliner offers accommodation for 65 passengers, while a passenger/cargo or all-cargo derivative is the Mk 1000C. The first customer airline was LTU. Subsequently the F28 received certification to allow its operation from unpaved runways. The total number of Mk 1000/1000Cs produced was 97, including 18 for Garuda Indonesian Airways. These, with seven later Mk 3000s and eight Mk 4000s, make Garuda the operator of the largest number of Fellowships.

The first 'stretched' version of the Fellowship was the Mk 2000, with accommodation for 79 passengers in a lengthened fuselage. Only 10 were produced, six going to Nigeria Airways (all remaining in use today). The current versions of the Fellowship are the Mk 3000 and Mk 4000. Each is powered by two 4 490-kg (9,900-lb)st Mk 555-15P turbofan engines. They carry more fuel in strengthened wings, have higher weights and other modifications. The Mk 3000 represents the current short-fuselage Fellowship, with Mk 1000 accommodation or with an alternative executive luxury interior, but the Mk 4000 can seat 85 persons in a fuselage that is more than 2.13 metres (7 feet) longer. The maximum cruising speed of the current versions is 843 km/h (523 mph) and the range for the Mk 4000 on a long haul route is 2 085 km (1,295 miles). More than 190 Fellowships of all versions have been ordered over the years by airlines around the world.

Less commercial success was attained by the VFW-Fokker VFW 614, another short-range airliner accommodating only 44 passengers. Of German origin, the VFW 614 made its maiden flight in July 1971 and entered service with the Danish airline Cimber Air in 1975. Others were delivered to TAT and Air Alsace. However, production ceased at the end of 1977. Of distinct design, its most recognizable feature is the position of the two 3 302-kg (7,280-lb)st Rolls-Royce M45H Mk 501 turbofan en-

Plate II

British Aerospace 146-100

cutaway drawing key

1 Radome
2 Weather radar scanner
3 Radar mounting
4 ILS aerial
5 Oxygen bottle, capacity 400 Imp gal (1 812 l)
6 Sloping front pressure bulkhead

7 VOR flush aerial
8 Nose undercarriage wheel bay
9 Nosewheel leg strut
10 Twin nosewheels
11 Pitot tube
12 Rudder pedals
13 Instrument panel
14 Windscreen wipers
15 Instrument panel shroud
16 Windscreen panels

17 Overhead switch panel
18 First officer's seat
19 Centre control pedestal
20 Control column handwheel
21 Side console panel (area navigation system)
22 Cockpit floor level
23 Captain's seat

24 Direct vision window/flight deck emergency exit
25 Folding observer's seat
26 Flight deck bulkhead
27 Air conditioning ducting
28 Starboard galley unit
29 Forward service door
30 Main cabin divider
31 Port side forward toilet compartment
32 Forward entry door
33 Door latching handle
34 Escape chute stowage

35 Underfloor radio and electronics equipment bay
36 Machined doorway cut-out main frames
37 Nose section/forward fuselage skin joint strap
38 Door frame support structure
39 Entry vestibule
40 Cabin attendant's folding seat
41 Six-abreast passenger seating
42 VHF aerial
43 D/F loop aerial
44 Cabin wall trim panels
45 Air conditioning ducting
46 Forward cargo hold door
47 Forward underfloor cargo hold
48 Seat rail support structure

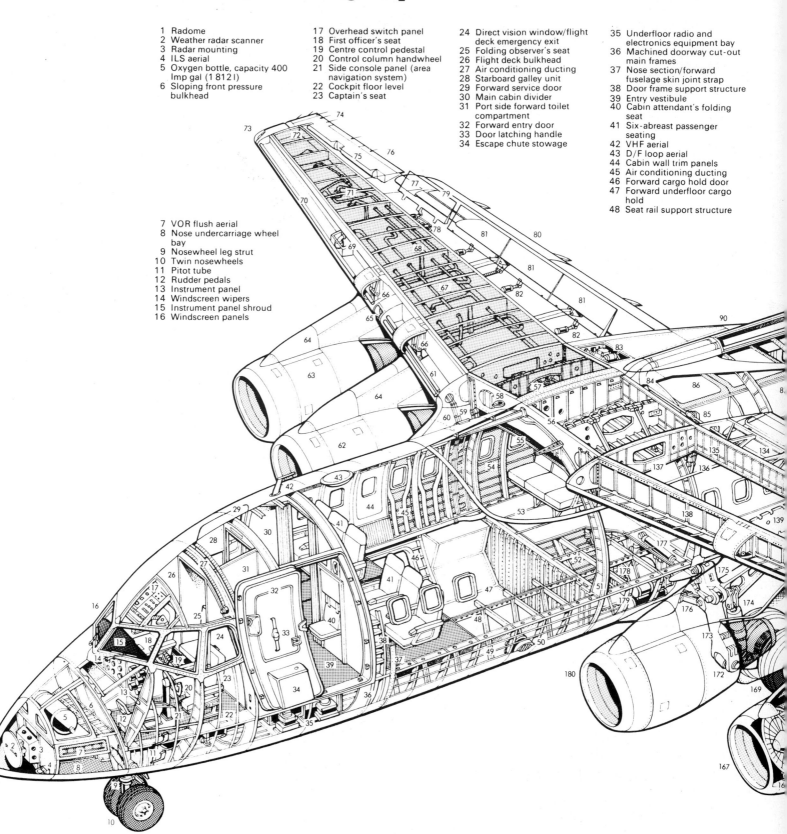

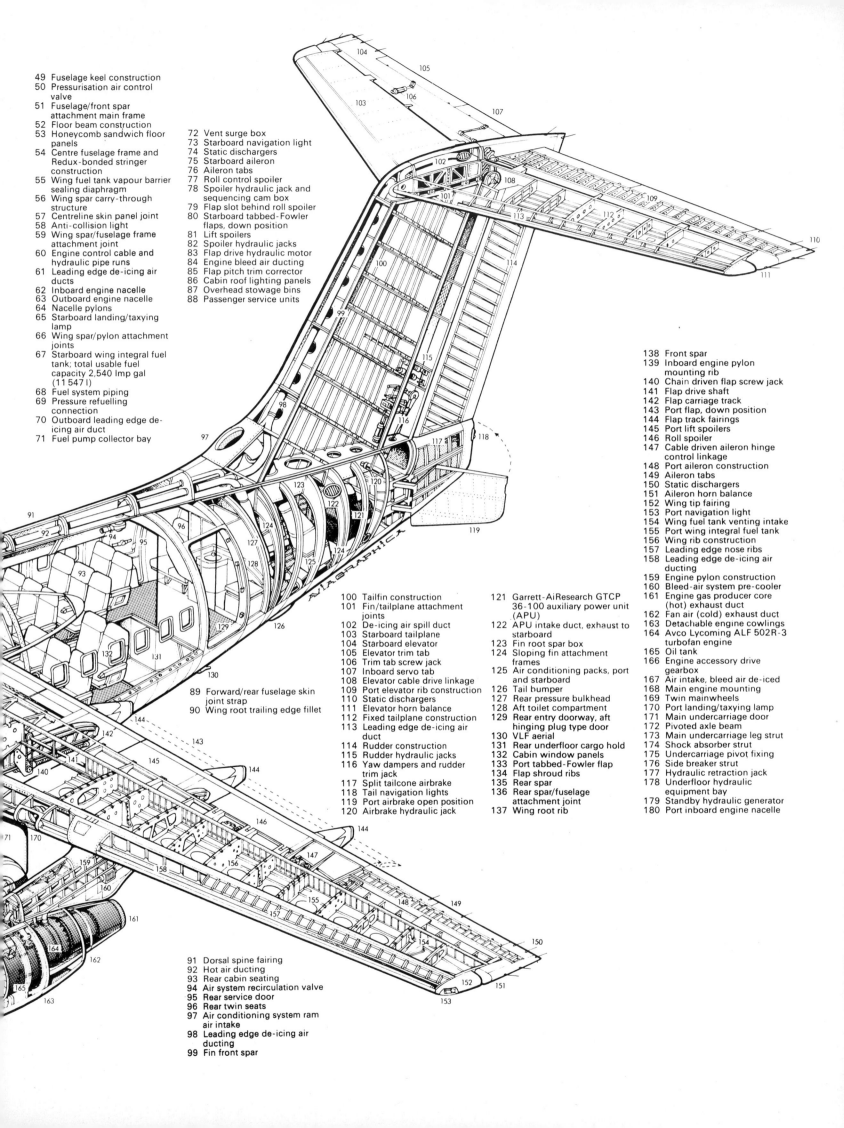

49 Fuselage keel construction
50 Pressurisation air control valve
51 Fuselage/front spar attachment main frame
52 Floor beam construction
53 Honeycomb sandwich floor panels
54 Centre fuselage frame and Redux-bonded stringer construction
55 Wing fuel tank vapour barrier sealing diaphragm
56 Wing spar carry-through structure
57 Centreline skin panel joint
58 Anti-collision light
59 Wing spar/fuselage frame attachment joint
60 Engine control cable and hydraulic pipe runs
61 Leading edge de-icing air ducts
62 Inboard engine nacelle
63 Outboard engine nacelle
64 Nacelle pylons
65 Starboard landing/taxying lamp
66 Wing spar/pylon attachment joints
67 Starboard wing integral fuel tank; total usable fuel capacity 2,540 Imp gal (11 547 l)
68 Fuel system piping
69 Pressure refuelling connection
70 Outboard leading edge de-icing air duct
71 Fuel pump collector bay

72 Vent surge box
73 Starboard navigation light
74 Static dischargers
75 Starboard aileron
76 Aileron tabs
77 Roll control spoiler
78 Spoiler hydraulic jack and sequencing cam box
79 Flap slot behind roll spoiler
80 Starboard tabbed-Fowler flaps, down position
81 Lift spoilers
82 Spoiler hydraulic jacks
83 Flap drive hydraulic motor
84 Engine bleed air ducting
85 Flap pitch trim corrector
86 Cabin roof lighting panels
87 Overhead stowage bins
88 Passenger service units

89 Forward/rear fuselage skin joint strap
90 Wing root trailing edge fillet

100 Tailfin construction
101 Fin/tailplane attachment joints
102 De-icing air spill duct
103 Starboard tailplane
104 Starboard elevator
105 Elevator trim tab
106 Trim tab screw jack
107 Inboard servo tab
108 Elevator cable drive linkage
109 Port elevator rib construction
110 Static dischargers
111 Elevator horn balance
112 Fixed tailplane construction
113 Leading edge de-icing air duct
114 Rudder construction
115 Rudder hydraulic jacks
116 Yaw dampers and rudder trim jack
117 Split tailcone airbrake
118 Tail navigation lights
119 Port airbrake open position
120 Airbrake hydraulic jack

121 Garrett-AiResearch GTCP 36-100 auxiliary power unit (APU)
122 APU intake duct, exhaust to starboard
123 Fin root spar box
124 Sloping fin attachment frames
125 Air conditioning packs, port and starboard
126 Tail bumper
127 Rear pressure bulkhead
128 Aft toilet compartment
129 Rear entry doorway, aft hinging plug type door
130 VLF aerial
131 Rear underfloor cargo hold
132 Cabin window panels
133 Port tabbed-Fowler flap
134 Flap shroud ribs
135 Rear spar
136 Rear spar/fuselage attachment joint
137 Wing root rib

138 Front spar
139 Inboard engine pylon mounting rib
140 Chain driven flap screw jack
141 Flap drive shaft
142 Flap carriage track
143 Port flap, down position
144 Flap track fairings
145 Port lift spoilers
146 Roll spoiler
147 Cable driven aileron hinge control linkage
148 Port aileron construction
149 Aileron tabs
150 Static dischargers
151 Aileron horn balance
152 Wing tip fairing
153 Port navigation light
154 Wing fuel tank venting intake
155 Port wing integral fuel tank
156 Wing rib construction
157 Leading edge nose ribs
158 Leading edge de-icing air ducting
159 Engine pylon construction
160 Bleed-air system pre-cooler
161 Engine gas producer core (hot) exhaust duct
162 Fan air (cold) exhaust duct
163 Detachable engine cowlings
164 Avco Lycoming ALF 502R-3 turbofan engine
165 Oil tank
166 Engine accessory drive gearbox
167 Air intake, bleed air de-iced
168 Main engine mounting
169 Twin mainwheels
170 Port landing/taxying lamp
171 Main undercarriage door
172 Pivoted axle beam
173 Main undercarriage leg strut
174 Shock absorber strut
175 Undercarriage pivot fixing
176 Side breaker strut
177 Hydraulic retraction jack
178 Underfloor hydraulic equipment bay
179 Standby hydraulic generator
180 Port inboard engine nacelle

91 Dorsal spine fairing
92 Hot air ducting
93 Rear cabin seating
94 Air system recirculation valve
95 Rear service door
96 Rear twin seats
97 Air conditioning system ram air intake
98 Leading edge de-icing air ducting
99 Fin front spar

The French airline Air Inter received all ten Dassault-Breguet Mercures and continues to operate them.

gines, which are carried in pods on over-wing pylons. The maximum cruising speed is 704 km/h (438 mph) and the range is 1 574 km (978 miles).

The year 1971 was also the year in which France became a competitor in the twin-engine, short- to medium-range airliner field, with the first flight of the Dassault-Breguet Mercure in May of that year. Intended basically to rival American-produced 'twins' by offering a high seating capacity (for up to 162 passengers) plus freight holds designed to accommodate standard Boeing 727 containers or other loads, the venture was not a commercial success. However, 10 Mercures were built for Air Inter, a French domestic operator, and these remain in use today with that airline. Like the Boeing 737, the Mercure is powered by two U.S. Pratt & Whitney JT8D engines carried in underwing pods, this time as 7 030-kg (15,500-lb)st JT8D-15s. These give a maximum cruising speed of 926 km/h (575 mph) and a maximum range of 2 084 km (1,295 miles) while carrying 150 passengers. Proposals to produce a follow-on version were later abandoned.

The latest short-range airliner to come onto the world scene is the British Aerospace 146. It is unusual because it is powered by four turbofan engines (3 039-kg; 6,700-lb st Avco Lycoming ALF 502R-3s) installed in pods beneath high-mounted wings. It also has a T-tail. Passengers are accommodated within a wide fuselage, and operating noise

levels are low. Two versions are available. The Series 100, of which the prototype first flew in September 1981, is the short-fuselage version with seating for between 71 and 93 passengers. It can operate from semi-prepared runways that are short in length. The first were ordered by the British airline, Dan-Air.

The BAe 146 Series 200 has a fuselage length some 2.39 metres (7 feet 10 inches) longer than that of the Series 100, making the overall length of the Series 200 28.55 metres (93 feet 8 inches). Accommodation has also been increased to between 82 and 109 passengers and the maximum take-off weight has been raised. The maximum cruising speed is similar to that of the Series 100, at 778 km/h (483 mph), but its range is longer at 1 853 km (1,150 miles). The first Series 200 made its maiden flight in August 1982 and deliveries began with the first of four ordered by Air Wisconsin. Pacific Express has ordered six Series 200s and among the airlines that have placed options for aircraft of this type is Dan-Air. Unlike the Series 100, this longer and heavier airliner requires a longer paved runway.

Easily possessing the smallest passenger accommodation of any airliner in this chapter is the Soviet Yakovlev Yak-40, known to NATO as *Codling*. A short-range airliner, it is normally fitted out for 27 passengers, although a high-density layout can allow for 32 passengers. The minimum number carried is normally 16. First flown in

October 1966, it first entered passenger services with Aeroflot in September 1968. Production ended only after more than a thousand had been built for Soviet use and for export, including a number with air-ambulance interiors, executive interiors or for military use. Only 20.36 metres (66 feet 9½ inches) in length, the Yak-40 is powered by three 1 500-kg (3,307-lb)st Ivchenko AI-25 turbofan engines, two mounted on the rear fuselage sides and one carried in the tail. Its maximum cruising speed is

Top: Dan-Air BAe 146 Series 100.

Above: Yakovlev Yak-40 flown by Aeroflot.

Left: The longer and higher-capacity BAe 146 Series 200, in the livery of Air Wisconsin.

550 km/h (342 mph) and its maximum range is 2 000 km (1,240 miles). Interestingly, it was the first civil transport aircraft to come from the Yakovlev bureau, which is best known for its fighters and bombers, and was designed to supersede the piston-engined Lisunov Li-2, a Soviet-built version of the U.S. DC-3. It can, therefore, take off and land on grass airstrips. It has been estimated that approximately 80 per cent of all Yak-40s built continue in airline service.

With the experience of designing and producing the Yak-40, Yakovlev set about the design of a much larger airliner of similar configuration. The resulting Yak-42 first flew as a prototype in March 1975 and first entered service in production form on Aeroflot's Moscow-Krasnodar domestic route in 1980. Due to the vast area of the Soviet Union, the Yak-42 was designed to operate in a wide range of climatic conditions and in areas where facilities are limited. It is a short- to medium-range airliner, also used in the Soviet Union as a feederliner to transport passengers from remote areas to airports on major routes.

In the long term it is possible that production of the Yak-42 could exceed that of the

Boeing 727, so far easily the world's best-selling airliner. However, this can be speculation only, as production has only been underway for a comparatively short time. The first Yak-42s to be operated outside Aeroflot went to Aviogenex of Yugoslavia. Each Yak-42 has normal accommodation for 100 or 120 passengers, making it a more than adequate Tu-134 replacement. Power is provided by three 6 500-kg (14,330-lb)st Lotarev D-36 turbofan engines. Its maximum cruising speed is 810 km/h (503 mph) and its range is 900 to 3 000 km (559 to 1,864 miles).

The Yak-40 represented the Soviet Union's first airliner with the triple jet-engine layout. Two years after its first flight as a prototype, Tupolev flew the prototype of its own 'triple' as the medium- to long-range Tu-154. Known to NATO as *Careless*, the basic Tu-154 is powered by three 9 500-kg (20,950-lb)st Kuznetsov NK-8-2 turbofan engines. These bestow a maximum cruising speed of 975 km/h (605 mph) and a maximum range with 95 passengers of 6 400 km (3,977 miles). Accommodation is provided for 128 to 167 passengers. Aeroflot inaugurated cargo/mail services with the

Similar in configuration to the Yak-40 but larger is the Yakovlev Yak-42.

Malev Tupolev
Tu-154B-2, photographed
at Madrid.

Tu-154 in May 1971, with regular passenger services beginning early the following year and international services (to Prague) that summer.

In 1975 Aeroflot introduced the improved Tu-154A on its scheduled passenger services. The main change involved the use of more powerful NK-8-2U turbofan engines, each rated at 10 500-kg (23,149-lb)st. The maximum take-off weight of this version was increased by 4 000 kg (8,818 lb) to 94 000 kg (207,234 lb), which allows an increase in the fuel carried. Maximum accommodation is for 168 passengers.

A third version of the Tu-154 appeared in 1977 as the Tu-154B, in its latest form now known as the Tu-154B-2. Other than a further increase in take-off weight of 4 000 kg (8,818 lb), most refinements have been associated with the aircraft's avionics. However, passenger accommodation has been increased to a maximum of 180, by the redesign of the cabin interior. While carrying the maximum payload, the Tu-154B has a range of 2 750 km (1,705 miles). Several hundred Tu-154s of all versions have been built, most of which have entered Aeroflot service. However, six other airlines fly the type, including Balkan Bulgarian Airlines which operates the largest Tu-154 fleet outside the U.S.S.R.

It is reported that the very latest version of the Tu-154 has the new designation Tu-164, indicating considerable changes. Apart from some redesign of the rear airframe, it is known that greater fuel economy has been achieved by the use of three 12 000-kg (26,455-lb)st Soloviev D-30KP turbofan engines, thereby offering increased range.

In September 1980 the first jet airliner of Chinese design and production flew for the first time as the Yunshuji-10, translated as Transport aircraft 10. It comes from the Shanghai works of the State Aircraft Factories and is therefore best known in the West as the Shanghai Y-10. Its four engines are, however, Pratt & Whitney JT3D-7 turbofans, as used by the state airline CAAC on its fleet of 10 Boeing 707-320B/Cs. These engines are pod-mounted below the wings, and in general appearance the Y-10 looks similar to a Model 707. It has important differences, however, not least of which is a wing span between those of the 707-120 and 707-320 and a length shorter than any Model 707. Accommodation allows for 124 to 178 passengers in civil form and it is likely that military versions will also be produced. Its maximum cruising speed is 917 km/h (570 mph) and it has a range of between 5 560 and 8 000 km (3,455 and 4,970 miles).

Twins, triples and quadruples

The introduction of the world's first wide-bodied airliner, in the massive form of the Boeing 747, heralded a gamut of other wide-bodied types from the U.S. and abroad. The Boeing Model 767 has already been described and is the latest American widebody. In 1970 two U.S. rival 'triples' made their maiden flights: the McDonnell Douglas DC-10 in August and the Lockheed L-1011 TriStar in November. Both can be described as all-purpose transports, suitable for short-haul routes or for medium and long ranges, according to version, with the DC-10 also offering convertible and all-cargo models.

The initial production version of the DC-10 was the Series 10, which began scheduled passenger services in August 1971 in American Airlines colours. Conceived as a version for domestic operations, it is powered by three 18 144-kg (40,000-lb)st General Electric CF6-6D or 18 597-kg (41,000-lb)st CF6-6D1 turbofan engines. Two engines are carried under the wings and the third above the rear fuselage. Today, American Airlines operates a DC-10-10 fleet of more than 30, the most operated by any one airline. The convertible passenger/cargo version of the Series 10 is known as the DC-10-10CF.

In 1972 McDonnell Douglas flew its new Series 30 version of the DC-10, intended for intercontinental services. Apart from a

change to more powerful CF6-50 series engines, the maximum take-off weight was substantially increased, from 206 385 kg (455,000 lb) to 259 450 kg (572,000 lb), with a resulting increase in payload and fuel capacity. The wing span was also increased and the undercarriage modified to accept the increase in weight. Later, the maximum take-off weight was further increased to 263 085 kg (580,000 lb), the heaviest of any DC-10 version. The maximum cruising speed is 908 km/h (564 mph), lower than for the Series 10, but its range with maximum payload has been greatly increased to 7 413 km (4,606 miles). All versions of the DC-10 can carry up to 380 passengers, although 255 or 270 is normal. Initial deliveries of the DC-10-30 were made to the

European airlines Swissair and KLM, the former receiving the greatest number. Swissair has 13 DC-10s, the largest European fleet. The Series 30CF convertible variant is also in service; operators include the U.S. airline World Airways, with eight, and Belgium's Sabena. Accommodation allows for passengers or up to 70 626 kg (155,700 lb) of freight.

A further increase in fuel capacity, by the installation of a new tank at the rear of the cargo compartment, has led to the DC-10-30ER (extended range). Existing Series 30s can be brought up to this standard using retrofit kits. Coupled with 24 494-kg (54,000-lb)st CF6-50C2B turbofans, the ER has a range of 10 620 km (6,600 miles). Swissair was the first customer.

Swissair McDonnell Douglas DC-10-30.

Prior to the first flight of a Series 30 in mid-1972, McDonnell Douglas flew the first Series 40, then known as the Series 20. Thus, the Series 40 was the second version of the DC-10. It is basically similar to the Series 30 intercontinental model, but with Pratt & Whitney engines as an alternative to General Electrics. Only two airlines operate Series 40s. These are Northwest Orient Airlines with a fleet of 22, which are powered by 22 407-kg (49,400-lb)st JT9D-20 turbofans, and Japan Air Lines with 18, powered by 24 040-kg (53,000-lb)st JT9D-59As.

Apart from the Series 30ER, the most recent version of the DC-10 is the Series 15. Intended as a longer range variant of the Series 10, it appeared in 1981. Power is provided by 21 092-kg (46,500-lb)st CF6-50C2F turbofans and the range is 6 850 km (4,258 miles), a considerable increase over that of the Series 10. The first operators are Mexicana and Aeromexico, the latter already an operator of the DC-10-30. More than 360 DC-10s of all versions had been delivered at the time of writing, with production continuing to fulfil orders.

Lockheed's TriStar is similar in configuration to the DC-10. In 1968 the company decided to use British Rolls-Royce RB.211 three-shaft high-bypass ratio turbofan engines for its new airliner and in the following year construction of the first TriStar began. Although the RB.211 is a fine engine and is equally at home on Boeing 747s and 757s, the cost of its development caused the collapse of the original Rolls-Royce Limited. The company was reformed in early 1971 with British government finance as Rolls-Royce (1971) Limited. These problems also caused Lockheed many headaches, but in April 1972 the first TriStar passenger service was inaugurated by Eastern Air Lines. The aircraft used was the L-1011-1 TriStar, the basic version with 19 050-kg (42,000-lb)st RB.211-22B turbofan engines and accommodation for up to 400 passengers. With a first-class and coach-class seating arrangement, the number of passengers carried is 256. Other early operators of the L-1011-1 were TWA, which currently has one of the largest fleets, together with Delta Air Lines, Eastern and the Japanese airline All Nippon Airways.

A variant of the L-1011-1 with a higher maximum take-off weight and increased fuel capacity became the L-1011-100. TWA received the largest number. With the L-1011-200, Lockheed offered a further increase in range to 6 671 km (4,145 miles) while carrying a maximum passenger load. The more powerful RB.211-524 engine, rated at 21 772 kg (48,000 lb)st or 22 680 kg (50,000 lb)st, depending on variant, also

A Mexicana DC-10-15 taking off on its first flight.

give performance benefits at take off and when operating in hot climates or from high-altitude airports.

The heaviest and longest-range version of the TriStar is the L-1011-500, powered by three 22 680-kg (50,000-lb)st RB.211-524B or RB.211-524B4 engines. Like the other versions, two of the engines are carried in pods under the wings and one in the rear fuselage. Weighing up to 231 330 kg (510,000 lb) at take off and with a maximum cruising speed and range of 973 km/h (605 mph) and 9 905 km (6,154 miles) respectively, the L-1011-500 can accommodate up to 330 passengers in a fuselage 4.11 metres (13 feet 6 inches) shorter than those of previous versions, at 50.05 metres (164 feet $2\frac{1}{2}$ inches). The first L-1011-500s to enter commercial service were those flown by British Airways in May 1979. With the delivery of the last few TriStars ordered, in 1984, production of this airliner will cease. The total number of TriStars built will then be nearly 250.

The first European wide-bodied airliner, and the first wide-bodied 'twin', is the short- to medium-range Airbus A300, the first prototype of which made its maiden flight in October 1972. Its development dates from the mid-1960s, when companies from the U.K. and France first got together to discuss such a transport aircraft. By September 1967, when a formal agreement was signed, Germany had joined the consortium. In 1969 Britain withdrew, with the result that the Airbus became mainly a project of France and Germany, in the form of the participating companies Aérospatiale and Deutsche Airbus respectively. (The latter is a company formed by MBB and VFW-Fokker.) Despite earlier events, Britain continued an important but diminished interest in the project by way of Hawker Siddeley's involvement as a private venture. Hawker Siddeley was responsible mainly for the aircraft's wings.

Airbus Industrie was formed in 1970 and now British Aerospace holds Britain's 20 per cent share in the programme. The major partners remain Aérospatiale and Deutsche Airbus, although Spain, too, has a 4.2 per cent interest, held by CASA. Fokker of the Netherlands is also participating in the A300 and A310 programmes, as are companies from Belgium and Yugoslavia. De Havilland Canada participates in the latest A320 programme.

Two A300 prototypes were built, known as A300B1s, with one large 22 225-kg (49,000-lb)st General Electric CF6-50A turbofan engine under each advanced-design wing. Both prototypes were French

One of the Lockheed L-1011-100s and -200s operated by Gulf Air, an airline with its head office in Bahrain.

registered, as Aérospatiale is responsible for the final assembly of the aircraft in addition to the manufacture of certain component parts, which include the nose section of the fuselage. The transportation of large component parts of the Airbus from their country of manufacture to France for assembly is carried out by Super Guppy freighters (detailed in Chapter Five). One B1 was later brought up to airline standard and was purchased for commercial use by the Belgian operator TEA (Trans European Airways). The B1 is shorter in length than production Airbus airliners, with a seating capacity for 302 passengers.

The initial production version of the Airbus A300 is the A300B2-100, first flown in mid-1973. Compared to the A300B1, it has a fuselage 1.12 metres (3 feet 8¼ inches) greater in length, at 52.03 metres (170 feet 8½ inches). Power can be provided by one of two types of engine, namely the 23 130-kg (51,000-lb)st General Electric CF6-50C or the 23 814-kg (52,500-lb)st CF6-50C2 turbofan, giving rise to the respective designations A300B2-101 and B2-103. The first example of this version to enter commercial service was introduced by Air France on its Paris–London route in May 1974. The maximum cruising speed of this short- to medium-range airliner is 911 km/h (567 mph), the range is 3 334 km (2,074 miles) while carrying 269 passengers, and the maximum accommodation is for 336 passengers in a high-density seating arrangement.

Longer range was introduced into the Airbus A300 with the availability of the A300B4-100. Based on the A300B2, it has increased fuel capacity and a higher maximum take-off weight. It was the first version fitted with Krueger flaps on the wing leading edges at the roots to improve performance at take-off. The engines listed for the A300B2-100 are joined by the option of the 24 040-kg (53,000-lb)st Pratt & Whitney JT9D-59A turbofan, leading to the respective designations of A300B4-100s with -50C, -50C2 and JT9D-59A engines as A300B4-101, A300B4-103 and A300B4-120. Eastern Air Lines has ordered the largest fleet of Airbus A300s; its 34 aircraft include 17 A300B4-103s. However, the first example of the B4 to be delivered went to Germanair, with whom commercial services began in June 1975. This airline became part of Hapag-Lloyd in 1977, which now has five A300B4-103s as part of its Airbus fleet, one of which is leased out. The B4-120 has a range of 4 820 km (2,990 miles) while carrying 269 passengers.

A version of the A300B2 with Krueger flaps and other B4-100 features, making it particularly suitable for operation in hot climates and to and from high-altitude airports, is the A300B2-200. With the same engine options as those listed for the B4-100, its model designations are A300B2-201, A300B2-203 and A300B2-220. The first example was an A300B2-203 delivered to South African Airways in November 1976. Four form part of this airline's fleet of seven

Facing page: Air Canada Lockheed L-1011-500 TriStar.

L-1011-500 TriStar flown by BWIA International, the national carrier of Trinidad.

43

A300s. The Swedish airline SAS has received four similar A300B2-320s with an increase in payload.

In April 1979 Air France received the first A300B4-200, a strengthened version of the B4-100 to make possible the highest take-off weight of any A300 version, at 165 000 kg (363,760 lb). Although payload is slightly lower than that for the B4-100, a range of 5 375 km (3,340 miles) can be attained while carrying 269 passengers or 4 115 km (2,555 miles) with maximum payload. JT9D-59B engines join the options, producing the A300B4-221. With the same engine options as listed previously, the model designations are A300B4-201, A300B4-203 and A300B4-220. Air France ordered a total of 10 B4-203s as part of its 23 A300 aircraft fleet and Eastern included the same model as part of its fleet.

Recently, advanced versions of the A300B2 and B4 have become available under the new -600 series designation. Although the -600 is a lengthened version to increase both the maximum number of passengers that can be carried and the cargo capacity (by adopting the rear fuselage section of the A310 in modified form), the resulting A300B2-600 and A300B4-600 have the same maximum take-off weights as the A300B2-200 and B4-200. Payload is, however, increased. This has been made possible by careful examination of ways to reduce weight, including the use of some composite materials. Power for these versions is provided by two 25 401-kg (56,000-lb)st Pratt & Whitney JT9D-7R4H turbofan engines, giving the model designations A300B2-620 and B4-620. Saudi Arabian Airlines ordered the first -600s, comprising 11 A300B4-620s. Others have been delivered to Eastern Air Lines and Thai International (comprising two B4-620s in its fleet of 12 A300s).

More than 250 A300s of all versions, including the C4 convertible freighter, have been ordered, with the number currently in commercial service approaching 200. Of these, the first with FFCC (forward facing crew cockpit) flight deck layouts have gone into service, beginning with examples of the A300B4-220 for Garuda Indonesian Airways in 1982. The FFCC allows operation of the aircraft by a flight crew of two instead of the usual three. It was fitting that this airline should receive the first FFCC-equipped A300s, as the company's president, Mr Wiweko Soepono, conceived the idea. Under his direction, Garuda was also responsible for carrying the greatest number of passengers by a Boeing 747, totalling 542. The FFCC cockpit arrangement has already been mentioned, and is now standard on the latest Boeing wide-bodied airliner and on the latest Soviet Tupolevs.

In April 1982 the first example of an Airbus A300 derivative made its maiden flight as the A310. Basically a shorter length Airbus, with new advanced-design wings of 43.90-metre (144-feet 0$\frac{1}{4}$-inch) span (instead of the A300's 44.84-metre/147-feet 1-inch span), a reduced-area tailplane and other changes, its maximum seating capacity is 255 passengers. Its cruising speed can be 895 km/h (556 mph) while carrying 237 passengers and its range is 4 725 km (2,935 miles) with 255 passengers. The range quoted is for an A310 fitted with two 21 772-kg (48,000-lb)st General Electric CF6-80A1 turbofan engines (as A310-202), the version selected by Lufthansa for its fleet of 25. Other engine options include the 22,680-kg (50,000-lb)st CF6-80A3 (as A310-203), the 21 772-kg (48,000-lb)st Pratt & Whitney JT9D-7R4D1 (as A310-221), or the 22 680-kg (50,000-lb)st Rolls-Royce RB.211-524B4 (as A310-240). Swissair, the other launch airline for the A310, has ordered 10 A310-221s. So far just over 100 A310s have been ordered. Commercial services followed certification of the airliner in 1983. Other versions of the A310 are the C-200 convertible passenger/cargo airliner and the F-200 freighter.

The latest airliner proposed by Airbus Industrie is the A320 (to date ordered by Air France). Although belonging to the same family of airliners as the A300 and A310, it is a very different aircraft. Only 37.41 metres (122 feet 8$\frac{3}{4}$ inches) in overall length and with a wing span of 34.48 metres (113 feet 1$\frac{1}{2}$ inches), it has an internal fuselage width of 3.72 metres (12 feet 2$\frac{1}{2}$ inches), wider than typical narrow-body airliners but much narrower than existing wide-bodied airliners. Accommodation will provide seating for between 150 and 179 passengers, depending on the version, and engine power will be in the class of the CFM International CFM56, at 10 886 kg (24,000 lb)st. Expected to be very economical to operate, the A320 is still in the design stage.

A Soviet airliner of similar type to the Airbus, though larger and powered by four 13 000-kg (28,660-lb)st Kuznetsov NK-86

Prototype Airbus A310, with Lufthansa livery on one side and Swissair on the other.

turbofan engines installed in pods under the wings, is the Ilyushin Il-86. This is known to NATO by the name *Camber*. Its development began in the late 1960s and the first flight of this first Soviet wide-bodied passenger airliner took place in December 1976. Aeroflot received its first Il-86 in the latter part of 1979 and inaugurated services on a domestic route in December 1980. International services began in July 1981, with a flight from Moscow to East Berlin in the German Democratic Republic. The first export customer is the Polish state airline LOT, which is reported to have ordered four.

As can be seen from the accompanying illustration, the Il-86 is a conventional wide-bodied airliner. It can accommodate a normal maximum of 350 passengers, plus the usual containerized cargo in lower deck holds. The cruising speed is 950 km/h (590 mph) and the range with the maximum fuel load is said to be approximately 4 600 km (2,858 miles). A version of the airliner with more powerful engines and an increased range is likely to follow.

Concorde goes it alone

In October 1980 Air France received the final production Concorde supersonic airliner, ending a production run which covered just 16 aircraft. Of these, 14 entered service in equal number with British Airways and Air France and two remained development aircraft with the two manufacturing companies involved in the Concorde Supersonic Transport programme, British Aerospace and Aérospatiale. A further four Concordes were built, comprising the original two prototypes and two pre-production aircraft, all of which are now on display in Britain and France.

Concorde is currently the world's only supersonic airliner. In the 1960s it appeared that there were to be three types of supersonic airliner in service: Concorde, Boeing's Model 2707 SST and the Tupolev Tu-144.

The four-engined
Ilyushin Il-86 wide-body
airliner.

The Boeing aircraft had been selected for U.S. government backing in 1966, originally as a swing-wing airliner but from 1968 with fixed gull wings as the Model 2707-300. President Nixon gave approval for the construction of two prototypes in 1969 but in the early 1970s the official backing was withdrawn and Boeing abandoned the project. Cruising speed of the Model 2707-300 was to have been approximately Mach 2.7 and seating was to have been provided for 250 passengers in the original short-fuselage version, with a 321-seater to follow.

Meanwhile, the Soviet Union had been working on its own Mach 2 + airliner as the Tupolev Tu-144. The first prototype Tu-144 became the first supersonic airliner to fly, on the last day of 1968, and regular services at supersonic speeds carrying mail and other cargoes began over a domestic route in December 1976. In November of the following year scheduled passenger services started, again on the route between Moscow and Alma-Ata in Kazakhstan. After more

than 100 flights had been made, Tu-144 operations were suspended (in 1978) following an accident to one Tu-144, fortunately not being used on regular service. Thirteen Tu-144s had been completed.

In 1979 a refined version of the airliner appeared as the Tu-144D, with new engines to improve range and lower the noise emission and operating costs. This version undoubtedly also accommodated up to 140 passengers and it was expected that earlier production Tu-144s would be brought up to this standard for service with Aeroflot. However, despite the expectation that the Tu-144Ds would enter into regular service in 1981–82, it now appears that this airliner is not being operated. Interestingly, two Tu-144s were recently photographed flying alongside the Soviet Union's latest strategic bomber, another Tupolev design known to NATO as *Blackjack*.

With knowledge of the Boeing Model 2707-300 and the Tu-144, the operating

Plate III

British Aerospace/ Aérospatiale Concorde

cutaway drawing key

1 Variable geometry drooping nose
2 Weather radar
3 Spring pot
4 Visor jack
5 'A'-frame
6 Visor uplock
7 Visor guide rails and carriage
8 Droop nose jacks
9 Droop nose guide rails
10 Droop nose hinge
11 Rudder pedals
12 Captain's seat
13 Instrument panel shroud
14 Forward pressure bulkhead
15 Retracting visor
16 Multi-layer windscreen
17 Windscreen fluid rain clearance and wipers
18 Second pilot's seat
19 Roof panel
20 Flight-deck air duct
21 3rd crew member's seat
22 Control relay jacks
23 1st supernumerary's seat
24 2nd supernumerary's folding seat (optional)
25 Radio and electronics racks (Channel 2)
26 Radio and electronics racks (Channel 1)
27 Plug-type forward passenger door
28 Slide/life-raft pack stowage
29 Cabin staff tip-up seat
30 Forward galley units (port and starboard)
31 Toilets (2)

42 Nosewheel leg
43 Shock absorber
44 Twin nosewheels
45 Torque links
46 Steering mechanism
47 Telescopic strut
48 Lateral bracing struts
49 Nosewheel actuating jacks
50 Underfloor air-conditioning ducts
51 Nosewheel door actuator
52 Nosewheel secondary (aft) doors
53 Fuselage frame (single flange)
54 Machined window panel
55 Underfloor forward baggage compartment (237 cu ft/6.72cm³)
56 Fuel lines
57 Lattice ribs
58 No 9 (port forward) trim tank
59 Single-web spar
60 No 10 (port forward) trim tank
61 Middle passenger doors (port and starboard)
62 Cabin staff tip-up seat
63 Toilets

77 Removable leading-edge sections, with:
78 Expansion joints between sections
79 Contents unit
80 Inlet control valve
81 Transfer pumps
82 Flight-deck air duct
83 No 8 fuselage tank
84 Vapour seal above tank
85 Pressure-floor curved membranes
86 Pre-stretched integrally machined wing skin panels
87 No 8 wing tank
88 No 4 forward collector tank
89 No 10 starboard forward trim tank
90 No 9 starboard forward trim tank
91 Quick-lock removable inspection panels
92 Spraymat leading-edge de-icing panels

103 Inspection panels
104 Cold-air unit
105 Fuel-cooled heat exchanger
106 Fuel/hydraulic oil heat exchanger
107 Fire-suppression bottles
108 Main spar frame
109 Accumulator
110 No 3 aft collector tank
111 Control linkage
112 "Z"-section spot-welded stringers
113 Riser to distribution duct
114 Anti-surge bulkheads
115 No 6 (underfloor) fuel tank
116 Machined pressurised keel box

32 Coats (crew and passengers)
33 Twelve 26-man life-rafts
34 VHF1 antenna
35 Overhead baggage racks (with doors)
36 Cabin furnishing (heat and sound insulated)
37 4-abreast one-class passenger accommodation
38 Seat rails
39 Metal-faced floor panels
40 Nosewheel well
41 Nosewheel main doors

64 Emergency radio stowage
65 Provision for VHF3
66 Overhead baggage racks (with doors)
67 Cabin aft section
68 Fuselage frame
69 Tank vent gallery
70 No 1 forward collector tank
71 Lattice ribs
72 Engine-feed pumps
73 Accumulator
74 No 5 fuel tank
75 Trim transfer gallery
76 Leading-edge machined ribs

93 Leading-edge anti-icing strip
94 Spar-box machined girder side pieces
95 No 7 fuel tank
96 No 7a fuel tank
97 Static dischargers
98 Elevon
99 Inter-elevon flexible joint
100 Combined secondary nozzles/reverser buckets
101 Nozzle-mounting spigots
102 Cabin air delivery/ distribution

117 Fuselage frame
118 Double-flange frame/floor join
119 Machined pressure-floor support beams
120 Port undercarriage well
121 Mainwheel door
122 Fuselage/wing attachments
123 Main spar frame
124 Mainwheel retraction link
125 Mainwheel actuating jack
126 Cross beam
127 Forked link
128 Drag strut

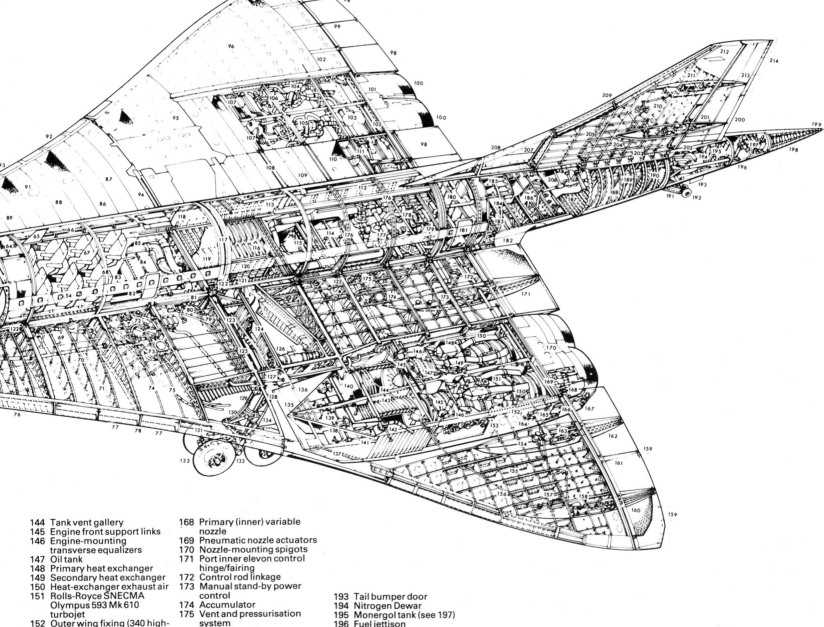

The sleek Concorde, the only supersonic airliner in regular use.

success of the Anglo-French Concorde is even more remarkable. The history of the Concorde dates from 1962, when agreements were signed regarding the development of the airliner by the British and French governments and the manufacturing companies involved in the project. The first prototype, known as Concorde 001, was assembled in France at Toulouse and flew for the first time in March 1969. The British prototype (002) took off on its maiden flight in April that year. The British Filton-built Concorde 01 became the first pre-production aircraft and the French 02 the second, flying initially in December

1971 and January 1973 respectively.

The first two production Concordes flew in December 1973 and February 1974 but remained with the manufacturers as development aircraft. Therefore, the first Concordes to enter airline service were the seventh and eighth to be built (Concordes 203 and 204). Interestingly, at one time the production future for the Concorde had looked very strong, with no fewer than 16 airlines having reserved option delivery positions on 74 aircraft. The subsequent failure to translate these options into delivered production aircraft cannot be seen as the fault of Concorde itself, which has

lived up to its promise.

The fifth and sixth production Concordes, in fact the ninth and tenth aircraft overall, first flew in October and November 1975 and were the first to be used on commercial services. These began on 21 January 1976, with Air France flying from Paris to Dakar and Rio de Janeiro and British Airways flying from London to Bahrain. The major breakthrough came on 24 May of the same year, when both airlines flew their first supersonic services to the United States, landing at Washington's Dulles International Airport. Meanwhile, Air France had started Concorde services to

Caracas. On 22 November 1977 both airlines opened services to New York. In December British Airways got together with Singapore Airlines to extend Concorde's Bahrain service to Singapore. In November 1977 and February 1978 respectively, Air France and British Airways began daily New York flights with Concorde, British Airways later increasing its services to 12 a week. In September 1978 Air France extended its Washington service to take in Mexico City. For a period the U.S. airline Braniff International was also involved with Concorde, operating a domestic service in conjunction with Air France and British Airways.

Concorde itself can cruise at above Mach 2, and at that speed it has a range of 6 230 km (3,870 miles). Accommodation is provided for 128 passengers, seated in a slender cabin with an internal width of 2.63 metres (8 feet $7\frac{1}{2}$ inches). The heart of the airliner is its four 17 260-kg (38,050-lb)st Rolls-Royce/SNECMA Olympus 593 Mk 610 turbojet engines, grouped in pairs under the ogival delta planform wings. Each wing has three elevons on the trailing-edge, which combine the functions of elevators and ailerons. The tail unit comprises a fin and rudder only. An interesting feature of the design is the aircraft's nose, which can be drooped hydraulically during take off and landing to improve forward vision for the pilots. A separate visor is raised hydraulically for cruising flight to fair the nose with the cockpit windscreen.

Development and manufacture of Concorde have given Britain and France a unique lead in advanced airliner technology. The fact that production was so limited does not detract from this. If the more conventional new airliners coming onto the aviation scene are going to prove typical of those requested by airlines for the remainder of this century, then the aspirations of those that backed supersonic development in Britain, France, the U.S.A. and the U.S.S.R. will be set aside for commercial priorities. But, artist impressions of airliners capable of supersonic cruising speeds (some in the 6 440 km/h; 4,000 mph range) continue to be produced. These, perhaps, indicate that one day airliners capable of flying between Los Angeles and Tokyo (or over similar routes) in times that require passengers to spend no more than $2\frac{1}{2}$ hours en route, may become commonplace.

3 The Past and the Future

Some of the airliners included in this chapter are among the oldest aircraft in commercial service today. Apart from well over 400 Douglas DC-3s, older piston-engined airliners employed by smaller airlines on passenger and/or freight services include the Curtiss C-46 Commando, Lockheed Constellation and Starliner, and the Convair Catalina amphibian. For the purpose of this chapter, passenger and freighter versions of older piston-engined airliners are detailed together.

Among the turboprop-powered airliners can be counted examples of the first such aircraft built, including the Vickers Viscount, Bristol Britannia, Lockheed Electra and Ilyushin Il-18. Although these date from past decades, airliners with turboprop engines are still being manufactured for a hungry market. Today, as in the past, it is the Soviet Union that produces the greatest number and range of turboprop-powered airliners, most of which are, however, employed mainly as freighters. The Soviet Union more than any other nation has been willing to accept the turboprop for major aircraft types, both military and civil, against the general trend of manufacturers abroad. Continuous development has left that nation with the world's most powerful turboprop engine, and has allowed aircraft with this form of engine to reach speeds close to those attained by aircraft with turbojet/turbofan engines.

It is easy to be mistaken into thinking that all large aircraft with propellers belong to bygone decades, even those powered by turboprop engines. Appearances can be very misleading. The fact is that a turboprop engine is not far removed from a turbofan. In very simple terms, these gas turbine engines each drive a form of propeller, easily visible on the turboprop and a shrouded multi-blade fan on the turbofan. It is because of the economy of operation offered by the turboprop, coupled with good range, that manufacturers in the U.S.A. and elsewhere are once again giving this type of engine another hard look. It is entirely possible that sometime in the future, possibly in the 1990s, a new range of large commercial and military transports will appear powered by prop-fan engines with multi-blade propellers. Very large transports powered by prop-fan engines driving perhaps 10-blade high-technology propellers at high speed have been mentioned, the engine/propeller arrangement reducing considerably the compressibility and noise problems normally associated with propeller-driven aircraft.

Piston power

In 1933 Boeing turned the commercial transport business upside down by producing its Model 247 airliner. This first truly modern airliner had low-mounted cantilever monoplane wings, enclosed cabins for the flight crew and passengers, a retractable undercarriage, and was of all-metal construction. Boeing could not keep pace with the number of airlines wishing to modernize their fleets resulting in the appearance soon after the first Model 247 of a rival from Douglas. From the Douglas DC-1 was developed the DC-2 and then the DC-3, the latter being offered in the form of the 14-passenger DST (Douglas Sleeper Transport) and 21-seat airliner. During the Second World War the DC-3 became a standard military transport; well over 10,000 were manufactured in military form and with military designations. When the several hundred DC-3s built for commercial service are added, this type has been the most widely flown transport aircraft in aviation history.

After the war many ex-military DC-3s, known also as C-47s and Dakotas, became available for purchase, together with a few newly built airliners. Two of the most important postwar conversions of ex-military aircraft were the DC-3C and DC-

3D, with reinforced structures and other changes. DC-3s were purchased by most airlines attempting to make a new beginning after the war. Each DC-3 normally accommodated between 21 and 28 passengers but many seated 36. Interestingly, the airliner was given several dates for withdrawal from service as it was considered below ICAO (International Civil Aviation Organization) standards, but over the years these were waived. Today the DC-3 and variants account for more than 400 of the world's airliners, used for passenger and freight services (although this represents a 50 per cent decrease from the figure reported in 1969).

The Dakota 4 version of the airliner is powered by two 1,200-hp Pratt & Whitney R-1830-90C or R-1830-90D piston engines. It can carry a maximum payload of 3 000 kg (6,620 lb), including 36 passengers, and has a cruising speed and range of 312 km/h (194 mph) and 2 430 km (1,510 miles) respectively. More than 170 airlines fly versions of the DC-3, most of which are small operators. One example of a larger airline still operating the type is Ethiopian Airlines, which counts nine in its fleet of airliners.

Because of the large number of DC-3s still flying, several attempts have been made to improve existing DC-3s by modification. One such modified type, produced by the Tri Turbo Corporation, was named the Tri Turbo-3, and was fitted with three 1,174-ehp Pratt & Whitney Aircraft of Canada PT6A-45 turboprops, the extra engine mounted in the fuselage nose. The latest conversion was produced by USAC (United States Aircraft Corporation), which, in July 1982, flew a version of the DC-3 with a lengthened fuselage and powered by two 1,254-ehp Pratt & Whitney Aircraft of Canada PT6A-45R turboprops. It is estimated that the economical cruising speed is 346 km/h (215 mph) and the payload is 5 955 kg (13,128 lb).

Douglas followed the DC-3 with the DC-4, which made its maiden flight as a four-engined airliner in mid-1938. The prototype did not match the requirements of interested airlines, resulting in a scaling-down and refinement of the design. In this

More than 400 Douglas DC-3s remain flying, this one in Peru.

51

form it first flew in February 1942. The U.S.A. by then was at war and the DC-4 left the production lines as the C-54 Skymaster military transport for the U.S.A.A.F. and R5D Skymaster for the U.S. Navy. A total of 1,163 military Skymasters was built, many of which became civil transports after the war. Douglas also produced 79 new commercial DC-4s after the war.

Today only 30 or so DC-4s remain in commercial use as passenger and cargo transports. As a passenger carrier, the DC-4 can accommodate up to 86 persons plus the usual freight carried in under-floor compartments. The cruising speed is 333 km/h (207 mph) and the range with the maximum payload of 9 695 kg (21,373 lb) is 1 850 km (1,150 miles). Apart from the use of four engines (1,450-hp Pratt & Whitney

Dominicana Douglas DC-6C, a conversion of the DC-6A for passengers or freight.

One of Air Haiti's two Curtiss C-46A Commandos.

R-2000-2SD-13G piston engines), an important feature of the DC-4 over the DC-3 is its nosewheel-type undercarriage, which leaves the fuselage level when the aircraft is at rest. This helps loading and unloading, which is especially important for those DC-4s employed as freighters with large doors and special floors.

In 1946 Douglas flew the prototype of a new transport, which had been ordered for military evaluation. Eventually the U.S.A.F. and U.S. Navy received 167 production examples under C-118/R6D Liftmaster designations. However, for the first time since the DC-2, most aircraft built as new were for commercial service. The new airliner became the long-range DC-6, a pressurized development of the DC-4 with a longer fuselage but similar span wing. Three versions were produced, totalling 537 aircraft, of which fewer than 100 remain in use today. These comprised the standard DC-6 with four 2,400-hp Pratt & Whitney R-2800 piston engines, the DC-6A freighter with a longer fuselage, and the DC-6B with the longest fuselage of all. The DC-6B, powered by four 2,400-hp R-2800-CB-16 or 2,500-hp R-2800-CB-17 piston engines, was the main production version, with accommodation for 108 passengers. A further version was produced by the conversion of the DC-6A, resulting in an airliner with similar accommodation to the DC-6B or which could be employed as a freighter. Today, DC-6s and DC-6Bs are the only versions flown, the latter with a maximum cruising speed of 507 km/h (315 mph) and a normal range with maximum payload of 4 835 km (3,005 miles).

Douglas also produced an enlarged and more powerful version of the DC-6, known as the DC-7, which first came onto the aviation scene in 1953. Three versions were built: the final version was known as the DC-7C Seven Seas, with accommodation for 65 to 105 passengers. Power for all versions was provided by four Wright R-3350 Turbo-Compound engines, each rated at 3,250 to 3,400 hp. However, whereas the smaller and shorter-range piston-engined airliners managed to find employment amidst the proliferation of subsequent jets, the intercontinental piston-engined airliners did not. Conversion of DC-7 passenger airliners into freighters helped prolong their useful life (producing the DC-7F freighter) but today only a handful of DC-7 types remain in commercial use.

Older than the DC-4, DC-6 and DC-7 is the Curtiss Commando, which first flew in prototype form as a pressurized and capacious airliner in 1940. But it was in unpressurized form that the Commando went into production as the C-46 military transport for service during the Second World War, each accommodating 40 troops, 33 stretchers or freight. Production totalled about 3,000 aircraft, of which many hundreds were converted for civil use after the war. Although many of these were fitted-out as 62-passenger airliners, the majority were put to use as freighters in several forms. These included the C-46D with two 2,000-hp Pratt & Whitney R-2800-51M1 piston engines and double doors for easy cargo loading and unloading. Today approximately 50 Commandos remain in commercial use in North and South America. The maximum cruising speed of the C-46D is 301 km/h (187 mph), its range is 1 883 km (1,170 miles) when carrying a 2 585 kg (5,700 lb) payload, and the maximum payload is 7 983 kg (17,600 lb).

Yet another airliner that got entangled in the Second World War was the Lockheed Constellation. Conceived as an intercontinental airliner for Transcontinental & Western Air (later TWA), with a payload of 2 722 kg (6,000 lb), the prototype was taken over by the U.S.A.A.F. The first flight was achieved in 1943. The 22 U.S.A.A.F. Constellations, known in military service as C-69s, were those ordered initially by airlines. After a year in military service these were returned to civil status. (Interestingly, C-69s ordered by the military were completed as civil aircraft, following the end of hostilities.)

A gracious-looking airliner with a long thin fuselage ending with a triple fin and rudder tail unit, the Constellation was well-received in commercial service. Several versions were produced, followed in turn by the longer Super Constellation and the final variant, the L-1649A Starliner. The latter aircraft was produced with four 3,400-hp Wright R-3350-988TC18EA-2 Turbo-Compound engines, allowing a cruising speed of 520 km/h (323 mph) and a range, while carrying the maximum payload, of 8 690 km (5,400 miles). Today, five Constellations and Super Constellations and a single Starliner remain in commercial use, mainly for long-haul freight transport.

Convair began a series of postwar airliners with the Convair-Liner 240, a series which commenced with the first flight of a CV-240 prototype in March 1947 and ended with the CV-990 Coronado (detailed previously). These marked the company's progression from airliners with piston engines to others with turbojets and then turbofans. The CV-240 was seen by Convair as a modern replacement for the DC-3. It offered a much increased maximum take-off weight of 22 544 kg (42,500 lb), accommodation for 40 passengers, a level fuselage (thanks to the nosewheel-type undercarriage) and the power of two 2,400-hp Pratt & Whitney R-2800-CA18 radial engines. It was built in substantial number but today only 20 or so are still in airline use.

Increased size and weight were introduced with the Convair-Liner 340, accommodating 44 passengers. Production of this model ended in 1955, with the delivery of two airliners to the Brazilian airline REAL. In the early 1980s fewer of this version

Nor-Fly of Norway operates two Convair 580s.

remain in commercial use than other Convair airliners, with just a handful in service with airlines in North, Central and South America.

Convair completed its range of postwar piston-engined airliners with the CV-440 Metropolitan of 1955. Based upon the Convair-Liner 340 and with two similar 2,500-hp R-2800-CB17 engines, it introduced new engine nacelles and other refinements. The cabin noise level for the 44 to 52 passengers was reduced, and the economical cruising speed and range were quoted as 465 km/h (289 mph) and 2092 km (1,300 miles) respectively. Despite fewer CV-440s being built than earlier aircraft by the close of production in 1958, more of these remain in use today than CV-240s and CV-340s added together (more than 40).

The remaining three Convair airliners in the series were all produced as turboprop conversions of the piston-engined models. U.S. engine manufacturer Allison became responsible for converting CV-340s and CV-440s into CV-580s, by replacing the original engines with two 3,750-eshp Allison 501-D13 turboprops. Well over 100 were produced, and of these Allegheny Airlines alone operated 42. More than 90 are still in commercial use.

The CV-600 and CV-640 were produced as conversions of the Convair-Liner 240 and Convair-Liner 340/CV-440 respectively,

ADSA-Aerolineas Dominicanas SA has a fleet of Martin 4-0-4s (as seen here) and a DC-3.

each re-engined under a joint programme with Rolls-Royce with two 3,025-ehp Dart RDa.10 Mk 542-4 turboprops. The first CV-600 flew in May 1965 and began commercial operations in November of that year, followed in December by services with the first CV-640. The CV-640 has a cruising speed of 482 km/h (300 mph) and a range of 1975 km (1,230 miles). Accommodation can be for up to 56 passengers.

Since the 1950s Convair has been a division of the General Dynamics Corporation and still has the tooling necessary to produce important components to support CV-240 to CV-990A airliners. The name Convair had been adopted a few years prior to this by the Consolidated Vultee Aircraft Corporation, itself formed in 1943 by a merger of the Consolidated Aircraft Corporation and Vultee Aircraft Incorporated. One product of the former Consolidated Aircraft Corporation had been the famous Catalina flying-boat/amphibian, which served extensively during the Second World War with several air forces, including those of the U.S.A., U.K., U.S.S.R., Australia and New Zealand. The Canadian Vickers works built 379 Catalinas, in that country known as Cansos, and some were used by the R.C.A.F. After they had run their course of military service, some Catalinas/Cansos found their way into civil use. In the early 1980s approximately seven are flown

commercially, carrying passengers or freight, mostly in Canada but with some in Chile. A further number are employed as water-bombers; Avalon Aviation for one uses Cansos. The PBY-5 Catalina has two 1,200-hp Pratt & Whitney R-1830 radial engines, carried on the leading-edge of the parasol wing. The maximum speed is about 282 km/h (175 mph) and the range is more than 3 200 km (2,000 miles). Avalon Aviation also converts Cansos/Catalinas into water-bombers for firefighting and has developed a turboprop-engined version with two Rolls-Royce Dart engines, known as Turbo-Cansos.

A rival for the Convair-Liner was Martin's 4-0-4, of which 101 of the 103 built went to Eastern Air Lines and TWA from 1951. Like the CV, it too was powered by two 2,400-hp R-2800 radial engines, although in the -CB16 version. It could boast a cruising speed of 450 km/h (280 mph) and a range of 1 738 to 4 184 km (1,080 to 2,600 miles). In the early 1980s more than a dozen remained in commercial use.

Similar in concept to the American Convair-Liner and Martin 4-0-4 was the Soviet Ilyushin Il-14. Known to NATO as *Crate*, it first appeared in 1953 and was produced in thousands in factories in the Soviet Union, East Germany and Czechoslovakia. Two main versions were produced as the 18- to 26-passenger Il-14P and the lengthened 24- to 28-passenger Il-14M; the latter became the major production version. Both East Germany and Czechoslovakia built the Il-14P, but Czechoslovakia went on to develop its own versions as the 32-passenger Avia 14-32A (based on the Il-14M), the Avia 14T freighter and the pressurized 42-passenger Avia 14 Salon with longer range by virtue of wingtip fuel tanks.

Today it is believed that well over 200 Il-14s remain in use as passenger and cargo transports. Of these, Aeroflot still has the largest number (probably converted passenger versions for use as freighters); other users include CAAC with more than 50 (being replaced by Xian Y-7s). Each is powered by two 1,900-hp Shvetsov ASh-82T piston engines, giving a maximum cruising speed and range of 318 km/h (198 mph) and 1 480 km (920 miles) respectively.

CAAC Ilyushin Il-14 at Guangzhou in China.

The turboprop revolution

In the 1940s, with war still raging in Europe and elsewhere, Britain set up the Brabazon Committee to form recommendations as to the types of commercial aircraft Britain should develop for postwar use. This early start was expected to give Britain a chance not only to catch up with the U.S. aircraft manufacturing industry but to lead the world. Although some aircraft built to its recommendations proved unsuccessful, such as the huge eight-engined Bristol Type 167 Brabazon airliner, others became world-beaters. The de Havilland Comet, the world's first turbojet-powered airliner, was one example and another was the Vickers Viscount.

In the early 1940s, turbojet engines were new enough but turboprop engines were an even more recent development. Rolls-Royce was engaged in the development of both types of engine during the Second World War and indeed an early form of turboprop was flight-tested on one of the Gloster Meteor jet-fighter prototypes. Further work led the company to produce the Dart which, in 1945, had a power rating of only 990-ehp. Interestingly, this turboprop engine remains in development and production today, with power ratings of 3,025-ehp in civil form and higher in military.

As the airliner recommended by the Brabazon Committee as the Type IIB, Vickers designed the Viscount. This was intended to be a short- to medium-range airliner, powered by four Dart turboprop engines. Work started in April 1945 and the prototype appeared in 1948. BEA was to be the launch airline but it had voiced serious doubts as to whether the airliner could be operated economically. It was under this cloud that the prototype first flew in July 1948. However, from the start it was clear that the Viscount was a superb aircraft, with high but economical performance.

BEA was delighted with what it saw, not least because the Viscount could be operated as a pressurized airliner capable of flying above bad weather, so giving passengers an exceptionally smooth and pleasant journey. This benefit was coupled with others offered by the turboprop engines. As a result, a new specification was drawn up for a version with increased all-up weight and accommodation for 43 passengers. A few days prior to this new aircraft's first

flight, as the Viscount 700 in August 1950, BEA placed an order for no fewer than 20 production Viscount 701s, an order subsequently to be increased.

With the Viscount, BEA flew the first commercial passenger service with a turbine-powered airliner in the world, of either turboprop or turbojet types. In this respect the Viscount beat Britain's Comet, introducing passengers to the advantages of flying the new generation airliners. The Viscount also proved a commercial success in terms of the number built, which exceeded 440 for operation in many countries including the United States. Various designations were used within the Series 700 type number, indicating delivery to different airlines, and passenger accommodation was provided for up to 63 persons.

The Series 700D introduced more powerful Dart engines and wing slipper fuel tanks, increased weights and accommodation for up to 59 passengers. Those Series 700Ds for U.S. customers became Series 770Ds. In July 1956 the Series 800 appeared, powered by 1,890-ehp Dart Mk 520 engines. A longer fuselage for up to 65 passengers was a feature of this version, with the associated increase in weight, but the range was reduced.

The most powerful version of the Viscount was built as the Series 810, powered by four 1,990-ehp Dart Mk 525 turboprop engines and with the longer fuselage of the Series 800 to accommodate up to 75 passengers. Convertible passenger/cargo interior layouts became available for the Series 800 and 810, designed by Scottish Aviation, with a maximum payload of 6 750 kg (14,900 lb) as a freighter. Production of the Viscount ended in the early 1960s, with the delivery of six to the recently reformed CAAC (Civil Aviation Administration of China), which still operated five in the early 1980s. The maximum cruising speed of the Series 810 is 576 km/h (358 mph) and the range is 2 775 km (1,725 miles). At the time of writing, more than 60 Viscounts remain in service with about 17 airlines, with the largest number operated in the U.K. by British Air Ferries (five) and British Midland Airways.

To meet BEA's requirement for a considerably larger airliner of Viscount type, Vickers evolved the Vanguard. The prototype made its maiden flight in January 1959. BEA and Trans-Canada Air Lines (which became Air Canada in 1964) both

Right: Afrek Bristol 175
Britannia.

One of Air UK's
Handley Page Herald
twin-turboprop airliners.

introduced the Vanguard into commercial service in early 1961. In 1968 BEA started converting Vanguards into Merchantman freighters, which remained in British Airways service throughout the 1970s.

The Vanguard was built to accommodate between 76 and 139 passengers. Power for the Type 952 was provided by four 5,545-ehp Rolls-Royce Tyne RTy 11 Mk 512 turboprop engines, giving a maximum cruising speed and range, with the maximum payload of 16 783 kg (37,000 lb), of 684 km/h (425 mph) and 2 945 km (1,830 miles) respectively.

Today there are approximately 10 Vanguard/Merchantman aircraft with airlines. The Indonesian airline Merpati Nusantara operates three passenger-carrying Vanguards. However, the largest number of aircraft are owned by the British airline Air Bridge Carriers, which has six freight-carrying Merchantman aircraft. Of these, three are normally in use at any one time and are based on the Vanguard 953C with 4,985-ehp Tyne Mk 506 engines. A cargo

door and other modifications were introduced by Aviation Traders during conversion.

Approximately the same number of Bristol 175 Britannia medium- to long-range airliners remain in service as Vanguards/ Merchantmen, although none with British airlines. The Britannia was developed to serve on BOAC's Empire routes and the prototype flew for the first time in August 1952. Several versions were produced, with various models of the Bristol Siddeley Proteus turboprop engine and with fuselages of varying lengths to accommodate between 82 and 133 passengers. With the much-developed Series 310 (actually known as a Series 312 in BOAC service), BOAC inaugurated the world's first service across the North Atlantic with turbine-powered airliners, beginning on 19 December 1957. Unfortunately for Bristol, although the Britannia was entirely successful from the point of view of design and performance, the appearance of turbojet airliners prevented a greater extent of service.

Production ended after 80 or so Britannias had been completed, a total which included 23 for the R.A.F. Twenty-two of these military Britannias were put up for sale in the mid-1970s and most Britannias in use today are probably of this type. The Britannia Series 310 and ex-R.A.F. aircraft are generally similar. Power is provided by four 4,445-ehp Proteus 765 turboprop engines mounted on the leading-edges of the long straight tapered wings. The maximum payload is 15 830 kg (34,900 lb), and the maximum cruising speed and range are 647 km/h (402 mph) and 6 868 km (4,268 miles) respectively. Only two Britannias are operated in Europe, by the Greek airline Afrek.

Another British turboprop airliner that first appeared in the 1950s was the short-range Handley Page Herald. Interestingly, the Herald had been designed to operate on the power of four piston engines, and it was with these fitted that the first prototype flew. However, the obvious success of turboprop-powered airliners and their impact upon airline operators led to a reappraisal of the engine arrangement, resulting in the selection of two Rolls-Royce Dart turboprops as standard. A Dart-engined prototype made its maiden flight in March 1958.

Several versions of the Herald were built or projected and examples of two of these are still widely flown. The initial Series 100 was the short-fuselage version, accommodating 44 passengers. BEA received three. A single example remains, formerly operated by British Air Ferries. The major production version became the Series 200, with a longer fuselage to accommodate up to 56 passengers. Power for this version comes from two 2,105-ehp Dart RDa 7 Mk 527 turboprops, bestowing a maximum cruising speed and range with maximum payload of 443 km/h (275 mph) and 1 125 km (700 miles) respectively. Of the Heralds still in commercial service in the early 1980s, two-thirds are of this version. The major operator of this version and of the Herald in general is Air UK, which has 10 Series 200s and a single Series 400. Another well-known operator is British Air Ferries, with two Series 200s.

The Series 400 is the version of the Herald originally supplied to the Royal Malaysian Air Force but withdrawn from military service in 1977 and acquired thereafter for commercial use. Eight were built, most of which continue to be flown.

The only turboprop airliner currently being manufactured in the U.K. with accommodation for more than 40 passengers is

BAe HS 748 operated in New Zealand by Mount Cook Line.

the British Aerospace HS 748. Of course,
other turboprop airliners are built in the
U.K., examples being the Shorts 330 and
360 and the Pilatus Britten-Norman Islander, but these are commuter/feederline
transports carrying fewer passengers and as
such are detailed in a later chapter.

Design of what became the Hawker
Siddeley 748 (later the BAe HS 748) began
in 1959, as a short- to medium-range
turboprop-powered airliner. The first
prototype made its maiden flight in mid-
1960 and the type was introduced into
service in Series 1 production form by
Skyways Coach Air in 1962. Only 18 Series
1 aircraft with 1,880-ehp Rolls-Royce Dart
514 engines were built. The Series 2 and 2A
followed, the former powered by two 2,105-
ehp Dart 531 engines and the latter with
either two 2,280-ehp Dart RDa.7 Mk 534-2
or Mk 535-2 engines (formerly known as
RDa.7 Mk 532-2L and Mk 532-2S respectively). The cruising speed of the Series 2A is
452 km/h (281 mph) and the range with the
maximum 58 passengers is 1 361 km (846
miles).

Series 2s and 2As make up the bulk of the
360 HS 748s so far sold to civil and military
customers (the latter including Andover
military transports for the R.A.F.; two used
by The Queen's Flight). Although the
Series 2A is still offered to customers, the
new Series 2B is the latest version of the HS
748. The engine power remains the same as
for the Series 2A, the RDa.7 Mk 536-2s
carried on the leading edges of the straight
tapered wings. The wings themselves have
increased span and the usual 7 degrees of
dihedral. These, coupled with the new
engines and other modifications and refinements to reduce drag, help make this model
well-suited for operation from high-altitude
airports and in hot climates. The first Series
2B was delivered to Air Madagascar in early
1980. Air Virginia operates the Series 2B
known under the U.S. name Intercity 748.

The very latest version of the HS 748 is
the Series 2B Super. This has a restyled
flight deck and galley and other changes,
the most significant of which have been
aimed at reducing the noise level of the
engines and vibration caused by the four-

blade propellers. The engines are fitted with so-called hush-kits, available also for installation on the engines of previous HS 748 models. A freighter version of the Series 2B is available. The HS 748 is also being assembled in India by Hindustan Aeronautics Limited (HAL), some of which are for use by Indian Airlines. The maximum range of the Series 2B while carrying a 3 660 kg (8,070 lb) payload is 2 630 km (1,635 miles).

British Aerospace is currently working on an advanced version of the HS 748 for service in the latter half of this decade. Known as the BAe ATP (Advanced Turboprop), it will represent a major redesign when it appears in 1985. Although based on the earlier airliner, the ATP will be lengthened to allow accommodation for up to 64 passengers, the nose of the fuselage will be restyled and the tailfin and rudder will be swept back. Power will be provided by two 2,520-ehp Pratt & Whitney Aircraft of Canada PW100/9 turboprop engines driving six-blade advanced propellers. In this form, the cruising speed is estimated to be 474 km/h (295 mph) and the range will be 1 390 km (863 miles) with a full passenger load.

Among the most successful turboprop-powered airliners ever built must be counted the Fokker F27 Friendship, a medium-range airliner originating in the Netherlands. Examples of the Friendship can be found in all parts of the world, including military versions for transport and specialized roles. The first prototype F27 took off for the first time in November 1955 as a 28-passenger airliner. The second

prototype had a higher seating capacity, further increased to a maximum of 52 for the first production version, the F27 Mk 100. This version remains in airline service, each aircraft powered by two 1,715-shp Rolls-Royce Dart RDa.6 Mk 514-7 turboprop engines carried under the high-mounted straight tapered wings.

Production of the F27 Mk 100 totalled 85. The first delivery took place in November 1958, to Aer Lingus. This airline began F27 operations during the following month. Simultaneously, the Friendship was produced under licence in the U.S.A. by Fairchild Industries, under F-27 designations initially. It was a Fairchild-built F-27 that was the first Friendship in commercial service, flown by West Coast Airlines from September 1958. F-27s were built with Mk 511 engines.

The first Friendship update came with the Mk 200, powered by two 2,050-shp Dart RDa.7 Mk 532-7 engines. Fairchild's equivalent became the F-27A, but with RDa.6 or the RDa.7 engines. A business version was also produced for the U.S. market as the F-27F. The Mk 200 built in the Netherlands remains available for purchase today, offered with 2,140-shp RDa.7 Mk 536-7R engines and airliner (44 or 48 passengers maximum) and executive transport (with conference room, rest room and lounge as standard) interiors.

The F27 Mk 300 was the initial Combiplane version, suitable for use as a cargo carrier or for a mixed passenger/cargo load. The cabin floor was strengthened and a large freight door fitted (in place of the standard door) on the port side of the

Five of Air UK's Fokker F27 Mk 200 Friendships on Pier A at Schiphol, Amsterdam.

forward fuselage to ease loading and unloading of cargo. Only 13 Mk 300s were built, the U.S. equivalent being the F-27B. The current Combiplane version is the Mk 400, but this is only built to order. It can accommodate 48 passengers, or a smaller number with cargo as a mixed load, or cargo only. Another cargo-carrying version, known as the Mk 700, was a modification of the Mk 100 and only one was built. Although the Combiplane versions have been less successful than the all-passenger versions in terms of numbers built, the Mk 400 continues to form the basis of the military transport derivative and a cartographic version for aerial survey work with two wide-angle cameras.

In late 1967 Fokker flew the prototype of its F27 Mk 500. Based on the Mk 200, the Mk 500 has an overall length of 25.06 metres (82 feet $2\frac{1}{2}$ inches), compared to 23.56 metres (77 feet $3\frac{1}{2}$ inches) for all other versions. A large freight door is standard. The accommodation provides for up to 60 passengers, although 52 is normal. The maximum take-off weight is also raised, to 19 050 kg (42,000 lb), an increase of 454 kg (1,000 lb) over the Mk 200. The typical

cruising speed of the Mk 500 is similar to that of previous versions, at 480 km/h (298 mph), but the range with the normal passenger load is 1 741 km (1,082 miles).

The most recent Fokker-produced commercial version of the Friendship dates from 1968. This is the Mk 600, which remains available for purchase. Reverting to the Mk 200 fuselage and using the standardized Mk 536-7R engines, it has accommodation for 44 passengers. However, this model also has features of the Combiplane, in so much as the purchaser has the option of buying a quick-change interior, enabling a speedy changeover from a passenger interior layout to a cargo-carrying interior. The large freight door of earlier versions is standard but the Mk 600 does not have the Combiplane's strengthened floor. Range for the Mk 600 is similar to that of the Mk 200, at 1 926 km (1,197 miles) while carrying 44 passengers.

Fairchild has not produced variants of the F27 for some years, having made available versions of the lengthened Mk 500 (as FH-227s) as well as standard length F-27s which included the powerful F-27J and M. By the early 1980s Fokker had sold

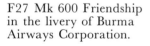

F27 Mk 600 Friendship in the livery of Burma Airways Corporation.

The Lockheed L.188A
Electra is commonly
used as a freighter.

537 Friendships, including 113 Mk 200s and 95 Mk 500s. Fairchild produced slightly more than 200 F-27s/FH-227s, of which 80 or so remain in use. Air UK operates one of the largest fleets of standard-length Friendships, with 14 F27-200s, while Air France has one of the largest fleets of Mk 500s. Recently, Air New Zealand and Garuda Indonesian Airways ordered the largest numbers of new Friendships, at six aircraft each.

In December 1957, Lockheed flew the first of its L-188 Electra medium-range airliners. The company had the advantage of big orders already placed by U.S. airlines, who were looking for a turboprop-powered airliner suited to domestic operations. Indeed, Lockheed had received its first order for the Electra two years earlier, when American Airlines had requested 35 off the drawing board. But American Airlines was not the first to put the Electra into service. This honour went to Eastern Air Lines, which introduced the airliner on 12 January 1959, 11 days before American Airlines services began.

The Electra was produced in two versions, totalling 165 aircraft. The last of these was delivered in May 1962 and today more than 80 remain in commercial service. However, most are used as freighters, having been converted by Lockheed Aircraft Services from the initial L-188A domestic Electra and the L-188C longer-range version that had been built to accommodate

between 66 and 99 passengers. Power is provided by four 3,750-ehp Allison 501-D13 turboprop engines, carried on the leading edges of the straight tapered wings. The maximum payload that can be carried is 12 020 kg (26,500 lb). The cruising speed is 652 km/h (405 mph) and a typical range is 4 458 km (2,770 miles).

In the same year that the Electra first flew, Ilyushin's follow-on to the Il-14 made its maiden flight (in July) as the Il-18. Larger and heavier than the Electra, the Il-18 entered service with Aeroflot in 1959. It is believed that more than 700 Il-18s were produced, of which 560 or so entered airline service. It has been reported that between entering service and 1979, those Il-18s flown by Aeroflot had accumulated 12 million hours in the air, carrying 235 million passengers.

Three versions of the Il-18 were produced for airline use. The basic version was the Il-18V, accommodating 90 to 110 passengers. This is the lowest-powered version, with four 4,000-ehp Ivchenko AI-20K turboprop engines carried on the leading edges of the straight tapered wings. The two follow-on versions were the Il-18D and Il-18E. Both were produced with 4,250-ehp AI-20M engines, the 'D' having additional fuel capacity which reduced accommodation from 90–122 passengers to a normal 65. Maximum cruising speed of the developed versions is 675 km/h (419 mph), the range of the Il-18D 3 700 km (2,300 miles).

Ilyushin Il-18 at
Chengdu in China, in
the colours of CAAC.

Approximately half the Il-18s built for
airline use remain in service today. Of these,
Aeroflot retains the largest fleet and the
majority of all remaining Il-18s. A number
have been modified into freighters for continued service with Aeroflot, at Moscow's
Factory 402. Changes include a stripped
interior with a reinforced floor and the
addition of a large cargo-loading door in the
rear fuselage. Other airlines that continue
to fly Il-18s (known to NATO as *Coots*)
include CAAC (being replaced by Xian
Y-7s), CSA, Interflug, LOT, Malev and
Tarom (all but the first being east European
airlines).

Many Soviet Antonov transports are included in the chapter dealing with freighters. However, the Antonov An-24 (NATO
Coke) is an exception, although this also is
widely operated as a freighter in its An-24T
and An-24RT versions. Development of the
An-24 began in 1958, as a modern replacement for piston-engined transports then
being operated by Aeroflot as feederliners.
The 44-seat prototype made its maiden
flight in 1960 and the first production An-
24s to serve with Aeroflot began short-haul
domestic services from Moscow in September 1963. Production ended in the
Soviet Union in 1978, after approximately

1,100 had been built. The majority of these remain in service with many airlines (more than 850, including about 150 of those An-24s exported), while others became military aircraft. Tarom of Romania is a major operator of exported An-24s, with more than 30 in service.

Because of its feederline role with Aeroflot, the An-24 was designed to be capable of operating from all types of runway, including natural. For cargo operations, it can be fitted with rocket units to boost power during take off in high temperatures while carrying the maximum payload. At the other end of the temperature scale, the An-24 has been operated to support stations in the Antarctic. It has a circular-section fuselage, high-mounted wings and dihedral on the tailplane only, which is slightly swept back.

Early production An-24s were of the Series I type, each powered by two 2,550-ehp Ivchenko AI-24 turboprop engines. Later production aircraft were of the Series II type and were produced in five basic versions. The standard version was built as the An-24V Series II. Based on the Series I, it has two similarly-rated AI-24A engines with water injection and was offered in 44- to 52-seat passenger, VIP, mixed passenger/cargo, convertible, and freighter versions. The maximum payload of this version is 5 500 kg (12,125 lb), the cruising speed is 450 km/h (280 mph) and the range can vary between 550 and 2 400 km (341 and 1,490 miles), depending on the payload/fuel carried.

A firefighting version of the An-24 was produced as the 'P' (for Pozharny). This appeared in 1971 and was intended to parachute firefighters into forest areas. To improve upon the high altitude and hot-

Ilyushin Il-18V flown by LOT-Polish Airlines.

Plate IV

De Havilland Canada Dash 7

cutaway drawing key

1 Radome
2 Weather radar scanner
3 Radar transmitter and receiver units
4 Nose electronics compartment
5 Radio and electronics racks
6 Front pressure bulkhead
7 Twin nosewheels
8 Nosewheel doors
9 Control runs beneath cockpit floor
10 Rudder pedals
11 Instrument panel
12 Windscreen wipers
13 Windscreen panels
14 Instrument panel shroud
15 Overhead switch panel
16 Co-pilot's seat
17 Control column handwheel
18 Pilot's seat
19 Nosewheel steering control
20 Pitot tubes
21 Circuit breaker panel
22 Cockpit bulkhead
23 Electrical distribution panel
24 Cabin roof control runs
25 Cabin trim panels
26 Rearward facing seat row
27 Seat attachment rails
28 Emergency exit window panel, port and starboard
29 Four-abreast passenger seating, 50-seats
30 VHF aerial
31 Fuselage frame and stringer construction
32 Floor beam construction

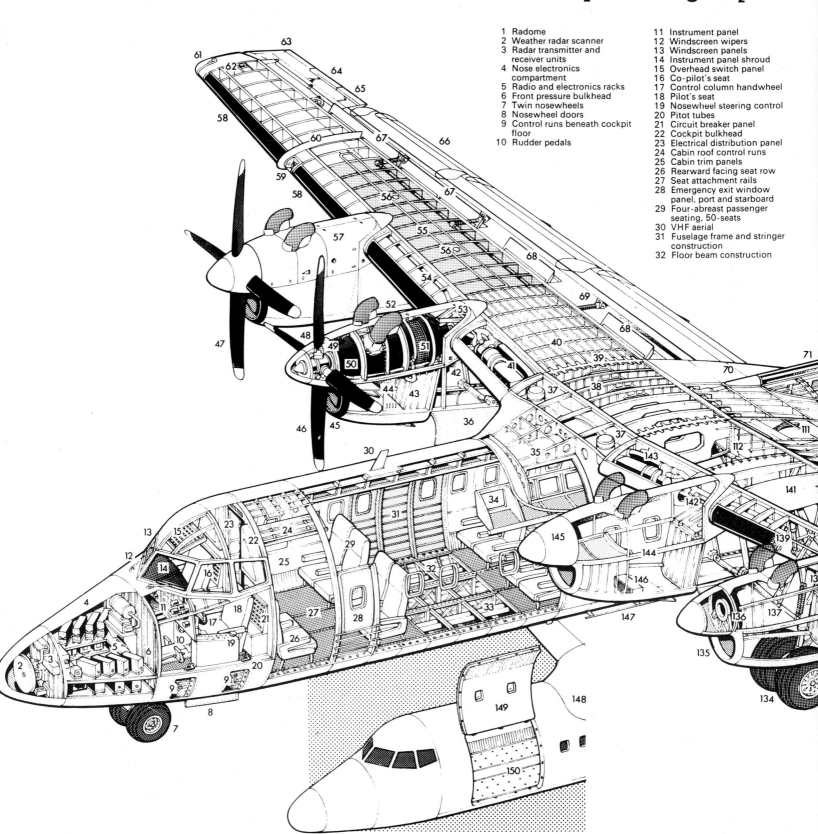

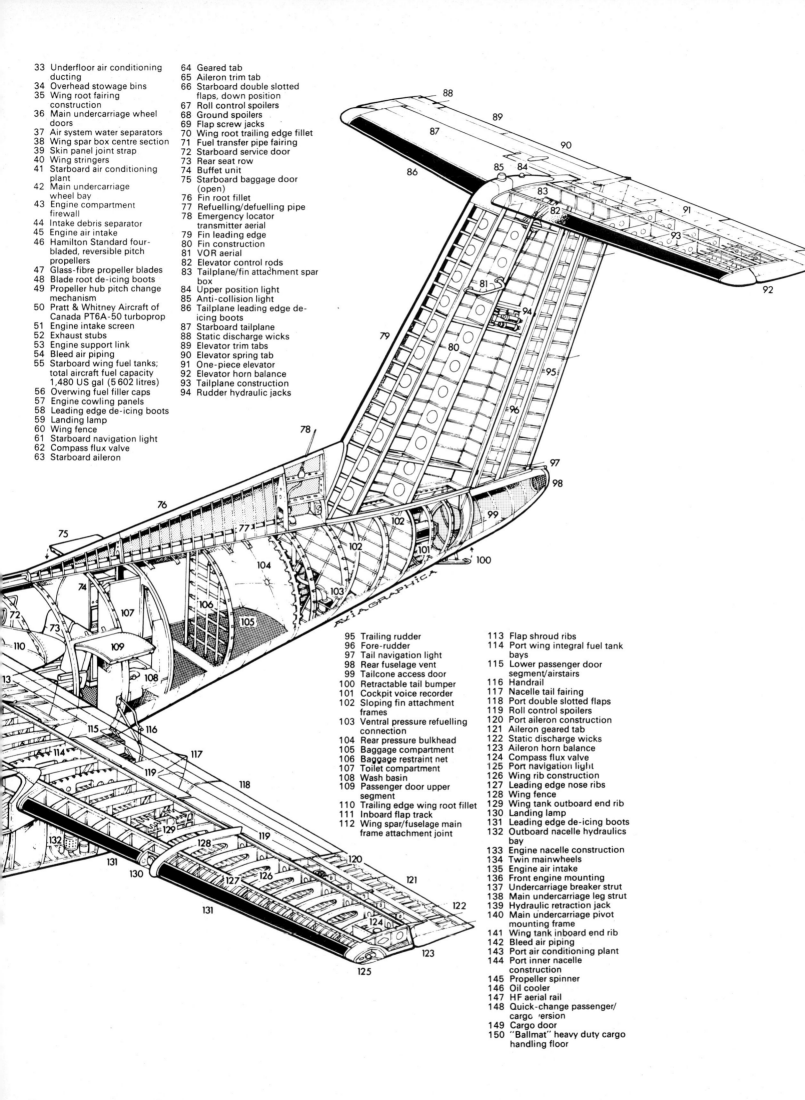

33 Underfloor air conditioning ducting
34 Overhead stowage bins
35 Wing root fairing construction
36 Main undercarriage wheel doors
37 Air system water separators
38 Wing spar box centre section
39 Skin panel joint strap
40 Wing stringers
41 Starboard air conditioning plant
42 Main undercarriage wheel bay
43 Engine compartment firewall
44 Intake debris separator
45 Engine air intake
46 Hamilton Standard four-bladed, reversible pitch propellers
47 Glass-fibre propeller blades
48 Blade root de-icing boots
49 Propeller hub pitch change mechanism
50 Pratt & Whitney Aircraft of Canada PT6A-50 turboprop
51 Engine intake screen
52 Exhaust stubs
53 Engine support link
54 Bleed air piping
55 Starboard wing fuel tanks; total aircraft fuel capacity 1,480 US gal (5 602 litres)
56 Overwing fuel filler caps
57 Engine cowling panels
58 Leading edge de-icing boots
59 Landing lamp
60 Wing fence
61 Starboard navigation light
62 Compass flux valve
63 Starboard aileron

64 Geared tab
65 Aileron trim tab
66 Starboard double slotted flaps, down position
67 Roll control spoilers
68 Ground spoilers
69 Flap screw jacks
70 Wing root trailing edge fillet
71 Fuel transfer pipe fairing
72 Starboard service door
73 Rear seat row
74 Buffet unit
75 Starboard baggage door (open)
76 Fin root fillet
77 Refuelling/defuelling pipe
78 Emergency locator transmitter aerial
79 Fin leading edge
80 Fin construction
81 VOR aerial
82 Elevator control rods
83 Tailplane/fin attachment spar box
84 Upper position light
85 Anti-collision light
86 Tailplane leading edge de-icing boots
87 Starboard tailplane
88 Static discharge wicks
89 Elevator trim tabs
90 Elevator spring tab
91 One-piece elevator
92 Elevator horn balance
93 Tailplane construction
94 Rudder hydraulic jacks

95 Trailing rudder
96 Fore-rudder
97 Tail navigation light
98 Rear fuselage vent
99 Tailcone access door
100 Retractable tail bumper
101 Cockpit voice recorder
102 Sloping fin attachment frames
103 Ventral pressure refuelling connection
104 Rear pressure bulkhead
105 Baggage compartment
106 Baggage restraint net
107 Toilet compartment
108 Wash basin
109 Passenger door upper segment
110 Trailing edge wing root fillet
111 Inboard flap track
112 Wing spar/fuselage main frame attachment joint

113 Flap shroud ribs
114 Port wing integral fuel tank bays
115 Lower passenger door segment/airstairs
116 Handrail
117 Nacelle tail fairing
118 Port double slotted flaps
119 Roll control spoilers
120 Port aileron construction
121 Aileron geared tab
122 Static discharge wicks
123 Aileron horn balance
124 Compass flux valve
125 Port navigation light
126 Wing rib construction
127 Leading edge nose ribs
128 Wing fence
129 Wing tank outboard end rib
130 Landing lamp
131 Leading edge de-icing boots
132 Outboard nacelle hydraulics bay
133 Engine nacelle construction
134 Twin mainwheels
135 Engine air intake
136 Front engine mounting
137 Undercarriage breaker strut
138 Main undercarriage leg strut
139 Hydraulic retraction jack
140 Main undercarriage pivot mounting frame
141 Wing tank inboard end rib
142 Bleed air piping
143 Port air conditioning plant
144 Port inner nacelle construction
145 Propeller spinner
146 Oil cooler
147 HF aerial rail
148 Quick-change passenger/cargo version
149 Cargo door
150 "Ballmat" heavy duty cargo handling floor

climate performance of the An-24V Series II, coupled with better take-off performance under normal operations, Antonov produced the An-24RV with a 900-kg (1,984-lb)st Type RU 19-300 auxiliary turbojet engine installed in an engine nacelle. This turbojet is also used to start the turboprop engines. The maximum take-off weight of the An-24RV is 21 800 kg (48,060 lb), compared to the An-24V's 21 000 kg (46,300 lb). The An-24T/RT are freighters.

Although production of the An-24 has ended in the Soviet Union, a version is currently in production in China as the Y-7. This is being manufactured at the Xian works under the Chinese name Yunshuji-7 and early examples were expected to enter service with CAAC in 1982.

Canada has been a major producer of turboprop-powered aircraft for many years, its products including a number of commercial airliners and freighters, military transports and other types. The new Turbo-Canso water-bomber conversion has already been mentioned and other types can be found in the chapters dealing with commuter aircraft and freighters. Both Canadian passenger-carrying airliners with turboprop engines to be detailed in this chapter come from de Havilland Canada, a company established in 1928 as an offshoot of the British de Havilland Aircraft Company.

The first of these is the de Havilland Canada DHC-5E Transporter, a civil version of the DHC-5D Buffalo military transport, which can fulfil both passenger-carrying and freighter roles. The Buffalo itself had been developed from the roughly similar-sized DHC-4 Caribou, a piston-engined transport that entered military service but which was also built in limited number as a 30-passenger or cargo commercial aircraft. Today a handful of Caribous are in airline service. The Transporter's two 3,133-shp General Electric CT64-820-4 turboprop engines are carried in nacelles below the high-mounted wing and the tailplane is carried on top of the fin and rudder. As the Buffalo was developed for STOL (short take-off and landing) operations, so the Transporter also has this ability, although it has to operate under civil safety regulations. Accommodation is provided for 44 passengers, with the cabin interior so designed that the seats can be stowed in the sides to make room for freight, which is loaded via a cargo loading door and rear-fuselage ramp. To speed this operation, a rapid changeover interior is available. Another interior option provides for 19 seats in an executive layout. The maximum cruising speed of the Transporter is 463 km/h (287 mph) and the range is between 185 and 3 185 km (115 and 1,980 miles).

Prior to the development of the Transporter but well after the Buffalo itself, de Havilland Canada began work on a new quiet STOL airliner for commercial operations over short-range routes. The resulting DHC-7 Dash 7 made its maiden flight in March 1975. Following the general configuration of the company's earlier turboprop-powered aircraft, the Dash 7 has

Facing page, top: De Havilland Canada DHC-5E Transporter, a civil version of the DHC-5D Buffalo.

Facing page, bottom: The Transporter has STOL performance, allowing it to take off in 290 m (950 ft) while carrying a 5 443-kg (12,000-lb) load.

Antonov An-24s of CAAC standing at Guangzhou.

a high-mounted wing under which are carried four 1,120-shp Pratt & Whitney Aircraft of Canada PT6A-50 turboprop engines. A T-tail is used. The circular-section fuselage accommodates 50 passengers as standard, although mixed passenger/cargo and freighter layouts are available. The maximum payload in any layout is 5130 kg (11,310 lb).

Services with the Dash 7 were inaugurated by Rocky Mountain Airways in 1978. At the time of writing, sales and option orders for the aircraft had reached 130. Air Wisconsin was among the first few airlines flying Dash 7s and currently has the largest fleet. Countries in which Dash 7s are flown include Abu Dhabi, Austria, Canada, Denmark, Greenland, Indonesia, Honduras, Papua New Guinea, Norway, the U.K., the U.S.A. and South Yemen. The cruising

De Havilland Canada DHC-7 Dash 7 STOL airliner operated by Alyemda in the People's Republic of Yemen.

speed is 428 km/h (266 mph) and range with 50 passengers is 1 279 km (795 miles).

In 1962 Japan added its name to the small number of countries that had produced a turboprop-engined airliner, with the appearance of the prototype NAMC YS-11. The decision to produce such an aircraft dated from 1956, and development was undertaken by a consortium of Japanese manufacturers. The initial version to come off the production line was the YS-11-100, a 60-passenger airliner which first went into commercial service with Toa Airways in 1965.

In 1967 an improved version appeared as the YS-11A, offering an increase in payload. Five variants of the YS-11A were produced subsequently, all but one available for the civil market. The first of these was the YS-11A-200. Like the others in the series, it is powered by two 3,060-ehp Rolls-Royce Dart Mk 542-10K turboprop engines carried on the low-mounted straight tapered wings. The maximum cruising speed and range of this version are 469 km/h (291 mph) and 1 094 to 3 218 km (680 to 2,000 miles) respectively. Seating is provided for up to 60 passengers.

Other versions of the YS-11A produced for the civil market were: the YS-11A-300, accommodating a mixed payload of passengers and cargo; the YS-11A-500 all-passenger version with the maximum take-off weight raised from 24 500 kg (54,013 lb) for the YS-11A-200 to 25 000 kg (55,115 lb); and the YS-11A-600, a mixed payload version of the YS-11A-500. The total number of aircraft built in the YS-11/11A series by the close of production in 1972 was

182. Of these, more than 100 remain in commercial service as short- to medium-range airliners. Since the YS-11 series, Japanese aircraft manufacturers have not produced an airliner of comparable size. The only twin turboprop aircraft currently in production of Japanese origin is the Mitsubishi MU-2, which is manufactured in the U.S.A. The MU-2 is a six- to nine-passenger business aircraft.

Scheduled to make its first flight as a prototype before the British Aerospace ATP is the ATR 42, a smaller twin-turboprop airliner currently under development by Aérospatiale of France and Aeritalia of Italy as a joint venture. Of very different appearance to the British aircraft and not based on a previous design, the ATR 42 will have a high wing, on the leading edge of which will be carried two 1,800-shp Pratt & Whitney Aircraft of Canada PW120 turboprop engines. A T-tail will be used. The undercarriage design is unusual for a civil transport of this type, with the main wheels retracting into a fuselage fairing.

Two versions of the ATR 42 are planned. The ATR 42-100 is the basic version with accommodation for 42 passengers, and is intended for regional stage routes of up to 1 300 km (807 miles). The ATR 42-200 will have seating for 49 passengers in a similar-length fuselage and is intended for stages of 1 450 km (900 miles). The maximum cruising speeds of the two versions are estimated to be 513 km/h (319 mph) and 510 km/h (317 mph) respectively. At the time of writing two ATR 42-100s and 24 ATR 42-200s had been ordered. Services with the airliner begin in late 1985 or early 1986.

Above: Dash 7 flown by the Danish airline Maersk Air.

Left: NAMC YS-11A-513, one of a large number of YS-11As operated by the Japanese airline All Nippon Airways.

4 Serving the City

For the benefit of this chapter, the heading *Commuter Airliners* also encompasses aircraft used for regional, feeder and third-level services. The demarcation between these services is not clearly defined, and is further complicated by the fact that some of the aircraft described in the previous chapter are used on regional as well as domestic services.

In an attempt to clarify the terms detailed above, the following can be considered a guideline. Domestic services are those operated within a country, normally by a state or large airline, between major cities and using large airliners with relatively high seating capacities. Regional services are scheduled operations over a small area, whilst commuter/feeder/third-level services are scheduled operations that link major cities on important routes with outlying populated areas. Aircraft used on regional or commuter/feeder/third-level services can be the same, typically (but not always) with fewer seats than airliners used on other forms of scheduled operations. To complicate the matter further, a number of aircraft operated by companies as business transports are also to be found within the

fleets of airlines flying third-level services. In the final analysis, deciding which aircraft to detail in this chapter has to be, to a small degree, a question of personal choice.

A number of the world's finest regional and commuter aircraft are produced in the United Kingdom, spearheaded by Shorts of Belfast. Short Brothers was among the first companies to put an aircraft into series production, when it received an order for six Flyers from the Wright brothers in 1909, and, before the Second World War, the company became synonymous with large flying-boats. Today the company has three aircraft types in production. One, whose design was initiated in 1959, is the well-known SC.7 Skyvan. The prototype first flew in January 1960.

The Skyvan first went into production in its Series 2 form, powered by two 730-ehp Turboméca Astazou XII turboprop engines. Although short in length, the fuselage was designed to be square in section, with an inside height and width of 1.98 metres (6 feet 6 inches). Loading and unloading when it is used as a freighter is aided by a wide rear door under the upswept rear fuselage. In 1968 the Series 2 was superseded by the

Short Skyvan Series 3 in the insignia of the Greek airline Olympic Airways.

Series 3, which remains the current civil version. This is powered by two 715-shp Garrett TPE331-201 turboprop engines carried under the high-mounted wings. It can accommodate up to 19 passengers or 2 085 kg (4,600 lb) of freight or vehicles of various types, or can be equipped as an air ambulance. The maximum cruising speed is 327 km/h (203 mph) and the range can be 1 115 km (694 miles). Because it has STOL performance, the distance necessary for take off can be as short as 213 metres (700 feet). More than 70 examples of this aircraft have been ordered over the years.

Apart from military versions of the Skyvan, Shorts has produced examples of the Skyvan Series 3A with a higher gross weight, and the de luxe Skyliner with a longer passenger cabin, but neither type is currently available.

Using the same design concept that produced the Skyvan, Shorts developed a larger twin turboprop transport as the 330, originally known as the Shorts SD3-30. This aircraft first flew in prototype form in August 1974 and commercial services were inaugurated by Time Air two years later. Like the Skyvan, the 330 (and its freighter-only derivative, the Sherpa) has a cabin interior width and height of 1.98 metres (6 feet 6 inches). However, the fuselage is considerably longer and with a more pointed nose, and accommodation is provided for 30 passengers. It can also be used to carry a mixed payload of passengers and cargo, or can be used for all-cargo operations, with bulky items being loaded through a large door on the port side of the forward fuselage. Only the Sherpa freighter has the very wide rear fuselage loading door.

Olympic also operates the Shorts 330-200, a larger wide-body transport.

Plate V

Shorts 330

cutaway drawing key

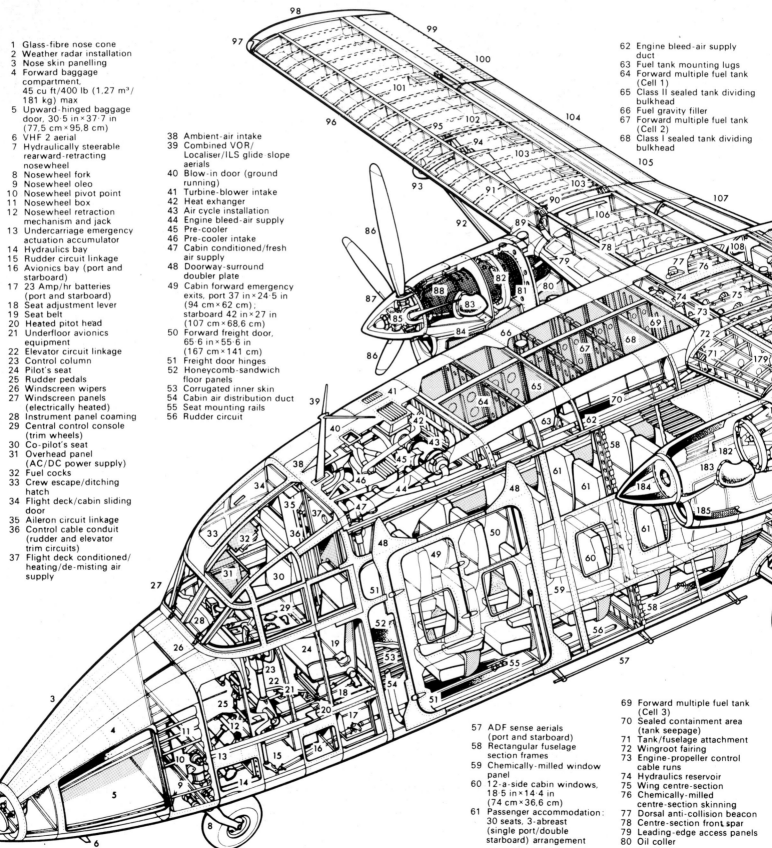

1 Glass-fibre nose cone
2 Weather radar installation
3 Nose skin panelling
4 Forward baggage compartment, 45 cu ft/400 lb (1,27 m³/ 181 kg) max
5 Upward-hinged baggage door, 30·5 in × 37·7 in (77,5 cm × 95,8 cm)
6 VHF 2 aerial
7 Hydraulically steerable rearward-retracting nosewheel
8 Nosewheel fork
9 Nosewheel oleo
10 Nosewheel pivot point
11 Nosewheel box
12 Nosewheel retraction mechanism and jack
13 Undercarriage emergency actuation accumulator
14 Hydraulics bay
15 Rudder circuit linkage
16 Avionics bay (port and starboard)
17 23 Amp/hr batteries (port and starboard)
18 Seat adjustment lever
19 Seat belt
20 Heated pitot head
21 Underfloor avionics equipment
22 Elevator circuit linkage
23 Control column
24 Pilot's seat
25 Rudder pedals
26 Windscreen wipers
27 Windscreen panels (electrically heated)
28 Instrument panel coaming
29 Central control console (trim wheels)
30 Co-pilot's seat
31 Overhead panel (AC/DC power supply)
32 Fuel cocks
33 Crew escape/ditching hatch
34 Flight deck/cabin sliding door
35 Aileron circuit linkage
36 Control cable conduit (rudder and elevator trim circuits)
37 Flight deck conditioned/ heating/de-misting air supply

38 Ambient-air intake
39 Combined VOR/ Localiser/ILS glide-slope aerials
40 Blow-in door (ground running)
41 Turbine-blower intake
42 Heat exhanger
43 Air cycle installation
44 Engine bleed-air supply
45 Pre-cooler
46 Pre-cooler intake
47 Cabin conditioned/fresh air supply
48 Doorway-surround doubler plate
49 Cabin forward emergency exits, port 37 in × 24·5 in (94 cm × 62 cm); starboard 42 in × 27 in (107 cm × 68,6 cm)
50 Forward freight door, 65·6 in × 55·6 in (167 cm × 141 cm)
51 Freight door hinges
52 Honeycomb-sandwich floor panels
53 Corrugated inner skin
54 Cabin air distribution duct
55 Seat mounting rails
56 Rudder circuit

57 ADF sense aerials (port and starboard)
58 Rectangular fuselage section frames
59 Chemically-milled window panel
60 12-a-side cabin windows, 18·5 in × 14·4 in (74 cm × 36,6 cm)
61 Passenger accommodation: 30 seats, 3-abreast (single port/double starboard) arrangement

62 Engine bleed-air supply duct
63 Fuel tank mounting lugs
64 Forward multiple fuel tank (Cell 1)
65 Class II sealed tank dividing bulkhead
66 Fuel gravity filler
67 Forward multiple fuel tank (Cell 2)
68 Class I sealed tank dividing bulkhead

69 Forward multiple fuel tank (Cell 3)
70 Sealed containment area (tank seepage)
71 Tank/fuselage attachment
72 Wingroot fairing
73 Engine-propeller control cable runs
74 Hydraulics reservoir
75 Wing centre-section
76 Chemically-milled centre-section skinning
77 Dorsal anti-collision beacon
78 Centre-section front spar
79 Leading-edge access panels
80 Oil coller

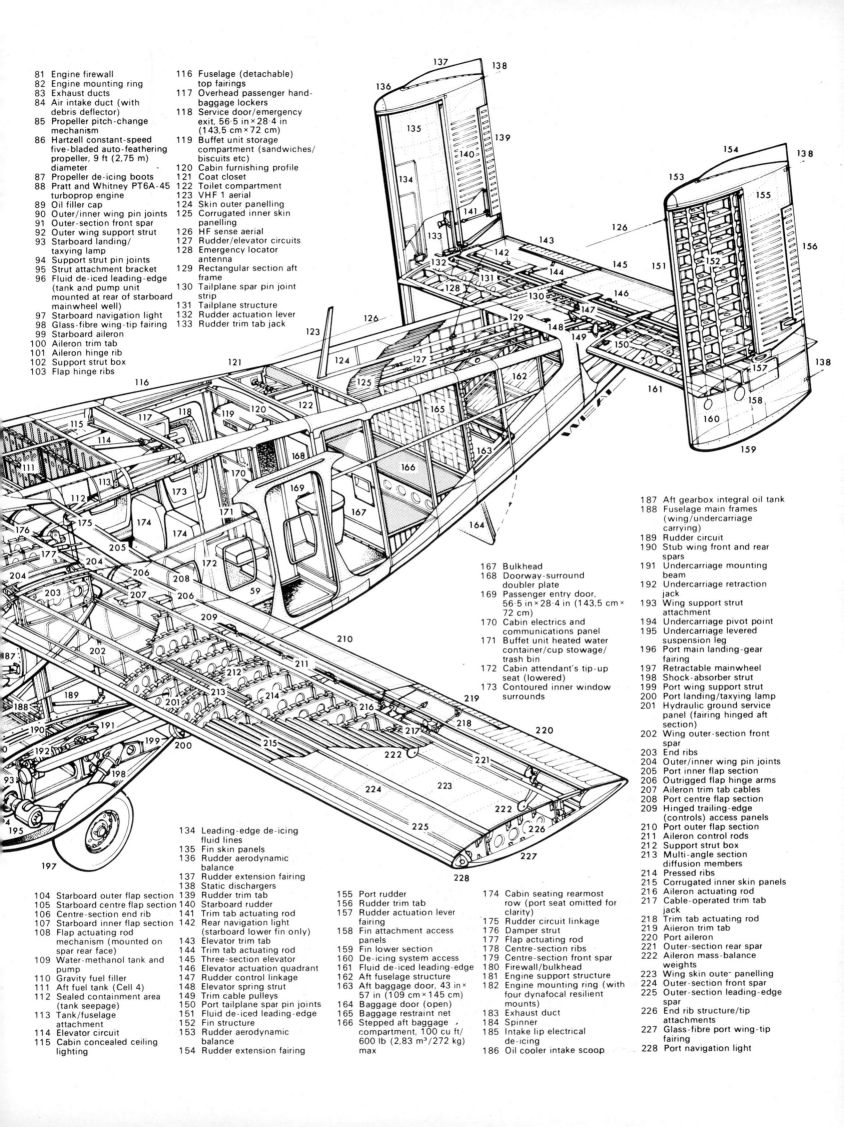

81 Engine firewall
82 Engine mounting ring
83 Exhaust ducts
84 Air intake duct (with debris deflector)
85 Propeller pitch-change mechanism
86 Hartzell constant-speed five-bladed auto-feathering propeller, 9 ft (2,75 m) diameter
87 Propeller de-icing boots
88 Pratt and Whitney PT6A-45 turboprop engine
89 Oil filler cap
90 Outer/inner wing pin joints
91 Outer-section front spar
92 Outer wing support strut
93 Starboard landing/taxiing lamp
94 Support strut pin joints
95 Strut attachment bracket
96 Fluid de-iced leading-edge (tank and pump unit mounted at rear of starboard mainwheel well)
97 Starboard navigation light
98 Glass-fibre wing-tip fairing
99 Starboard aileron
100 Aileron trim tab
101 Aileron hinge rib
102 Support strut box
103 Flap hinge ribs

104 Starboard outer flap section
105 Starboard centre flap section
106 Centre-section end rib
107 Starboard inner flap section
108 Flap actuating rod mechanism (mounted on spar rear face)
109 Water-methanol tank and pump
110 Gravity fuel filler
111 Aft fuel tank (Cell 4)
112 Sealed containment area (tank seepage)
113 Tank/fuselage attachment
114 Elevator circuit
115 Cabin concealed ceiling lighting

116 Fuselage (detachable) top fairings
117 Overhead passenger hand-baggage lockers
118 Service door/emergency exit, 56·5 in × 28·4 in (143,5 cm × 72 cm)
119 Buffet unit storage compartment (sandwiches/biscuits etc)
120 Cabin furnishing profile
121 Coat closet
122 Toilet compartment
123 VHF 1 aerial
124 Skin outer panelling
125 Corrugated inner skin panelling
126 HF sense aerial
127 Rudder/elevator circuits
128 Emergency locator antenna
129 Rectangular section aft frame
130 Tailplane spar pin joint strip
131 Tailplane structure
132 Rudder actuation lever
133 Rudder trim tab jack

134 Leading-edge de-icing fluid lines
135 Fin skin panels
136 Rudder aerodynamic balance
137 Rudder extension fairing
138 Static dischargers
139 Rudder trim tab
140 Starboard rudder
141 Trim tab actuating rod
142 Rear navigation light (starboard lower fin only)
143 Elevator trim tab
144 Trim tab actuating rod
145 Three-section elevator
146 Elevator actuation quadrant
147 Rudder control linkage
148 Elevator spring strut
149 Trim cable pulleys
150 Port tailplane spar pin joints
151 Fluid de-iced leading-edge
152 Fin structure
153 Rudder aerodynamic balance
154 Rudder extension fairing

155 Port rudder
156 Rudder trim tab
157 Rudder actuation lever fairing
158 Fin attachment access panels
159 Fin lower section
160 De-icing system access
161 Fluid de-iced leading-edge
162 Aft fuselage structure
163 Aft baggage door, 43 in × 57 in (109 cm × 145 cm)
164 Baggage door (open)
165 Baggage restraint net
166 Stepped aft baggage compartment, 100 cu ft/600 lb (2,83 m³/272 kg) max

167 Bulkhead
168 Doorway-surround doubler plate
169 Passenger entry door, 56·5 in × 28·4 in (143,5 cm × 72 cm)
170 Cabin electrics and communications panel
171 Buffet unit heated water container/cup stowage/trash bin
172 Cabin attendant's tip-up seat (lowered)
173 Contoured inner window surrounds

174 Cabin seating rearmost row (port seat omitted for clarity)
175 Rudder circuit linkage
176 Damper strut
177 Flap actuating rod
178 Centre-section ribs
179 Centre-section front spar
180 Firewall/bulkhead
181 Engine support structure
182 Engine mounting ring (with four dynafocal resilient mounts)
183 Exhaust duct
184 Spinner
185 Intake lip electrical de-icing
186 Oil cooler intake scoop

187 Aft gearbox integral oil tank
188 Fuselage main frames (wing/undercarriage carrying)
189 Rudder circuit
190 Stub wing front and rear spars
191 Undercarriage mounting beam
192 Undercarriage retraction jack
193 Wing support strut attachment
194 Undercarriage pivot point
195 Undercarriage levered suspension leg
196 Port main landing-gear fairing
197 Retractable mainwheel
198 Shock-absorber strut
199 Port wing support strut
200 Port landing/taxiing lamp
201 Hydraulic ground service panel (fairing hinged aft section)
202 Wing outer-section front spar
203 End ribs
204 Outer/inner wing pin joints
205 Port inner flap section
206 Outrigged flap hinge arms
207 Aileron trim tab cables
208 Port centre flap section
209 Hinged trailing-edge (controls) access panels
210 Port outer flap section
211 Aileron control rods
212 Support strut box
213 Multi-angle section diffusion members
214 Pressed ribs
215 Corrugated inner skin panels
216 Aileron actuating rod
217 Cable-operated trim tab jack
218 Trim tab actuating rod
219 Aileron trim tab
220 Port aileron
221 Outer-section rear spar
222 Aileron mass-balance weights
223 Wing skin outer panelling
224 Outer-section front spar
225 Outer-section leading-edge spar
226 End rib structure/tip attachments
227 Glass-fibre port wing-tip fairing
228 Port navigation light

One of the latest users of the Shorts 330-200 is Thai Airways.

Early versions of the Shorts 330 are powered by 1,156-shp Pratt & Whitney Aircraft of Canada PT6A-45B turboprop engines. These have been superseded by 1,198-shp PT6A-45R engines on the current Shorts 330-200. This later version has a maximum cruising speed of 352 km/h (218 mph) at a gross weight of 9 525 kg (21,000 lb) and its range, with 30 passengers on board, is 890 km (553 miles). A total of 112 Shorts 330s had been ordered at the time of writing.

Shorts further strengthened its hand in the regional/commuter market in 1981, with the appearance of the Shorts 360. In many respects this airliner is similar to the 330. Using the same type of wide-bodied square-section and unpressurized fuselage, although with a cabin interior width and height of 1.93 metres (6 feet 4 inches), it is nevertheless different in several important respects. The fuselage is longer to provide accommodation for up to 36 passengers and a large amount of baggage, the wings and struts are strengthened, the 330's twin fins and rudders give way to a conventional tail unit, and power for production aircraft is provided by two 1,327-shp Pratt & Whitney Aircraft of Canada PT6A-65R turboprop engines. The aircraft was conceived to offer advantages over other aircraft operating typical stage routes for commuter services and, as such, has a range (with reserve fuel for diversions and hold) with 36 passengers of 425 km (265 miles). This range is significantly increased when the aircraft carries its maximum fuel load. The stated break-even load factor for this airliner is less than 40 per cent.

The prototype Shorts 360 made its maiden flight in mid-1981 and Suburban Airlines of Pennsylvania introduced the airliner into commercial service in late 1982. At the time of writing a total of more than 30 Shorts 360s had been ordered. The cruising speed is 391 km/h (243 mph).

Another British success story has been the series of feederline transports of the Islander range, conceived by Britten-Norman to fulfil a similar role to that once performed

Left: The highly
successful Pilatus Britten-
Norman BN-2B Islander.

by aircraft like the de Havilland Dragon
Rapide biplane. The company had been
founded in 1955 as an agricultural aircraft
equipment specialist and thus the development of the Islander was a new venture.

In June 1965, Britten-Norman flew the
prototype of its Islander. Subsequent initial
production aircraft were known as BN-2s,
followed from mid-1969 by the refined BN-
2A. This remained the standard production
model until 1978, by which time Britten-
Norman (Bembridge) Limited had become
a member of the Fairey Group and
remained so until that company's close-
down, after which it again traded as Britten-
Norman (Bembridge) Limited. The BN-2A
was available with various options including standard or extended wings, the
standard fuselage nose or an extended nose
with baggage space, and a choice of
Lycoming engines.

In general configuration, the BN-2A is
similar to earlier and later models, with a
rectangular-section fuselage accommodating nine passengers, and a high-mounted
wing under which are carried two 260-hp
Lycoming O-540-E4C5 or 300-hp IO-540-
K1B5 piston engines. The cruising speed
with the more powerful engines and the
airframe with standard-span wings and a
short nose is 290 km/h (180 mph). Optional
equipment choices make the aircraft
suitable for other roles.

Since 1979 the standard version of the
Islander has been the BN-2B, with sub-
variants indicating the engines fitted (as
detailed for the BN-2A) and the use of
auxiliary fuel tanks in the extended wing-

tips. In the same year the Swiss company
Pilatus Flugzeugwerke AG acquired
Britten-Norman and all products of the
company are now known under the title
Pilatus Britten-Norman. The BN-2B is able
to land at a heavier weight and has improvements to the interior design of the
cabin. The nine passengers and the pilot sit
in pairs. The maximum cruising speed of
the BN-2B with the 300-hp engines is
264 km/h (164 mph), and the range varies
from 1 136 to 1 677 km (706 to 1,042 miles)
with the 300-hp engines, depending on
whether standard or extended-span wings
are fitted.

A version of the Islander with turboprop
engines is known as the BN-2T Turbine
Islander. It is powered by two 400-shp
Allison 250-B17C engines and offers customers a reduced level of noise. The first
production BN-2T was delivered in late
1981. The maximum cruising speed is

Prototype Shorts 360
36-passenger wide-body
transport with a single
fin and rudder.

similar to that of the BN-2A and the range is up to 1 253 km (778 miles) with auxiliary fuel (available in extended wingtips and underwing tanks, as for other Islanders). Civil and military versions of the Islander series have been delivered to approximately 120 different countries, with the actual number delivered exceeding 1,000. In addition to British production, Islanders have been built in Belgium (the main producer during the period of the Fairey Group's involvement), Romania and the Philippines.

In September 1970 the first flight was made by the prototype Trislander, an enlarged triple-engined version of the Islander, intended to accommodate 17 passengers. Compared to the Islander, the Trislander's fuselage was lengthened by 2.29 metres (7 feet 6 inches), the wings were given the extended span as standard and the tail unit was modified to have a high-mounted tailplane and to carry the third engine. Other changes included a new undercarriage. Deliveries of production aircraft began in early 1971, with the first going into commercial service with Aurigny Air Services operating in the Channel Islands. Under Pilatus Britten-Norman, the last of 73 Trislanders was delivered in 1982. Since June of that year the American company International Aviation Corporation (IAC) has taken over production of the Trislander under the new name Tri-Commutair. The cruising speed is 267 km/h (166 mph) and the maximum range is 1 610 km (1,000 miles).

In 1970 the famous British aircraft manufacturing company, Handley Page, ceased trading. It had only recently begun delivering examples of its twin-turboprop feederline transport known as the Jetstream Mk 1, the prototype of which had made its initial flight in 1967. The Mk 1 had been delivered with two 840-ehp Turboméca Astazou engines but already a new version was being developed with more powerful 996-ehp Astazou XVI C2 turboprops as the Jetstream

BN-2T Turbine Islander, powered by two Allison 250-B17C turboprop engines.

One of the Pilatus
Britten-Norman BN-2A
Mk III Trislanders in
service with Trans-
Jamaican Airlines Ltd.

The first BAe Jetstream
31 went to the West
German airline
Contactair.

200. After the close of Handley Page, Scottish Aviation eventually took over the Jetstream 200 (from Jetstream Aircraft Limited, which had followed Handley Page). The Jetstream 200 is a 12- to 18-passenger aircraft with a cruising speed of 454 km/h (282 mph) and a range of 2 224 km (1,382 miles). Some Mk 1s were uprated to this standard and other Jetstreams have been fitted with various engines in the U.S.A.

In the late 1970s Scottish Aviation became part of British Aerospace, the newly formed British nationalized aircraft company. In December 1978 it was announced that a new version of the Jetstream was to be developed and in early 1980 a converted Mk 1 flew as the prototype of the Jetstream 31. The first production Jetstream 31 made its maiden flight two years later, in March 1982. By the end of that year, seven had been ordered by airlines in the U.K., U.S.A., West Germany and Norway. The first went to German operator Contactair.

The Jetstream 31 is powered by two 900-shp Garrett TPE331-10 turboprop engines,

The first United Kingdom airline to fly the Jetstream 31 is Peregrine Air Services.

The interior layout of a Jetstream 31 Commuter.

One of many Riley Turbo Skyliners flown by Prinair of Puerto Rico.

carried on the low-mounted wings. The maximum cruising speed is 488 km/h (303 mph) and the range varies according to the version. The Commuter can carry 18 passengers over a distance of 1 167 km (725 miles) or a maximum of 19 passengers. The Corporate has a much greater range but has accommodation for only eight to 10 passengers in a revised luxury executive interior, similar to that of the HS 125. The other non-

military version is the Executive, which is intended to transport company personnel between factories and has mostly forward-facing seats.

In 1945 and 1950 de Havilland flew the prototypes of its Dove twin-engined transport and Heron four-engined transport respectively. Both used de Havilland Gipsy Queen engines and the Dove had the honour of being the first postwar British civil transport aeroplane. A total of 540 Doves was built in several versions, including the Dove Series 8A or Dove Custom 600 executive version for the U.S. market. Most Doves built were exported. In the U.S.A. some Doves were converted to use turbocharged and turboprop engines (the former by Riley as the Turbo-Exec 400, featuring 400-hp Lycoming IO-720s). With normal accommodation for between eight and 11 passengers, the maximum cruising speeds of the Dove 8 and Riley Turbo-Exec 400 are 338 km/h (210 mph) and 459 km/h (285 mph) respectively.

The Heron was produced as a 14- to 17-seat companion to the Dove, with four engines and larger overall dimensions. The main production version was the Heron 2, powered by 250-hp Gipsy Queen 30 Mk 2 piston engines and with a cruising speed and typical range of 307 km/h (191 mph) and 1 900 km (1,180 miles) respectively. Production totalled more than 140 and variants were produced in Mexico, Japan, Canada and the U.S.A. by engine conversion. The best known of the conversions was produced as the Riley Turbo Skyliner, powered by four 290-hp Lycoming IO-540-K1C5 supercharged engines.

A worldwide industry

Aircraft of commuter type are built in more than a dozen other countries. From Australia comes the GAF (Government Aircraft Factories) Nomad, which is enjoying considerable success in civil and military forms. Typical of many commuter-type aircraft, the Nomad has a rectangular fuselage and high-mounted strut-braced wings, though the bases of the struts are mounted on fairings that house the main undercarriage units when retracted. The fairings themselves are carried at the ends of stub wings.

The prototype Nomad flew for the first time in July 1971 as a STOL utility transport and the initial production versions were the N22 and the lengthened N24. The current standard and production versions are the N22B and N24A, the 12/13-passenger and lengthened 16/17-passenger versions of the Nomad respectively, each powered by two 420-shp Allison 250-B17C turboprop engines. The N22B is available in Commuter/Cargo, Surveymaster and Medicmaster forms, while the N24A has Commuterliner, Cargomaster and Medicmaster variants. In addition the Nomad N22B is offered with a twin float undercarriage as the Floatmaster, and in amphibious form. One hundred and forty-two N22Bs and N24As had been ordered at the time of writing, for use in 16 countries. The cruising speed of the current versions with wheel undercarriages is 311 km/h (193 mph), and the range can be 1 352 km (840 miles).

Brazil has become one of the most important centres of production in recent years, following the founding of Empresa Brasileira de Aeronáutica SA, better known simply as EMBRAER. This organization can now claim to be one of the top 11 aircraft manufacturing companies in the world in terms of annual production. Probably the company's most famous product is the EMB-110 Bandeirante, a twin-turboprop light general-purpose transport developed to meet a specification issued by the Brazilian Ministry of Aeronautics. The first prototype with a military designation flew for the first time in October 1968. Since 1972, production aircraft have gone to civil operators and the military, with the 400th delivered (to Southeastern Airlines in the U.S.A.) in the early spring of 1982.

Many versions of the Bandeirante have been produced. The current civil versions are the unpressurized EMB-110P1 and EMB-110P2. The former is an 18-seat commuter airliner or cargo transport with a quick-change interior, and the latter is a 21-seat commuter airliner. Higher weight

GAF N24A Commuterliner.

Left: Bush Pilots Airways (BPA) GAF N22B Nomad.

versions are the EMB-110P1/41 and P2/41.
The maximum cruising speed of the EMB-110P2 is 413 km/h (257 mph) and the range
is 2 001 km (1,244 miles). These performances are achieved on the power of two 750-
shp Pratt & Whitney Aircraft of Canada
PT6A-34 turboprop engines, which are the
standard engines for current versions. A
pressurized version of the EMB-110 is the
P3, which is under development as a 19-
passenger commuter airliner with a T-tail
and powered by two 1,173-shp PT6A-65
engines.

In 1976 EMBRAER flew the prototype
of a smaller twin-turboprop transport with
a T-tail, known as the EMB-121 Xingu.
Now to be found in civil and military
service, the basic version is the EMB-121A
Xingu I, which is powered by two 680-shp
Pratt & Whitney Aircraft of Canada PT6A-
28 turboprops and carries nine passengers.
Its maximum cruising speed is 450 km/h
(280 mph) and its typical range is 2 270 km
(1,410 miles). Xingu I transports can be
modified to EMB-121A1 Xingu II standard
by the substitution of more powerful
750-shp PT6A-135 engines. However,
production-built Xingu IIs have two short
strakes under the tailcone. The maximum
cruising speed of the Xingu II is 480 km/h
(298 mph).

Prior to the first flight of a Xingu II, in
September 1981, EMBRAER flew the
prototype of an enlarged Xingu which has
since been designated EMB-121B Xingu
III. This has pressurized accommodation
for seven or nine passengers. It is powered
by two 850-shp PT6A-42 engines that allow
a maximum cruising speed and range, with
a 900 kg (1,984 lb) payload, of 502 km/h
(312 mph) and 2 224 km (1,382 miles) re-

spectively. This aircraft can be regarded as the most important follow-on to the Xingu I (with the Xingu II regarded as an improved Xingu I).

Very significant to EMBRAER's future is the company's latest transport, the 30-passenger EMB-120 Brasilia. A big brother to the Bandeirante, the Brasilia prototype made its maiden flight in 1983. By that time well over 100 options for the Brasilia had been placed by 23 potential operators. These are from Brazil, Australia, Colombia, Finland, France, Mexico, the U.K. and the U.S.A. – continuing the company's tradition of exporting the majority of its aircraft built. Furthermore, with the vast area of

Brazil, the Brasilia is likely to play an important role in domestic operations.

The Brasilia is more like an enlarged Xingu than a Bandeirante, with a circular-section fuselage and a T-tail. The tailplane is swept back. Power is provided by two 1,500-shp Pratt & Whitney Aircraft of Canada PW115 turboprop engines. As an alternative to the 30-passenger interior, the Brasilia can be configured to accommodate 24 or 26 passengers plus 900 kg (1,984 lb) of cargo, all cargo up to a weight of 3 178 kg (7,006 lb), or as an executive transport. To facilitate the loading and unloading of cargo, a large door has been incorporated into the rear fuselage. The maximum cruising speed is estimated to be 543 km/h (337 mph) and its range, with a full passenger load, is estimated to be 1 010 km (628 miles) with reserves.

For many years Canada has been a major producer of small utility aircraft suitable for passenger, cargo and other operations. Many of these have STOL capability and are equally at home on wheel, float or ski undercarriages to assist in operations in areas of Canada where surface communications are poor and the climate extreme.

In 1946 de Havilland Canada produced its first aircraft of original design as the DHC-1 Chipmunk, a highly successful tandem-seat trainer. In August 1947 it followed its earlier success with the first of a long line of STOL utility transports, known as the DHC-2 Beaver. Production of the Beaver continued into the 1960s, covering military and civil versions of the Beaver Mk I and finally 60 Turbo-Beaver Mk IIIs. The Mk I, of which more than 1,650 were produced (over 1,000 for military use), was

The EMB-110P1 Bandeirante accommodates 19 passengers or 1 747 kg (3,850 lb) of cargo. This P1 is operated by Alas Chiricanas from Panama.

built with a 450-hp Pratt & Whitney R-985-SB3 radial piston engine as standard. It has high-mounted wings, accommodation for the pilot and seven passengers or cargo, and can utilize all three types of undercarriage mentioned above.

The Turbo-Beaver appeared in 1963 and 60 were built, each powered by a 578-ehp Pratt & Whitney Aircraft of Canada PT6A-6 or a 579-ehp PT6A-20 turboprop engine. This version proved to have the highest speed, with a maximum cruising speed of 252 km/h (157 mph), compared to the Beaver's maximum speed of 225 km/h (140 mph). The ranges for the Beaver and Turbo-Beaver are 1,090 km (677 miles) with reserves and 1 252 km (778 miles) respectively. The Turbo-Beaver carries 10 passengers or 815 kg (1,800 lb) of cargo.

De Havilland Aero Services has recently begun offering a retrofit kit to operators of the Beaver Mk I, which can bring the aircraft up to Turbo-Beaver standard. Apart from the PT6A-20 engine and new propeller, it includes a plug to lengthen the fuselage to allow two more seats, and strengthening of the airframe. With these modifications, the aircraft has improved take-off, landing and climbing performances.

With the success of the Beaver, de Havilland Canada lost little time developing a larger aircraft on the same lines. The result was the DHC-3 Otter, of which 460 were delivered to military (more than 80 per cent) and civil customers from 1952. It is similar in configuration to the Beaver but enlarged and has a fuselage capable of

EMBRAER EMB-121A1 Xingu II.

accommodating 10 or 11 passengers, cargo
or stretchers. The power plant selected was
the 600-hp Pratt & Whitney R-1340-S1H1-
G or S3H1-G piston engine. An amphibious
undercarriage joined the other undercarriages available. As a landplane, the Otter
has a maximum cruising speed of 212 km/h
(132 mph) and a range of 1 520 km (945
miles).

In 1965 de Havilland Canada produced
its first small twin-turboprop STOL transport as the DHC-6 Twin Otter. Despite the
name, it bears no resemblance to the single-
engined Otter. The Twin Otter is a much
more modern aircraft, with only its strut-
braced constant-chord wings bearing any
likeness to that of earlier DHCs. Because the
Twin Otter is twin-engined, the fuselage has
a pointed nose. The tail unit, compared to
that of the Otter, is angular, with a slightly
swept fin and rudder and a mid-mounted

constant-chord tailplane. Power for the
latest Series 300 version is provided by two
652-ehp Pratt & Whitney Aircraft of
Canada PT6A-27 turboprop engines carried in the leading-edges of the wings.

The first two production versions of the
Twin Otter were the Series 100 and 200; 115
of each were built. Both were built with two
579-ehp PT6A-20 engines but the latter
aircraft was produced with a longer fuselage
nose in landplane form. The standard production version since 1969 has been the
Series 300, making up the majority of the
800 or so Twin Otters sold to customers in
74 countries. Available with a wheel, ski or
float undercarriage (in floatplane form with
a shorter fuselage nose), it is powered by two
652-ehp Pratt & Whitney Aircraft of
Canada PT6A-27 turboprops and has seating for 20 passengers. Other interior layouts
provide for freighter (up to 1 941 kg; 4,280

Left: Front view of the
EMB-120 Brasilia.

Right: De Havilland Canada DHC-2 Beaver floatplane.

Below: De Havilland DHC-3 Otter at the Poplar Hill Indian reserve near the Manitoba/Ontario border.

lb load), air ambulance, executive, survey and other roles. The maximum cruising speed of the Series 300 is 338 km/h (210 mph) and the range, with a 1 134-kg (2,500-lb) payload, is 1 297 km (806 miles).

The latest de Havilland Canada short-haul transport is the DHC-8 Dash 8, which made its maiden flight as a prototype in 1983. In terms of seating capacity and overall size, the Dash 8 is larger than the Twin Otter but smaller than the Dash 7. Even before its maiden flight, 40 production aircraft had been ordered, the majority by customers from the U.S.A. Two versions have been announced. The first is the standard 32- to 36-seat Commuter, which is also available in mixed passenger/cargo form. The maximum cruising speed and normal range of the Commuter are 500 km/h (310 mph) and 1 056 km (656 miles) respectively. The Corporate is the version for non-scheduled use by companies and will normally accommodate up to 24 passengers. Its range can be longer than that of the Commuter but the power plant remains the standard two 1,800-shp Pratt & Whitney Aircraft of Canada PW120 turbo-prop engines. In general appearance, the Dash 8 looks similar to a twin-engined Dash 7.

Another Canadian company, Canadair, is marketing a commuter transport which is also suited for cargo carrying and for use as a business aircraft. Known as the Challenger, it is based on the LearStar 600, an aircraft conceived by William P. Lear Sr.

De Havilland Canada DHC-2 Turbo-Beaver Mk III floatplane.

Above: NorOntair operates a fleet of Twin Otter Series 300s in northern Ontario.

Right: One of many de Havilland Canada DHC-6 Twin Otter Series 300s ordered by ACES (Aerolineas Centrales de Colombia SA).

of Learjet and Lear Fan fame. Changes were introduced into the design before a prototype CL-600 flew in September 1979.

Unlike the de Havilland aircraft previously mentioned, the Challenger is a low-wing, T-tailed jet, powered by two rear fuselage-mounted 3 400-kg (7,500-lb)st Avco Lycoming ALF502L-2 or ALF502L-3 turbofan engines in its initial CL-600 form. Fifty CL-600s had been delivered by the spring of 1982. Orders for the Challenger at the time of writing totalled about 150, including some for the CL-601 version. This later model, which made its maiden flight as a prototype in April 1982, is basically similar to the CL-600 but has winglets fitted to the tips of the advanced-technology swept wings and is powered by higher-rated General Electric CF34-1A engines. Passenger accommodation in both versions provides seating for up to 19 persons. The maximum payload of the CL-600 is 3 733 kg (8,230 lb), which is greater than the CL-601's payload despite the aircraft's lower maximum take-off weight.

Aircraft of Chinese design and manufacture have been appearing over recent years as possible replacements for Chinese-built aircraft of foreign origin. One such aircraft is the small Y-11, a twin-engined general-purpose aircraft produced at the Harbin works. The Y-11 is believed to have first appeared in 1975 and early production examples were employed in an agricultural role in 1977. However, the cabin can be utilized for other purposes, thereby allowing the Y-11 to undertake the transportation of seven or eight passengers, cargo weighing up to 870 kg (1,918 lb), or stretchers in an air ambulance role. The two 285-hp Huosai-6A radial engines provide the Y-11 with a cruising speed of 190 km/h (118 mph) and a range of 400 to 995 km (248 to 618 miles).

In July 1982 the first flight took place of an enlarged version of the Y-11, powered by

Artist's impression of the de Havilland Canada DHC-8 Dash 8 short-haul transport.

two Pratt & Whitney Aircraft of Canada PT6A turboprop engines. In its latest form the aircraft is known as the Y-11T2, and has 620-shp PT6A-27s. The fuselage has been lengthened to allow an increase in the number of passengers carried (to 17), and for other roles the payload has been increased to 1 700 kg (3,748 lb). The performance of the Y-11T is considerably higher than that of the Y-11.

The Czechoslovakian L-410 Turbolet is a twin-engined general-purpose transport. Amongst its civil and military users is Aeroflot, with whom it is a standard feeder-liner. It is produced by Let Národní Podnik at Kunovice, whose earlier products have included the L-200 Morava four/five-seat light aircraft. Its design was started in 1966, with the intention of producing an aircraft capable of flying from grass and sand airstrips as well as from paved and other runways, and the aircraft has proved capable of operating in snow and ice and in extreme temperatures.

The initial production version of the Turbolet was the L-410A. This passenger or cargo transport is powered by two Pratt & Whitney Aircraft of Canada PT6A-27

Above: L-410UVP Turbolet.

Right: Canadair CL-600 Challenger commuter, cargo and business aircraft.

turboprop engines carried under the high-mounted wing. The 39 built have proved to have the highest performance of the series. The first production examples were delivered to the Czech domestic airline Slov-Air in September 1971. The L-410AF was delivered to Hungary for photographic survey work and was followed by the L-410M with two 730-ehp Walter M 601A turboprop engines. This version, accommodating up to 17 passengers or cargo, has a cruising speed of 365 km/h (227 mph) and a range, with a 760-kg (1,675-lb) load, of 1 160 km (720 miles). Aeroflot began flying the L-410M in 1979, over routes in Siberia. Production totalled 110 aircraft.

The latest version of the Turbolet is the L-410UVP, which has been the basic passenger and cargo version since 1979. Other roles can include air ambulance and

firefighting, typical uses for general-purpose aircraft of this size. The L-410UVP is, however, much more than a re-engined L-410M. Apart from the similarly rated Walter M 601B engines (a refined M 601A of increased diameter), this version has a greater wing span, a lengthened fuselage, a revised tail unit with tailplane dihedral, cockpit improvements and many other refinements. Performance is similar to that of the L-410M, although the maximum payload is lower at 1 310 kg (2,888 lb).

France has surprisingly few aircraft to contribute to this chapter, although the Dassault-Breguet Mystère-Falcon business jets undertake other relevant roles. The three aircraft of French origin covered here are all related and all come from Nord-Aviation, a company that later became part of Aérospatiale. The N 262 was developed

Canadair CL-601 Challenger with higher-rated General Electric engines and winglets.

89

Mohawk 298, a re-engined Aérospatiale N 262.

Facing page: Dornier first flew its four/six-seat piston-engined Do 27 in 1955. One of the few in commercial use is this Do 27 B-3, which is flown by Rheingau Air Service on its sightseeing charter flights.

as a pressurized short-range airliner from the piston-engined Max Holste MH-250 Super Brousard and subsequent twin-turboprop MH-260 (Nord-Aviation having produced the airliner following its take-over of Max Holste in 1961). The prototype N 262 made its maiden flight in 1962. Two versions were produced, the N 262 Series A and B, the latter becoming the first in commercial service when Air Inter began operating the only four built in 1964.

The standard production version was the N 262 Series A, powered by two 1,080-ehp Turboméca Bastan VIC turboprop engines carried on the leading-edge of the high-mounted wing. Improved versions were produced as the N 262 Series C and D, but these became known as Frégates. The main difference between the Frégate and the Series A and B was the use of more powerful 1,145-ehp Bastan VII engines mounted on wings with raked tips. The Series D had been intended as the military derivative of the commercial Series C. In total, 110 N 262/Frégates were built, of which 67 were Series As.

Just prior to the close of N 262 production in 1975, Allegheny Airlines, as an important user of the N 262 Series A, worked with Aérospatiale on a conversion of the airliner to use 1,120-shp Pratt & Whitney Aircraft of Canada PT6A-45 turboprop engines. The resulting re-engined aircraft became known as the Mohawk 298 and the airline put the first into service in 1977. Today 25 N 262-type/Mohawk 298 airliners remain in commercial service, including a large number with Ransome Airlines (Mohawk 298s), one of the original operators of the N 262. Accommodating up to 29 passengers or passengers and cargo, the Mohawk 298 has a cruising speed of 396 km/h (246 mph) and its range is 1020 km (633 miles).

Like France, West Germany's aircraft of commuter type all come from a single manufacturer, in this case Dornier. The first of these is the Do 28 D Skyservant, a STOL general-purpose transport that was produced in civil and military guise but which had little similarity to its earlier Do 28 namesake or the Do 27 predecessor. First flown in February 1966, the prototype was followed

Above: Dornier Do 28 B-1 seven-passenger, twin piston-engined, utility aircraft.

Right: The 10-seat Dornier 128-6, the twin-turboprop variant of the new Do 128-2.

by seven Do 28 Ds and then the first major production version, the Do 28 D-1. The Do 28 D-2 became the standard production version from 1971 until the close of production at the end of the decade. Heavier than earlier versions, the D-2 Skyservant uses the rectangular-section fuselage and high-mounted wing of the D-1 and is powered by two 380-hp Lycoming IGSO-540-A1E piston engines carried on the stub wings that support the undercarriage. Accommodation is provided for 12 to 14 passengers or cargo. The maximum cruising speed is 306 km/h (190 mph) and the range with the maximum payload is 1 050 km (652 miles). Production of the Skyservant included more than 120 for the Federal German Air Force and Navy.

Dornier's replacement aircraft for the Do 28 D-2 Skyservant is the Dornier 128-2, which is similar in both configuration and size, and is powered by similar engines. However, it has a slightly higher empty weight and normal accommodation is provided for eight or nine passengers or cargo, although five stretchers and five other persons can be carried. Its maximum cruising speed is 304 km/h (189 mph) and its range with the maximum amount of fuel (which includes two auxiliary fuel tanks carried

under the wing) is 2 875 km (1,786 miles). The Dornier 128-2 has been on the market since 1980.

In 1978 Dornier flew a Do 28 D-2 fitted with two Avco Lycoming LTP 101 turboprop engines, calling the modified aircraft the Do 28 D-5X Turbo Skyservant. Although this did not enter production, with the launch of the Dornier 128-2 has come a turboprop derivative, known as the Dornier 128-6. Power plant for the production version, which became available to civil and military customers in 1981, is two 400-shp (derated) Pratt & Whitney Aircraft of Canada PT6A-110 engines. The maximum take-off weight of this version is 4 350 kg (9,590 lb), considerably higher than for the 128-2 and resulting in the need for a strengthened undercarriage. The maximum cruising speed and range with a maximum fuel load are 330 km/h (205 mph) and 1 825 km (1,134 miles) respectively.

In March and May 1981 Dornier flew the prototypes of the new 228 commuter and utility aircraft, in 228-100 and 228-200 forms respectively. The Dornier 228 bears some resemblance to the Dornier 128 but has a new greater-span Dornier-developed supercritical wing with raked tips, a

Dornier Do 28 D-2 Skyservant.

The new Dornier 228-100 15-passenger airliner in the livery of the first operator, AS Norving Flyservice of Norway.

lengthened fuselage with a longer nose, a retractable undercarriage, and is powered by two 715-shp Garrett TPE331-5 turbo-prop engines carried under the wing. The basic version of the Dornier 228 is the 228-100, with accommodation for 15 passengers. It is equally suited to mixed passenger/cargo operations or all-cargo, in the latter form carrying a 2 373-kg (5,231-lb) load. The maximum cruising speed and range with 15 passengers are 432 km/h (268 mph) and 1 970 km (1,224 miles) respectively.

The 19-passenger 228-200 has an overall length of 16.56 metres (54 feet 4 inches), compared to the 228-100's 15.04 metres (49 feet 4 inches). It has a higher empty weight but a similar maximum take-off weight, resulting in a lower passenger or cargo payload capability. The range of this version when carrying 19 passengers is

1 150 km (715 miles). The first Dornier 228-100 was delivered in early 1982, going to AS Norving Flyservice of Norway, followed mid-year by the first 228-200 to Jet Charters in Australia. By the beginning of that year, Dornier had received orders for 23 228s from operators in eight different countries.

A twin-turboprop STOL transport of very different configuration to any other so far described is the IAI Arava. This Israeli aircraft has a circular-section fuselage, the rear section of which can swing open to provide unobscured access to the main cabin. This design feature is particularly useful when the aircraft is being used for carrying cargo or vehicles, or for loading stretchers when used as an air ambulance or medical clinic, or for loading chemicals for rainmaking, and so on. The strut-braced high-mounted wings are of constant-chord and carry the twin tail booms that extend from the rear of the engine nacelles. A twin fin and rudder and linking tailplane comprise the tail unit.

The prototype Arava made its maiden flight in November 1969 but the initial civil version, the IAI 102, was not certificated until 1976. This version has accommodation for 20 passengers as a commuter airliner, 12 in VIP form, or it can be configured for carrying cargo or other duties. Five years after certification a total of 10 had been sold, most going to Argentina. One of these has been used as a water-bomber.

In 1980, a new civil version of the Arava was certificated as the IAI 101B. Produced with American customers in mind, it uses two 750-shp Pratt & Whitney Aircraft of Canada PT6A-36 turboprop engines. The cargo version is known as the Cargo Commuterliner. The first 18-seat airliner was acquired by Key West Airlines, and the first Cargo Commuterliner went to Airspur.

Soon after certification of the civil IAI 102, the company began testing a lengthened version known as the IAI 202. Other changes were related mainly to the wings, which carried more fuel and had boundary layer fences and winglets. Power was provided by PT6A-36 engines. The airframe modifications were evolved to reduce induced drag by a substantial amount. IAI subsequently produced a winglet modification kit, which became available to customers operating Aravas, with large dorsal and smaller ventral surfaces. The maximum cruising speed of the civil Arava is probably about 319 km/h (198 mph) at 3000 metres (10,000 feet).

The first of the Italian aircraft to be described is the Piaggio P.166, an unusual light transport with gull wings and the engines/propellers installed as 'pushers'. This wing form and engine configuration was not new to Piaggio when the P.166

Below: Nineteen-passenger Dornier 228-200.

Bottom: IAI 202 Arava with winglets.

prototype took off for its first flight in 1957, as a similar arrangement had been featured on the company's P.136 five-seat light amphibian that appeared soon after the end of the Second World War. Early civil production versions of the P.166 were all powered by two Lycoming piston engines. Four versions were produced: the six- to eight-seat P.166, which was the major production version with two 340-hp Lycoming GSO-480 engines; the P.166 Portofino with 380-hp Lycoming IGSO-540 engines, a lengthened fuselage nose and with an improved cabin for up to 10 passengers; the similar 12-passenger P.166C; and the longer-range P.166-DL2 with integral wingtip fuel tanks. Production of these four piston-engined versions totalled 32, five, two and four respectively.

In July 1976 a new lease of life for the aircraft came with the introduction of a civil turboprop-engined version of the P.166-DL2, known as the P.166-DL3. Powered by two 599-shp Avco Lycoming LTP 101-600

turboprop engines, it has standard accommodation for eight passengers or can have interior changes to accommodate stretchers as an air ambulance or to carry cargo. Higher-rated LTP 101-700A1A engines are also available for this aircraft. With either engine type, the maximum cruising speed is 370 km/h (230 mph) and the range can be 2 038 km (1,266 miles).

In 1970 General Avia Costruzioni Aeronautiche Sri was founded to develop to prototype stage aircraft designed by Dott Ing Stelio Frati, for subsequent manufacture by other companies. One such aircraft is the SF.600 Canguro, the prototype of which made its maiden flight at the close of 1978. SIAI-Marchetti began production of the Canguro in 1981 and currently offers it in two forms. The SF.600 is the piston-engined version with two 350-hp Avco Lycoming TIO-540-J engines carried under the high-mounted constant-chord wing. Nine passengers can be accommodated, or other interiors allow for stretchers as an air

R. Piaggio P.166-DL3 in Alitalia insignia.

96

Prototype SIAI-Marchetti SF.600TP Canguro.

ambulance or cargo weighing up to 1 050 kg (2,315 lb). Its cruising speed is estimated to be 285 km/h (177 mph) and its range 2 400 km (1,490 miles). The turboprop version is known as the SF.600TP and is powered by two 420-shp Allison 250-B17C engines. Accommodation remains similar but the cruising speed is 290 km/h (180 mph) and the range can be 2 250 km (1,398 miles). Its empty weight is less than the piston-engined SF.600 and its take-off weight higher. The first Canguros were received by customers in 1983.

A joint venture by CASA of Spain and PT Nurtanio of Indonesia has produced the CN-235 commuter airliner, managed under a new company known as Airtec (Aircraft Technology Industries). PT Nurtanio was founded in 1976 and since then has manufactured the CASA Aviocar under licence. The company also produces the MBB BO 105 and Aérospatiale Puma/Super Puma under licence. Its involvement in this project with CASA is, therefore, explained, and the company has the added advantage of being able to contribute its half of CN-235 components from a brand new manufacturing plant which requires no artificial heating or lighting (and so reduces manufacturing costs) because of its near-equatorial latitude.

The prototype CN-235 was expected to

fly in 1983. It is a 34/38-passenger airliner with a circular-section pressurized fuselage and a high-mounted wing. Power is provided by two 1,700-shp General Electric CT7-7s, a type of engine similar to that selected for the Saab-Fairchild 340 joint-venture airliner (detailed later in this chapter). It can also be configured for mixed passenger/cargo or freighter operations. The loading and unloading of bulky items or containers is aided by a wide ramp that forms part of the underside of the upswept rear fuselage. The maximum cargo load is estimated to be 4 500 kg (9,921 lb). Production examples of the CN-235, of which a large number have been ordered or reserved by option, are expected to be delivered to customers in 1984. The maximum cruising speed of the CN-235 is estimated to be 454 km/h (282 mph).

CASA's own C-212 Aviocar first appeared in 1971. It had been developed primarily to fulfil a military transport role as a replacement for outdated transports then serving with the Spanish Air Force, including a number of Junkers Ju 52/3ms. Its STOL performance allows it to take off from and land on short unprepared airstrips. The first production version was the C-212-5 Series 100, comprising five variants. Of these, the C-212C was produced as the commercial transport,

Right: CASA C-212 Series 200 Aviocar, flown by Air Tungaru of the Republic of Kiribati.

Merpati Nusantara Air Lines Series 200 Aviocars, built in Indonesia and awaiting delivery.

powered by two 776-ehp AiResearch TPE 331-5-251C turboprop engines carried in the leading edge of the tapered high-mounted wing. Accommodation is provided for up to 19 passengers or 2 000 kg (4,410 lb) of cargo. The latter can include vehicles which are loaded into the cabin via a hinged ramp which forms the under-surface of the upswept tail.

Excluding development aircraft, CASA built 125 C-212-5 Series 100s and PT Nurtanio of Indonesia produced a further 29 under licence, which include military examples. The first C-212C for commercial use was delivered in July 1975 and the small number built included one for Air Logistic Company in Alaska, two for the Royal Thailand Rain Industry and several for Merpati Nusantara Air Lines. The maximum speed of the Series 100 is 359 km/h (223 mph) and the range with a full load is 480 km (298 miles).

The standard civil and military version since 1979 has been the higher weight C-212 Series 200 Aviocar, powered by two 900-shp Garrett TPE 331-10-501C turboprop engines. Accommodation is provided for 26 to 28 passengers, or alternative interior layouts allow the aircraft to be used as a VIP transport or as a freighter for 2 770 kg (6,106 lb) of cargo. Both the Series 100 and 200 can perform air ambulance duties. The maximum cruising speed of the Series 200 is 365 km/h (227 mph) and its range with a full load is 408 km (253 miles). With the maximum amount of fuel carried, range can increase four-fold. Already more Series 200s have been ordered than Series 100s, for commercial and military operations.

In an historic step, Saab-Scania of Sweden and Fairchild Industries of Maryland, U.S.A., have jointly designed, developed and are manufacturing a twin-engined commuter airliner and corporate transport (up to 22 seats) as the Saab-Fairchild 340. The first 340 off the assembly line at the newly constructed factory at Linköping, Sweden, appeared in October 1982 in the livery of Air Midwest. The first flight was achieved in January 1983. Fairchild is responsible for marketing the airliner in the North American continent (Canada, the U.S. and Mexico) and Saab-Scania to all other customers. To date each company has orders and reserving options for more than 50 340s, of which approximately one-quarter are for the corporate

version. One of the latest orders for the corporate version has come from Philip Morris Incorporated, which ordered three 14-seat examples.

The Saab-Fairchild 340 is a conventionally configured pressurized airliner, with low-mounted straight-tapered wings. Power is provided by two advanced 1,630-shp General Electric CT7-5A turboprop engines on the commuter version and 1,600-shp General Electric CT7-7Es in corporate form. These bestow an estimated maximum cruising speed and range (when carrying a full passenger load of 34 persons) of 508 km/h (315 mph) and 1 686 km (1,048 miles) respectively. The aircraft has been designed to be simple to maintain and economical in operation. The first aircraft will be in commercial use in 1984.

A single-engined utility transport aircraft that has achieved great success in both civil and military forms is the Swiss Pilatus PC-6, known in piston-engined form as the Porter (also the name for piston and turboprop-engined PC-6s built under licence in the U.S.A. by Fairchild) and as the Turbo-Porter when installed with a turboprop. It can operate as a STOL transport in greatly varying climatic conditions and in

The Saab-Fairchild 340 first flew on 25 January 1983. This photograph was taken three days later, when the undercarriage was retracted for the first time.

Above: Pilatus PC-6
Turbo-Porter STOL
utility transport.

Right: Chinese-built
Y-5, based on the
Antonov An-2.

difficult terrain, whether from snow-covered high-altitude airstrips near ski resorts, from sand, or as a floatplane from water. It achieves its STOL performance from the double-slotted flaps on the trailing edge of the high-mounted and strut-braced constant-chord wings and from the high-power of its engine. The undercarriage wheels can be of the low-pressure oversized type, particularly suited for operating from soft ground. The rectangular-section fuselage has accommodation for seven to 10 passengers, or it can be quickly adapted for carrying cargo or for other uses such as agricultural crop spraying, surveying, glider towing and water bombing.

The first PC-6 Porter prototype made its maiden flight in May 1959 and the initial production version was built with a 340-hp Lycoming GSO-480 piston engine. An uprated piston-engined version appeared as the PC-6/350 Porter, with a 350-hp IGO-540 engine. Turboprop power was introduced in 1961, with the availability of the PC-6/A Turbo-Porter. This version was initially given a 523-shp Turboméca Astazou IIE or IIG engine, and was followed by two other versions with 573-shp Astazous.

The first of the 'B' series Turbo-Porters was the PC-6/B-H2, the first of three versions using Pratt & Whitney Aircraft of Canada PT6A turboprops. This and the next version were produced with engines of 550 shp, and both came onto the aviation scene in 1964. The version of the Turbo-Porter available today is the PC-6/B2-H2, powered by a 680-shp PT6A-27 turboprop engine. The maximum cruising speed is 259 km/h (161 mph) and the maximum range without the use of auxiliary underwing fuel tanks is 1 050 km (652 miles). Take-off at sea level at maximum weight can be achieved in a distance of 110 metres (360 feet). Turbo-Porters with AiResearch TPE 331 turboprop engines of about 575 shp were also produced, as PC-6/C models. More than 450 Porters/Turbo-Porters have been delivered to customers in more than 50 countries since 1961, and production of the PC-6/B2-H2 continues today.

The Aero Industry Development Center–Chinese Air Force, or AIDC/CAF of Taiwan, produces under licence the Northrop F-5 Tiger II tactical fighter for the Chinese Nationalist Air Force and in the past has been responsible for the manufacture of other aircraft of foreign origin.

However, one aircraft of its own design is the XC-2, a twin-engined high-wing transport equally suited to commercial and military use.

The prototype made its maiden flight in 1979 but its status today is not clear. It is powered by two 1,451-ehp Avco Lycoming T53-L-701A turboprop engines and in civil form can accommodate 38 passengers or 3 855 kg (8,500 lb) of cargo, with the capability of rapid changeover from one interior layout to another. A mixed passenger/cargo layout is also possible. A loading and unloading ramp is provided under the upswept rear fuselage. The maximum cruising speed and its range with a full load are estimated to be 370 km/h (230 mph) and 480 km (298 miles) respectively.

Where Antonovs reign supreme

Other than the Yak-40, a short-haul airliner discussed in a previous chapter, all the aircraft of Soviet origin in this chapter come from the Antonov Bureau. However, Antonovs are even more prominent in the freighter role and can also be found among agricultural types.

In August 1947 the first flight took place of an aircraft that combined the engine power of a modern light aircraft with the biplane wings of the prewar era. Designated An-2 by Antonov and later given the reporting name *Colt* by NATO, it had been built to the requirements of the Soviet ministry of agriculture and forestry. In the following year the aircraft entered production, powered by a nose-mounted 1,000-hp Shvetsov ASh-62 radial engine.

Major production of the An-2 did not end in the Soviet Union until the early 1960s, and even then others were built in An-2M form. Soviet production totalled well over 5,000 aircraft. These were put into service as military general-purpose biplanes, and in civil form as passenger, VIP and cargo transports, air ambulance and survey aircraft, agricultural sprayers and dusters, and for many other roles. Today Soviet-built An-2s remain in widespread use in the Soviet Union and in those countries that received export versions.

As Soviet production of the An-2 was winding down, so the Polish PZL company began high-volume production at its factory at Mielec. By 1982 PZL Mielec had far exceeded Soviet production of the biplane,

PZL Mielec An-2
skiplane.

having produced more than 9,200 for military and civil operation. Of those exported to 14 countries, nearly 90 per cent were delivered to the Soviet Union. When production in Poland comes to an end in 1985, it will mark the completion of the greatest number of general-purpose transports and related variants of a single design ever produced. The total number will have to include An-2s built in China, latterly as Shijiazhuang Y-5s, the name indicating the location of the Y-5 factory.

Polish-built An-2s include the basic 12-adult and two-children An-2P passenger airliner, the An-2T passenger or cargo version, and the mixed traffic An-2TP. A floatplane version of the An-2T is the An-2LW and the five-seat VIP transport is designated An-2PK. The An-2R agricultural version is mentioned in a later chapter. These are but some of the An-2 variants produced in Poland. Soviet-built An-2s include the An-2M and S agricultural aircraft, An-2V floatplane and An-2L water-bomber. The An-2P is powered by an ASz-621R radial engine. This engine was developed in the Soviet Union as the Shvetsov ASh-62 from the American Wright R-1820 Cyclone, and also powers the remaining Lisunov Li-2s, the Soviet-produced version of the Douglas DC-3. The maximum speed of the An-2P is 258 km/h (160 mph) and the typical range is 900 km (560 miles). The unequal-span biplane wings of the An-2 have slotted trailing-edge flaps, and the upper wings have leading-edge slots, allowing the aircraft to take off from a runway in 150 metres (492 feet), a distance increased only to 170 metres (558 feet) when taking off from grass. Despite the An-2's antiquated appearance, it remains highly prized as one of the only aeroplanes capable of flying to relatively inaccessible parts of the Soviet Union.

A neat little general-purpose transport aircraft from Antonov made its maiden flight in 1958 as the An-14 Pchelka (NATO named *Clod*). It is a strut-braced high-wing monoplane, with a twin fin and rudder tail unit and two piston engines. A few hundred were produced between 1965 and the end of the decade for Aeroflot and for military service. As a passenger transport it accommodates eight persons, reduced to five in VIP form. Interior changes allow the aircraft to be used for agricultural work, or it can be configured as an air ambulance or freighter. The developed version is powered by two wing-mounted 300-hp Ivchenko AI-14RF engines, which bestow a normal cruising speed and range of 180 km/h (112 mph) and 650 to 800 km (404 to 497 miles) respectively.

By scaling up the An-14 and powering it with two turboprop engines, Antonov has produced the An-28. This is known to NATO as *Cash*. The prototype made its first flight in 1969 but it was not until 1975 that a pre-production An-28 flew in definitive form. Like the An-14, it is a strut-braced high-wing aircraft with a non-retractable undercarriage and twin tail unit. Power is provided by two 960-shp Glushenkov TVD-10B turboprop engines, which allow a cruising speed of 337 km/h (209 mph) and a range, with a payload of 1 750 kg (3,858 lb),

of 560 km (348 miles). The overall length of the An-28 is 13.10 metres (42 feet $11\frac{3}{4}$ inches), compared to the An-14's 11.44 metres (37 feet $6\frac{1}{2}$ inches). In the longer fuselage can be accommodated up to 20 passengers, passengers and cargo, or cargo only, or it can be configured for other roles. Loading of bulky items is aided by a ramp under the upswept rear fuselage.

Manufacture of the An-28 is being undertaken by PZL Mielec, with the first Polish aircraft to appear in 1983. It is expected to be operated extensively over short-haul routes by Aeroflot and may supersede the remarkable An-2 biplane over some of these. Take-off and landing distances are kept short by the use of single-slotted ailerons that droop with the double-slotted flaps.

Other Antonov transports capable of carrying passengers include the An-26 and An-32. However, both of these are primarily freighters, with the former offering accommodation for up to 40 persons on tip-up seats along the sides of the main cabin and the latter accommodating 39 passengers. Both aircraft are described in the following chapter, which is concerned with freighters.

The second Soviet-built Antonov An-28 in Aeroflot colours.

Above: The Volpar
Turboliner, the final
evolution of the Beech
Model 18 by Volpar.

Right: Beechcraft
Commuter 1900. Note
the taillets and
horizontal surfaces below
the tailplane.

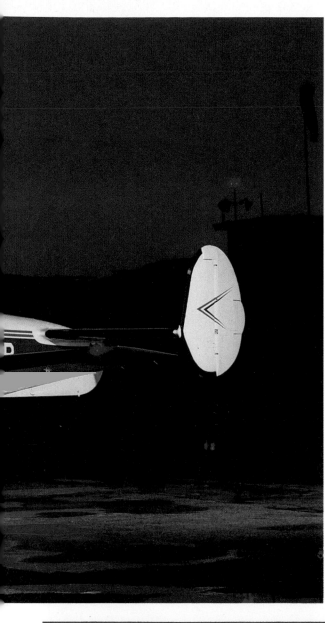

Birthplace of the commuter airliner

The United States of America is recognized as the birthplace of commuter air travel. Much of that nation's aircraft industry is connected with the manufacture of light, business and commuter-type aircraft, and the U.S.A. potentially offers foreign manufacturers their largest export market.

Most of the nation's requirements are satisfied by aircraft of American origin, whether low-capacity piston-engined aircraft or sleek jets with greater passenger accommodation. The types detailed in the following paragraphs represent some of the aircraft manufactured in the U.S.A. that are engaged as commuter airliners. Others that are employed commercially to a limited degree can be found in the chapter dealing with business aircraft. The latter usually fly non-scheduled charter services.

Three U.S. aircraft manufacturers dominate the world light aircraft scene. These are the Beech Aircraft Corporation, Cessna Aircraft Company and the Piper Aircraft Corporation. By 1982 the three companies had, between them, produced well over 341,000 aircraft. One of the oldest aircraft from these companies to remain in commercial use is the Beechcraft 18, the prototype of which first flew in 1937. Several versions were produced with alternative piston engines and other options including either a

Beechcraft Commuter C99 prototype.

tailwheel- or nosewheel-type undercarriage. The Model H18 Super 18, which appeared in 1962 and ended the Beechcraft 18 production run in 1969, was built with two 450-hp Pratt & Whitney R-985-AN-14B piston engines, accommodation for nine passengers, and a cruising speed and maximum range of 354 km/h (220 mph) and 2460 km (1,530 miles) respectively. A turboprop conversion of the Beechcraft 18 was produced by Volpar as the Turbo 18, accommodating two extra passengers and powered by 705-ehp AiResearch TPE 331-1-101B engines. These increase the cruising speed to 451 km/h (280 mph). The same company also produced a lengthened version of the Turbo-18 for 15 passengers; it is known as the Turboliner.

In 1966 Beech flew the prototype of a modern unpressurized light transport as the Model 99. Production examples were delivered from 1968 with two 550-ehp Pratt & Whitney Aircraft of Canada PT6A-20 turboprop engines. A follow-on version became the Model 99A with PT6A-27 engines and this in turn was superseded by

Right: Cessna Model 402C, available in Utililiner and Businessliner forms.

Below: Cessna Titan third-level airliner and business transport.

the B99 Airliner and B99 Executive. The B99 Airliner was produced as a 15-passenger aircraft for third-level scheduled services and was installed with two 680-shp PT6A-28 turboprop engines. The executive version became the eight to 17-seat B99 Executive. The cruising speed of the B99 Airliner is 459 km/h (285 mph) and a typical range is 1 339 km (832 miles).

Production of the B99 Airliner and Executive ended in the 1970s, by which time 164 had been produced for more than 60 operators. In a bid to put a Beech aircraft back in the commuter aircraft market, the company has produced the new Commuter C99. This is based on the B99 Airliner but has a higher level of standard equipment, is powered by two 715-shp PT6A-36 turboprop engines, and has the same passenger or cargo area accommodation as the B99 Airliner. The maximum take-off weight is higher. Its cruising speed of 461 km/h (287 mph) and range of 1 686 km (1,048 miles) with the maximum amount of fuel carried, compare favourably with those of the B99 Airliner. Delivery of production Commuter C99s began in 1981.

A considerably larger commuter airliner has also been developed by Beech as part of the company's drive to regain old markets, the first prototype of which made its first flight in September 1982 as the pressurized Commuter 1900 Airliner. This is a newly designed aircraft with low-mounted wings, a T-tail, and is powered by two 1,000-shp Pratt & Whitney Aircraft of Canada PT6A-65B turboprop engines. Accommodation is provided for 19 passengers as standard. The estimated maximum cruising speed is 487 km/h (303 mph) and the range with the maximum payload of 1 814 kg (4,000 lb) is 1 390 km (860 miles). The first production Commuter 1900 Airliner was scheduled to make its maiden flight in early 1983.

In the same year that Beech flew its Model 99 prototype, the Model 402 third-level airliner appeared from Cessna. This first became available as a nine- to 10-seat passenger or cargo aircraft which, with the subsequent introduction of an executive version as the Businessliner, became known as the Utililiner. Today Cessna continues to offer the Utililiner and Businessliner in basic and higher-standard Mk II forms under the model designation Model 402C. The two 325-hp Continental TSIO-520-VB turbocharged engines give the Model 402C a maximum cruising speed of 394 km/h (245

Piper Cheyenne III commuter and corporate transport.

mph) and a typical range of 1 695 km (1,053 miles). The success of the Model 402 since its introduction has meant that 1,480 had been produced by the spring of 1982.

The Model 402 is just one in a range of aircraft from Cessna of fairly similar type. Another in the range is the Titan, originally known as the Model 404. Of increased span and length compared to the Model 402, it has the potential of a substantial increase in the revenue ton-miles performed on a given amount of fuel. Power is provided by two 375-hp Continental GTSIO-520-M piston engines. The prototype Model 404/Titan made its initial flight in February 1975 and between 1976 and 1982 a total of 378 had been sold. Production was then suspended temporarily.

Three principle versions of the Titan were built. These comprised the Titan Ambassador, with seating for eight passengers, the Titan Courier for passenger or cargo operations, and the Titan Freighter all-cargo version. Mk II variants of all three types and the Titan Ambassador Mk III indicate higher standards of avionics and equipment. The maximum cruising speed of the Titan is 402 km/h (250 mph) and typical range is 2 501 km (1,554 miles).

The first Piper aircraft to be detailed is the pressurized PA-42 Cheyenne III, the third and much-modified aircraft of the Cheyenne series, with accommodation for up to nine passengers as a commuter airliner and corporate transport. Delivered to

Nine/ten-passenger Piper T-1020, supported by the company's Airline Division.

Piper Chieftain eight-passenger commuter airliner.

Turboprop-powered Piper T-1040.

Other aircraft from Beech and Piper used commercially include the eight/15-seat and pressurized Beechcraft Super King Air B200 (right) and the Piper Cherokee (below).

customers from 1980, it is by far the largest Cheyenne and the first to feature a T-tail. Power is provided by two 720-shp Pratt & Whitney Aircraft of Canada PT6A-41 turboprop engines. Its cruising speed and typical range with auxiliary fuel are 537 km/h (334 mph) and 3 706 km (2,303 miles) respectively.

Prior to the appearance of the Cheyenne III, Piper had introduced its PA-31-350 Chieftain, a lengthened derivative of the Navajo, accommodating a flight crew of two and eight passengers as a commuter airliner or fewer passengers in greater luxury in its executive form. The cruising speed and typical range are 409 km/h (254 mph) and 1 714 km (1,065 miles) on standard fuel respectively, on the power of the two 350-hp Avco Lycoming TIO-540-J2BD turbocharged engines. About 500 Chieftains are in service with airlines operating commuter services.

To support its commuter airline customers, Piper formed an Airline division in 1981. This decision was brought about not only because of the appearance of two new Piper commuter airliners, the T-1020 and T-1040, but also to support Chieftains already in airline use. The T-1020, which went into service in 1982, is a derivative of the Chieftain and accommodates nine or 10 passengers. The main difference is the use of a strengthened undercarriage and doors, to take account of the great many short flights and the resulting heavy use made of these components during commuter services.

The T-1040 is the turboprop-powered companion of the T-1020. It first flew in July 1981, more than two months before the T-1020. The first production delivery was made in the spring of the following year. Its seating capacity is the same as that for the T-1020, as it too is based on the Chieftain fuselage but married to the same two 500-shp Pratt & Whitney Aircraft of Canada PT6A-11 turboprops, the fuselage nose, the tail unit and wings of the Piper Cheyenne I. The maximum take-off weight is 907 kg (2,000 lb) higher than that of the T-1020, at 4 082 kg (9,000 lb), yet the empty weight is only 79 kg (174 lb) greater. The maximum cruising speed is 437 km/h (272 mph) and its range with a full load is 1 093 km (679 miles). A freighter version is also available to customers, capable of carrying a cargo of nearly 1 315 kg (2,900 lb). Further room is provided by an optional cargo pod.

Of very different type to the U.S. aircraft so far mentioned is the Gulfstream I, which was produced between 1958 to 1969 as a 10- to 14-passenger twin-turboprop executive transport. A total of 200 Gulfstream Is was delivered to customers. In the late 1970s the Grumman American Aviation Corporation, which produced the Gulfstream I and built several other types of aircraft as a subsidiary of the Grumman Corporation, was taken over by American Jet Industries and became known thereafter as the Gulfstream American Corporation. One result of this take-over was interest in a possible 37-passenger commuter airliner version of the Gulfstream I. In October 1979 a Gulfstream I, with its fuselage lengthened considerably to accommodate the extra passengers, made its first flight as a Gulfstream American G159C Gulfstream I-C.

The wing span and engines remained the same as for the original executive transport, the latter comprising two 1,990-ehp Rolls-Royce Dart Mk 529-8X turboprops. Because of the modifications, the maximum cruising speed was reduced to 571 km/h (355 mph) and the range was 804 to 4 023 km (500 to 2,500 miles), depending on the number of passengers and fuel carried. The concept proved a success and the first Gulfstream I-C was delivered to Air North in late 1980. Several more have since been acquired by other airlines.

Having successfully launched its new airliner, Gulfstream American took over Rockwell International's General Aviation Division in 1981, renaming it the company's Commander Division. The aircraft produced are Commander Jetprop business types. Gulfstream American Corporation has recently been renamed Gulfstream Aerospace Corporation.

In 1947 Grumman itself had flown the prototype of its Albatross utility amphibian, which entered service with the U.S.A.F., U.S. Navy and others from 1949. Hundreds were produced, some of which were modified to HU-16B standard, with increased wing span and higher weight. Accommodation in this version is provided for 22 passengers or 12 stretchers.

Another Cessna aircraft used commercially is the six-seat Cessna 185 Skywagon, seen here as a Mount Cook Line skiplane.

To the initial order of Resorts International, Grumman has undertaken the task of converting HU-16B Albatross amphibians into 28-seat commuter amphibians. This work involves a complete check of the airframe and replacement of some component parts, overhaul of the two 1,475-hp Wright R-1820 radial engines, conversion of the interior to the new commercial standard, and other changes including new avionics. The prototype conversion by Grumman, in fact on an ex-Navy UF-2 Albatross, took off for the first time in February 1979.

It is anticipated that Grumman will convert 13 HU-16B Albatross amphibians to G-111 commuter standard for Resorts International. More than half this number had been delivered by early 1982. Of these, Resorts International's commuter operator, Chalks International, operates a number of G-111s. One of the first seven conversions

Chalks International G-111 commuter amphibian.

has been sold to an operator in Indonesia. Grumman has already bought in more than 50 HU-16Bs for modification to commercial standard, which could be just the beginning. The G-111 has a speed and range with a full passenger load of 382 km/h (237 mph) and 506-750 km (314-466 miles) respectively.

In August 1969 the Swearingen Aviation Corporation flew the prototype of a pressurized commuter airliner known as the Metro. This entered production and was followed by the refined Metro II, which has accommodation for 20 passengers and was also made available in all-cargo form. Power for the Metro II is provided by two 940-shp AiResearch TPE 331-3UW-303G turboprop engines, carried on the leading edges of the low-mounted wings.

In 1979 Swearingen Aviation became a subsidiary of Fairchild Industries and is now known as the Fairchild Swearingen

Corporation. It currently offers the Metro III as an 18-passenger commuter airliner, powered by two 1,100-shp Garrett TPE 331-11U-601G turboprop engines carried on greater-span wings. Many other refinements have been incorporated into the Metro III, which has a maximum cruising speed and range with a full passenger load of 515 km/h (320 mph) and 1610 km (1,001 miles) respectively. Compared to the Metro II, the Metro III's maximum take-off weight is substantially increased. Twenty-six airline operators had received more than 230 Metro series commuter airliners by June 1982. One operator, COMAIR, received two Metro IIIs early in 1983.

The latest version of the Metro is the Metro IIIA. As its designation indicates, it is a derivative of the Metro III, powered by two 1,100-shp Pratt & Whitney Aircraft of Canada PT6A-45R turboprop engines and has a revised undercarriage and other changes. Delivery of production Metro IIIAs began in 1983.

The final aircraft to be outlined in this chapter is also the latest to appear in the United States and can probably claim to be the largest-capacity commuter airliner. This is the Commuter Aircraft Corporation CAC-100, the prototype of which appeared in 1983. The Commuter Aircraft Corporation was founded to develop and market this airliner, with manufacture taking place at the company's new factory in Ohio. Delivery of production aircraft is to begin in 1984.

The CAC-100 is a 22.69-metre (74-feet 5½-inch)-span airliner, with an overall length of 21.63 metres (70 feet 11½ inches). It has pressurized accommodation for 50 or 60 passengers, making it particularly suitable for use on busy commuter routes. Power is provided by four 1,409-ehp Pratt & Whitney Aircraft of Canada PT6A-65R turboprop engines, which are expected to bestow a cruising speed and range (with 50 passengers) of 569 km/h (354 mph) and 1 186 km (737 miles) respectively.

5 Freighters

There are three methods of transporting cargo by air. The first is for ordinary passenger-carrying airliners to carry cargo in their underfloor holds. Although this is important as a method of transporting smaller amounts of cargo, and financially important to the airline operator, these aircraft are not true freighters in the accepted sense.

The second method involves an airliner that can be used for either passenger, mixed traffic or all-cargo operations. Such aircraft can be a single model which is offered with a choice of passenger interior or one for carrying freight, or one of the 'combis' or 'convertibles'. A combi carries both passengers and cargo in the main cabin areas. It can have a removable bulkhead that separates the two for possible all-passenger operation. A convertible is an aircraft designed to be operated either in all-passenger or all-cargo forms as markets dictate, sometimes with a quick-change interior to speed the passenger/cargo changeover process. This QC interior can include palletized seating. A large number of the aircraft mentioned in previous chapters are of the 'second method' type and will not be described again. Examples of these are the Fokker F27 Mk 600 Friendship and the Boeing 747-200C Convertible.

The third method is by actual freighter, an aircraft with no other purpose than to transport cargo by air. Freighters come in three forms. The first is the purpose-designed freighter, conceived and built for cargo carrying. Aircraft of this type can be those built for commercial use or modified ex-military transports. The second type of freighter is the purpose-built cargo-only version of an existing passenger airliner; one such example is the Boeing Model 747-200F. The third type is the older airliner, originally produced for passenger services but now outdated and converted for freighting. Aircraft of the latter type include examples of the Douglas DC-3, DC-4 and DC-6, the Ilyushin Il-14 and, to some extent, the Il-18 and the Lockheed Electra, and the Vickers Vanguard. The Vanguard, as detailed in Chapter Three, became the Merchantman in freighter form, capable of

Typical of older airliners used for freighting is the Ilyushin Il-18V, this one flown by LOT.

carrying large cargo pallets or other loads up to a maximum weight of approximately 18 500 kg (40,785 lb). The British airline Air Bridge Carriers has the largest fleet of Merchantman transports.

Among the older purpose-built freighters that continue to operate commercially are types of British, Canadian, French and American origin. One British type is the remarkable Bristol Type 170 Freighter, designed during the Second World War and produced and operated thereafter as a passenger and freight transport. Few who travelled across the Channel by Silver City Freighter, having seen their car driven up a ramp and between the aircraft's nose doors, will forget the experience. Today, Freighters continue to give reliable service in the U.K. and New Zealand. The British operator is Instone Air Line, which operates two from Stansted in Essex. These are ex-R.N.A.F. Freighter Mk 31s, each powered by two 1,980-hp Bristol Hercules 734 engines and with a speed and typical range of 362 km/h (225 mph) and 1 320 km (820 miles) respectively. With the maximum payload of approximately 5 400 kg (11,900 lb), a range of about 483 km (300 miles) is normal. They are often employed as blood-

stock transports, carrying perhaps eight horses and 10 accompanying grooms. Other transport tasks can include the transportation of oil and mineral exploration equipment and men.

Safe Air is the Freighter operator of New Zealand, and this company is one of the few airlines that count the Hawker Siddeley Argosy in their fleets. Another Argosy operator is Air Bridge Carriers, and IPEC of Australia is a third. Designed in commercial and military forms as a high-capacity freighter, the Argosy prototype appeared in 1959 as an Armstrong Whitworth type. Delivery of Argosy 650 Series 100 initial

Above: One of Air Bridge Carriers' Merchantman freighters with support equipment.

Top: Instone Air Line Bristol Freighter Mk 31, an ex-R.N.A.F. transport.

Right: Air Bridge Carriers' Argosy, with its nose cargo door swung open. Loads can include bloodstock or cattle, in twelve stalls or six pens respectively.

One of the ex-R.A.F. Shorts Belfasts operated by Heavylift Air Cargoes.

In January 1964 Short Brothers flew the prototype Belfast, a giant freighter intended to be offered to the military and for commercial use. In the event only the R.A.F. received production aircraft, using 10 as Belfast C.Mk 1s until they were withdrawn from service as a defence economy measure. This withdrawl left the R.A.F. without a single long-range heavy transport in service but, at the same time, released the aircraft for purchase by commercial operators. Five were acquired by HeavyLift Air Cargoes, a British airline based at Stansted Airport in Essex. These have been modified for civil use by Marshall of Cambridge (Engineering) Limited, the first entering service in March 1980. By 1982 three Belfasts were in use. The first commercial charter flight by a HeavyLift Belfast saw two of Bristow Helicopters' Pumas transported from England to Perth, Australia.

Powered by four 5,730-ehp Rolls-Royce Tyne RTy.12 turboprop engines, the Belfast in commercial form has a maximum take-off weight of 104 325 kg (230,000 lb). Its maximum payload is an impressive 34 020 kg (75,000 lb). The cruising speed is 510 km/h (316 mph) and its range can vary from 1 575 km (975 miles) with a full load to approximately 6 205 km (3,855 miles) with a 10 000 kg (22,040 lb) payload.

In France, Nord produced the Noratlas twin-tailboom transport, which entered military service with several air forces as a short- to medium-range troop carrier and freighter. Today a handful of Noratlas freighters are operated in civil form in

production aircraft began to a U.S. airline in 1962. BEA became a major operator of the later Series 220, its Argosy 222s being delivered from 1965.

The Argosy is a high-wing freighter, powered by four 2,230-ehp Rolls-Royce Dart Mk 532/1 turboprop engines. It is of large size and can carry up to 12 000 kg (26,455 lb) of cargo, loaded through the nose and rear fuselage. The twin fin and rudder tail unit is supported on twin booms. The normal cruising speed is 451 km/h (280 mph) and the range can vary from 780 km (485 miles) with a full load to a long range with a lighter payload.

Ecuador and Mozambique, each powered by two 2,040-hp SNECMA-built Bristol Hercules radial engines. They are capable of transporting a substantial amount of cargo, which is loaded at truck height via the hinged rear-fuselage door. Its maximum speed is approximately 400 km/h (250 mph).

In Canada, by extending the fuselage of the Bristol Britannia 300, modifying the wings to allow 5,730-ehp Rolls-Royce Tyne RTy.12 Mk 515/10 turboprop engines to be fitted, and introducing other changes, Canadair produced its CL-44. This was the largest aircraft produced in Canada and 39 were built (including 12 for the R.C.A.F.).

The first CL-44 made its maiden flight in 1960 and 27 CL-44D4s were produced as swing-tail commercial freighters for American operators. Four aircraft were modified as CL-44Js, for service as 189-passenger transatlantic airliners with Loftleidir Icelandic. Modifications included increasing the length of the fuselage by 4.57 metres (15 feet). These were subsequently renamed Canadair 400s. Loftleidir no longer operates this airliner; nor does Cargolux which took over the type. But 13 CL-44 series aircraft remain in commercial service, including ex-military aircraft without the swing tail for cargo loading, known as CL-44-6s. The cruising speed and range are 621 km/h (386 mph) and 5 245 km (3,260 miles) respectively, the latter while carrying a payload of 27 200 kg (60,000 lb).

One of the most surprising freighters is the U.S. Aero Spacelines Guppy, which has been produced in several forms with a

Jaguar International airframe assemblies are loaded on board a Belfast destined for India.

variety of fuselage diameters. These include the Pregnant Guppy, Super Guppy, Guppy-101, Mini Guppy and Guppy-201. As originally conceived, the Guppy was intended to be a freighter with an enormous cargo-carrying fuselage, capable of accommodating even the largest of outsized cargoes. Using the Boeing C-97/Stratocruiser transport as the basis of the aircraft, a huge new upper fuselage was added. The first such aircraft appeared in 1962 as the Pregnant Guppy and this aircraft, together with

the even larger Super Guppy, were employed by NASA and the U.S. Department of Defense to transport sections of Saturn rockets in support of the U.S. space programme.

Having established that the Guppy had a market, Aero Spacelines produced other versions for commercial use. The Guppy-201, with the Super Guppy (T-34 engines), is the grandaddy of them all. It was produced with a cargo hold width of 7.65 metres (25 feet 1 inch), a height of 7.77 metres (25 feet 6 inches), and a length of 33.99 metres (111 feet 6 inches). The first Guppy-201 flew in August 1970. Power is provided by four 4,912-eshp Allison 501-D22C turboprop engines, providing a cruising speed of 407 km/h (253 mph) and a range of 813 km (505 miles) with the maximum payload.

Two Guppy-201s are operated by Aeromaritime, the charter subsidiary of UTA. These fly in support of the European Airbus Industrie programme, transporting sections of aircraft from their various points of manufacture to the Toulouse assembly plant. Even bulky A300 fuselage sections fit easily into the hold, loaded via the swing-open fuselage nose which incorporates the flight deck. Interestingly, in service with Aeromaritime these are known as Super Guppies. Such is their worth that two more

Aéromaritime flies Airbus A300 and A310 sections to Toulouse for assembly in giant Super Guppy transports.

Right: The first of two new French-built Super Guppy outsized transports for Airbus Industrie.

Above: Transall C-160s
flown in Indonesia in
connection with the
transmigration
programme.

aircraft of the same type have been acquired. These were built in France.

France was also one of the partners (with
Germany) in the Transall C-160 medium-
range tactical military transport programme, under which the air forces of
France, West Germany, Turkey and South
Africa received production examples of the
C-160 from the latter 1960s. Four French C-
160 Fs were subsequently modified into
mail carriers and these have been operated
by Air France. Each is now designated C-
160 P and can carry up to 13 500 kg (29,735
lb) of mail. Power is provided by two 6,100-
ehp Rolls-Royce Tyne RTy.20 Mk 22
turboprop engines, bestowing a cruising
speed and range of 492 km/h (306 mph) and
1 175 km (730 miles) with a full load
respectively.

In 1981 the first flight took place of the
first second-series C-160 military transport;
various improvements had been made to
the avionics and the range had been extended. Three were also delivered to the
government of Indonesia, which is using
them to carry volunteer families and their
goods from Java and Bali to new homes on
other less-populated islands as part of a
transmigration programme.

Also used in connection with the Indonesian transmigration programme are
Lockheed L-100-30 Hercules transports
operated by Pelita Air Service. Each Pelita
Hercules can transport 128 persons plus
their belongings, thereby contributing
greatly to the many thousands of family
groups that find new homes each month.
Commercial use of the Hercules, which is in
worldwide use as a medium- to long-range
military transport, began in the latter
1960s. Today there are two versions available from Lockheed. The first is the L-100-
20, which first flew in April 1968. It is 2.54
metres (8 feet 4 inches) longer than the

119

L-100 initial version of the commercial Hercules. The latter had been based on the military C-130E. It has a length of 29.78 metres (97 feet 9 inches) and is powered by four 4,050-ehp Allison 501-D22 turboprop engines. Recipients of the L-100-20 have included TAAG-Angola Airlines and Philippine Aero Transport.

By lengthening the fuselage of the commercial Hercules further, to give a new overall aircraft length of 34.37 metres (112 feet 9 inches), Lockheed produced its latest version, the L-100-30. Power is provided by four 4,508-ehp Allison 501-D22A turboprop engines (as used on the L-100-20) and the maximum payload has been increased to 23 014kg (50,738 lb). Typical cruising speed is 583 km/h (363 mph) and the range with a full payload is 3 226 km (2,005 miles). Operators of this version include Safair Freighters and Transamerica Airlines. Transamerica's 12 aircraft comprise the largest L-100-30 fleet in operation at the present time.

Bottom: The Soviet Union's largest transport aircraft in use is the giant Antonov An-22 Antheus, capable of carrying very heavy loads including the heaviest vehicles.

Below: LOT-Polish Airlines Antonov An-12B, photographed at London's Heathrow airport.

Aeroflot's vast fleet of transports

Soviet-built Antonov and Ilyushin freighters are flown in many countries, but Aeroflot, as the world's largest airline, operates the greatest number of each type. Roughly equivalent to the U.S. Hercules is the Antonov An-12, known to NATO as *Cub*, and currently in large-scale military service with the air forces of 15 countries. Production An-12s entered Soviet military service in 1959 and by the close of production in 1973 more than 900 had been built. The military An-12 has lost some of its former importance with the Soviet forces but, of those An-12s built, a proportion went into service with Aeroflot and other airlines. Today more than 260 continue civil operations, not including those manufactured at the Hanzhong works in China for CAAC as Yunshuji-8s or Y-8s.

The An-12 is powered by four 4,000-ehp Ivchenko AI-20K turboprop engines, which allow a maximum cruising speed and range with full payload of 670 km/h (416 mph) and 3 600 km (2,236 miles) respectively. The equivalent Chinese-built engines are known as Wojiang-6s. As a freighter, the maximum load that can be carried is 20 000 kg (44,092 lb). Interestingly, it has been reported that Chinese Y-8s have a higher maximum cruising speed and marginally longer range than An-12s. As an alternative to cargo, some aircraft are equipped to carry 96 passengers.

In early 1965 the prototype Antonov An-22 Antheus freighter made its first flight.

Antonov An-26 in Aeroflot markings, stopping off in England on its way to Cuba.

Many in the West were surprised at the sheer size of this aircraft, which has a wing span of 64.4 metres (211 feet 4 inches) and an overall length of approximately 58 metres (190 feet). Because of its extreme weight, the fuselage rests on main undercarriage units comprising 12 wheels and a twin-wheel nose unit. A twin fin and rudder tail unit is fitted. Until the first flight of the U.S.A.F.'s Lockheed C-5 Galaxy, the An-22 was the world's largest aeroplane by far. Two prototypes were initially operated on experimental services in Aeroflot livery before production aircraft proper entered Soviet military and Aeroflot use from 1967.

It is not known how many An-22s were built but a likely figure seems to be more than 100. Those of Aeroflot can carry payloads of up to 80 000 kg (176,350 lb) on domestic flights to underdeveloped areas such as Siberia. The cargo hold, which is 33 metres (108 feet 3 inches) in length and has a height and width of 4.40 metres (14 feet 5 inches), is loaded via a ramp under the upswept rear fuselage. Powered winches running on full-length rails facilitate loading of bulky and heavy items. The four massive 15,000-shp Kuznetsov NK-12MA turboprop engines, which are the most powerful turboprops in the world and which drive contra-rotating propellers, allow a maximum speed of 740 km/h (460

mph) and a range with a full payload of 5 000 km (3,100 miles). No other airline flies the An-22. It is known that an even larger transport has been developed in the Soviet Union. Whether this will be purely for military service or will also join Aeroflot is not clear.

Details of the Antonov An-24 (NATO *Coke*) and its Chinese-built equivalent are given in Chapter Three. However, two versions are specialized freighters and these are known as the An-24T and An-24RT. The former is similar to the An-24V Series II but has the main cabin stripped for cargo carrying. Cargo is loaded via a door positioned under the rear fuselage, which opens into the cabin. A powered winch that runs on a rail is used to lift items through the freight door and carry them along the cabin to their assigned position. A floor conveyor is also installed. The maximum amount of cargo that can be carried is 4 612 kg (10,168 lb). A greater load, weighing up to 5 700 kg (12,566 lb), can be carried by the An-24RT, a version with an auxiliary turbojet.

From the An-24 was developed the An-26 which, in civil form, is flown by Aeroflot and a few other airlines as a freighter. It uses An-24-type wings, which carry two more-powerful 2,820-ehp Ivchenko AI-24VT turboprop engines plus the auxiliary turbojet, but the fuselage is slightly longer, in-

Above: Cubana Antonov
An-26 photographed at
Grenada.

Right: Antonov An-32.

corporating various design changes. These
include a new forward section and replacement of the An-24T/RT's freight door with a
rear loading ramp under the upswept rear
fuselage. The latter permits the loading of
vehicles. This ramp can be moved clear of
the opening for direct loading of cargo from
trucks.

Two versions of the An-26 have been
produced, each of which is known to NATO
by the name *Curl*. The first is the standard
An-26, which appeared in the late 1960s
and uses a conveyor system for loading.
More recently the An-26B has become
available, which specializes in the transportation of three regular-sized freight pallets.
The maximum weight of cargo that can be
carried by the An-26 is 5 500 kg (12,125 lb),
slightly less than by the An-24RT. The

cruising speed and range with this payload
are 440 km/h (273 mph) and 1 100 km (683
miles) respectively. Civil operators other
than Aeroflot include TAAG-Angola Airlines and Tarom.

In 1974 Antonov flew the prototype An-
30. This has entered service with Aeroflot as
an aerial survey aircraft and is generally
similar in configuration to the An-24. It can
also be used as a freighter, but this is not its
primary role. The follow-on aircraft, the
An-32, was designed as a transport for cargo
or for up to 39 passengers/stretchers but at
the time of writing was not in civil use.
Based on the An-26 but with changes to the
tail unit, it is optimized for operation from
high-altitude airstrips or in hot climates. Its
two more powerful 5,180-ehp Ivchenko AI-
20M turboprop engines are carried on the

wings rather than under them, to ensure that these do not suffer damage during operation from natural airstrips. The prototype could be seen at the Paris Air Show of 1977. It has sported Aeroflot livery and there is every reason to expect this aircraft to enter civil service.

The very latest Antonov freighter is the An-72, an advanced STOL transport capable of carrying a payload of up to 10 000 kg (22,045 lb) and of operating to and from unprepared airstrips and in harsh weather. It is seen as a modern and more capable replacement for the An-26, with military and civil applications. It is the first Antonov to discard turboprops. Instead it has two high-positioned 6 500-kg (14,330-lb)st Lotarev D-36 turbofan engines, an engine type also to be found on the Yak-42. The T-tail is also a new feature for Antonov transports.

The prototype first flew in December 1977 and production aircraft appeared in the early 1980s. It has an An-26-type rear cargo ramp and a winch assists loading of bulky or heavy items. Typically, folding seats are fitted along the cabin walls, for 32 passengers. In a civil capacity, one purpose for these seats could be to allow work crews to accompany cargo. A similar seating arrangement is to be found in the An-26. The An-72, known to NATO by the name *Coaler*, has a maximum cruising speed and range with full payload of about 720 km/h (447 mph) and 1 000 km (620 miles) respectively. It can take off after a run of just 470 metres (1,542 feet).

Despite Antonov's dominance of freighter production in the U.S.S.R. over many years, arguably the most important freighter of recent years has come from Ilyushin. This is the impressive Il-76, known to NATO by the name *Candid* and built as a

Antonov An-72 twin-turbofan transport with STOL performance.

Left: Ilyushin Il-76 freighter.

Plate VI

Boeing 707-320C

cutaway drawing key

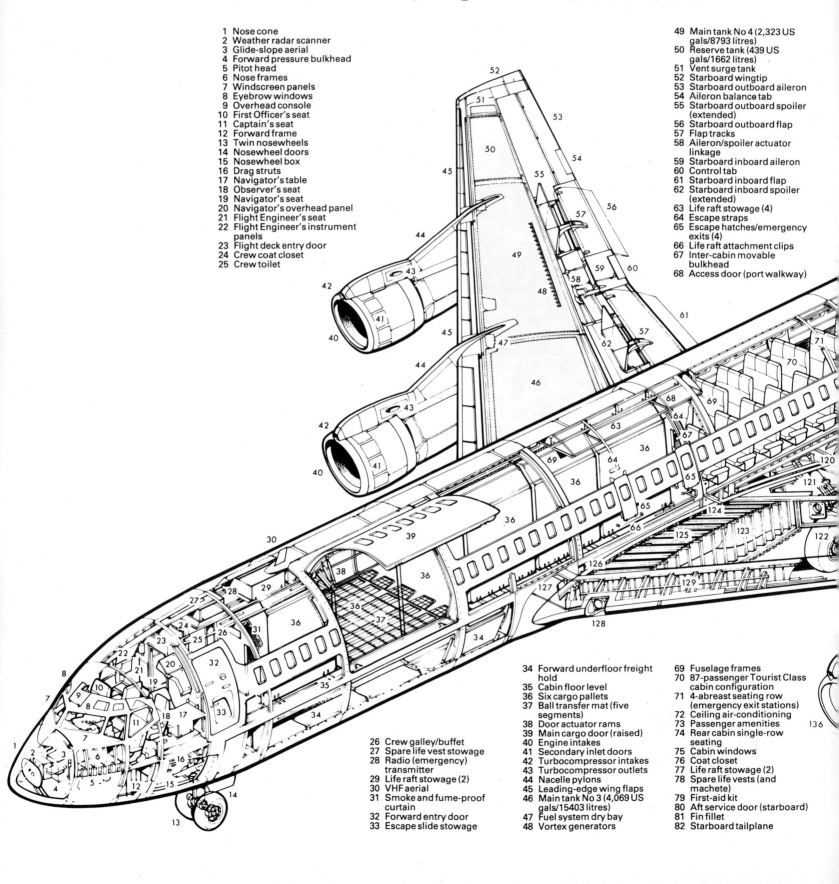

1 Nose cone
2 Weather radar scanner
3 Glide-slope aerial
4 Forward pressure bulkhead
5 Pitot head
6 Nose frames
7 Windscreen panels
8 Eyebrow windows
9 Overhead console
10 First Officer's seat
11 Captain's seat
12 Forward frame
13 Twin nosewheels
14 Nosewheel doors
15 Nosewheel box
16 Drag struts
17 Navigator's table
18 Observer's seat
19 Navigator's seat
20 Navigator's overhead panel
21 Flight Engineer's seat
22 Flight Engineer's instrument panels
23 Flight deck entry door
24 Crew coat closet
25 Crew toilet

26 Crew galley/buffet
27 Spare life vest stowage
28 Radio (emergency) transmitter
29 Life raft stowage (2)
30 VHF aerial
31 Smoke and fume-proof curtain
32 Forward entry door
33 Escape slide stowage

34 Forward underfloor freight hold
35 Cabin floor level
36 Six cargo pallets
37 Ball transfer mat (five segments)
38 Door actuator rams
39 Main cargo door (raised)
40 Engine intakes
41 Secondary inlet doors
42 Turbocompressor intakes
43 Turbocompressor outlets
44 Nacelle pylons
45 Leading-edge wing flaps
46 Main tank No 3 (4,069 US gals/15403 litres)
47 Fuel system dry bay
48 Vortex generators

49 Main tank No 4 (2,323 US gals/8793 litres)
50 Reserve tank (439 US gals/1662 litres)
51 Vent surge tank
52 Starboard wingtip
53 Starboard outboard aileron
54 Aileron balance tab
55 Starboard outboard spoiler (extended)
56 Starboard outboard flap
57 Flap tracks
58 Aileron/spoiler actuator linkage
59 Starboard inboard aileron
60 Control tab
61 Starboard inboard flap
62 Starboard inboard spoiler (extended)
63 Life raft stowage (4)
64 Escape straps
65 Escape hatches/emergency exits (4)
66 Life raft attachment clips
67 Inter-cabin movable bulkhead
68 Access door (port walkway)

69 Fuselage frames
70 87-passenger Tourist Class cabin configuration
71 4-abreast seating row (emergency exit stations)
72 Ceiling air-conditioning
73 Passenger amenities
74 Rear cabin single-row seating
75 Cabin windows
76 Coat closet
77 Life raft stowage (2)
78 Spare life vests (and machete)
79 First-aid kit
80 Aft service door (starboard)
81 Fin fillet
82 Starboard tailplane

136

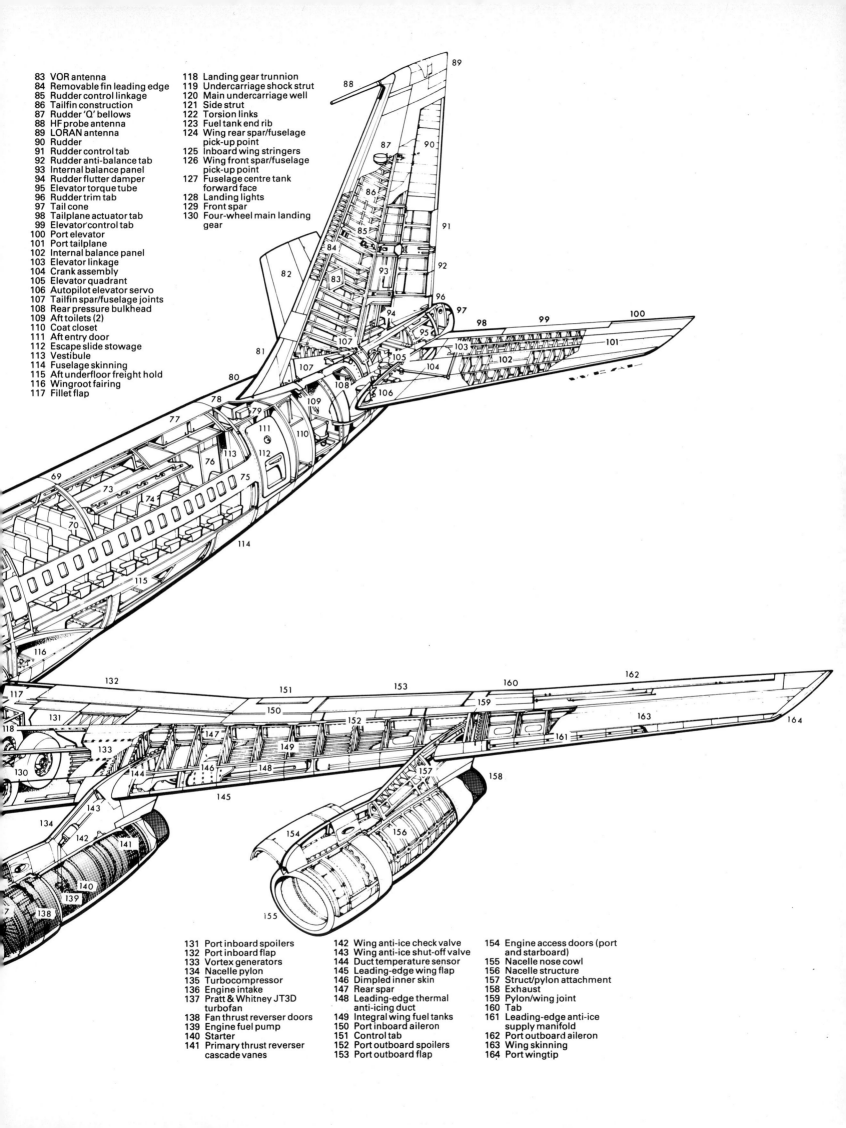

83 VOR antenna
84 Removable fin leading edge
85 Rudder control linkage
86 Tailfin construction
87 Rudder 'Q' bellows
88 HF probe antenna
89 LORAN antenna
90 Rudder
91 Rudder control tab
92 Rudder anti-balance tab
93 Internal balance panel
94 Rudder flutter damper
95 Elevator torque tube
96 Rudder trim tab
97 Tail cone
98 Tailplane actuator tab
99 Elevator control tab
100 Port elevator
101 Port tailplane
102 Internal balance panel
103 Elevator linkage
104 Crank assembly
105 Elevator quadrant
106 Autopilot elevator servo
107 Tailfin spar/fuselage joints
108 Rear pressure bulkhead
109 Aft toilets (2)
110 Coat closet
111 Aft entry door
112 Escape slide stowage
113 Vestibule
114 Fuselage skinning
115 Aft underfloor freight hold
116 Wingroot fairing
117 Fillet flap

118 Landing gear trunnion
119 Undercarriage shock strut
120 Main undercarriage well
121 Side strut
122 Torsion links
123 Fuel tank end rib
124 Wing rear spar/fuselage
    pick-up point
125 Inboard wing stringers
126 Wing front spar/fuselage
    pick-up point
127 Fuselage centre tank
    forward face
128 Landing lights
129 Front spar
130 Four-wheel main landing
    gear

131 Port inboard spoilers
132 Port inboard flap
133 Vortex generators
134 Nacelle pylon
135 Turbocompressor
136 Engine intake
137 Pratt & Whitney JT3D
    turbofan
138 Fan thrust reverser doors
139 Engine fuel pump
140 Starter
141 Primary thrust reverser
    cascade vanes

142 Wing anti-ice check valve
143 Wing anti-ice shut-off valve
144 Duct temperature sensor
145 Leading-edge wing flap
146 Dimpled inner skin
147 Rear spar
148 Leading-edge thermal
    anti-icing duct
149 Integral wing fuel tanks
150 Port inboard aileron
151 Control tab
152 Port outboard spoilers
153 Port outboard flap

154 Engine access doors (port
    and starboard)
155 Nacelle nose cowl
156 Nacelle structure
157 Struct/pylon attachment
158 Exhaust
159 Pylon/wing joint
160 Tab
161 Leading-edge anti-ice
    supply manifold
162 Port outboard aileron
163 Wing skinning
164 Port wingtip

Air New Zealand's single DC-8-50F freighter with its loading door raised.

medium- to long-range transport to replace the An-12. It was designed to meet the strictest requirements, which included the ability to fly 5 000 km (3,100 miles) with a 40 000 kg (88,185 lb) payload in less than six hours. It was also intended to be capable of operating in the harsh weather conditions experienced in some regions of the Soviet Union and to use short unpaved airstrips. All these requirements were met with the production Il-76T, which has a cruising speed of up to 800 km/h (497 mph) on the power of four 12 000-kg (26,455-lb)st Soloviev D-30KP turbofan engines, the more powerful companion of the Il-62M's engine.

The prototype Il-76 made its maiden flight in March 1971 and production Il-76Ts were put into service in the latter 1970s. A military version was also produced as the Il-76M, featuring the usual tail-gun armament. Aeroflot flies both the Il-76T and M (without the gun armament fitted but with the turret) production versions and is also using the Il-76T on international services between Moscow and Japan. Aeroflot is thought to operate more than 50 Il-76 aircraft and others are already in airline service in Iraq, Libya and Syria.

One of a series

The majority of freighters produced outside the U.S.S.R. are versions of passenger airliners, hence the sub-heading 'one of a series'. This applies equally to freighters still available for purchase and those produced as variants of aircraft no longer being built. When Douglas had its DC-6 and DC-7 series in production, it made available specialized freighter variants as the DC-6A and DC-7F, featuring cargo doors and strengthened floors. The company's later DC-8 jet series included the Series 54F and 55F freighter versions of the Series 50 intercontinental passenger airliner and 'F' freighter versions (also known as Jet Traders) of the Super Sixty series. Such is the importance of the DC-8 as a freighter that in 1976 McDonnell Douglas began modifying passenger DC-8s into freighters by stripping the passenger fittings of each, removing the cabin windows, installing a cargo handling system and providing a large cargo door. Many of these are now in commercial use, together with Super Seventy conversions of Super Sixty series freighters (see Chapter Two).

Included in McDonnell Douglas' DC-9 twin-turbofan airliner series are 'F' freighter versions with large cargo doors. The first freighter was acquired by Alitalia in 1968 as a Series 30F. The company's later DC-10 was made available in convertible passenger/cargo versions as the DC-10-10CF and DC-10-30CF but not in freighter-only form. However, with an all-cargo interior, the DC-10-30CF can accommodate up to 70 626 kg (155,700 lb) of freight.

Boeing probably has the most impressive record for the production of freighter versions of jet airliners, beginning with the Model 707-320C. Like the DC-10 CFs, this was offered (until recently) as a convertible passenger, mixed traffic or all-cargo aircraft, with a large cargo-loading door and the necessary modifications to the interior. It was, in fact, the last version of the Model 707 to be offered as new and the final aircraft was delivered in 1982 to the Moroccan government. In cargo-carrying configuration, the aircraft's basic weight is more than 2 270 kg (5,000 lb) lighter than when it is configured to accommodate 219 passengers. This means that its cargo payload can be as high as 40 324 kg (88,900 lb). The maximum cruising speed on the power of four 8 618-kg (19,000-lb)st Pratt & Whitney JT3D-7 turbofan engines is 973 km/h (605 mph) and its range, with a 36 287 kg (80,000 lb) cargo load, is 5 835 km (3,625 miles). Today Varig Brazilian Airlines operates one of the largest fleets of Model 707-320Cs, rivalled only by those of TMA

(Trans-Mediterranean Airways SAL) of Lebanon and Egyptair.

An actual freighter-only version of the Boeing Model 727 is offered as the 727-200F, one of only two versions of this triple-engined airliner still available for purchase. It was introduced in 1981, powered by Pratt & Whitney JT8D-17A turbofan engines. It is easily recognizable by its lack of cabin windows and the addition of a large cargo door on the port side of the forward fuselage. It can carry a payload of 28 622 kg (63,100 lb), a weight which includes the handling system. Eleven pallets of 2.24 by 3.17 metres (7 feet 4 inches by 10 feet 5 inches) can be accommodated which, for interest only, compares with 22 similar pallets for the larger DC-10-30CF and 13 for the 707-

Bottom: Air Canada DC-8-54F.

Below: Boeing 707-320C flown by Fast Air Carrier of Chile.

Above: Federal Express
Boeing 737-200C.

Right: Boeing 737-200C
of Air Nauru of Nauru
Island, Central Pacific,
being loaded with cargo.

320C. The first Model 727-200Fs were delivered to Federal Express in 1983. This airline has ordered a total of 15 to supplement the convertible versions of the Model 727-100 already operated. The airline also received a small number of Model 737-200Cs, the convertible passenger/cargo version of the 737-200, with an all-cargo payload of up to 17 223 kg (37,970 lb).

Amazing though it may seem, it is a fact that a freighter version of a standard passenger airliner has the greatest cargo capacity of any commercially operated aircraft, including those built in the Soviet Union. This, of course, is the Boeing 747-200F Freighter, capable of carrying a payload weighing an incredible 113 400 kg (250,000 lb) or of transporting 90 720 kg (200,000 lb) of freight over a distance of more than 8 060 km (5,000 miles). This impressive ability has made the 747-200F and earlier 747-100F much prized additions to the fleets of airlines with major cargo operations. Nearly 50 747-200Fs had been ordered at the time of writing.

The 747-200F Freighter has an external appearance similar to that of other 747-200 series versions but without side cabin windows. The major difference is that the fuselage nose is hinged to swing upward during cargo loading. This allows straight-through loading to the main hold and can be supplemented by a cargo door on the fuselage side. The lower holds are loaded via large doors. A mechanical cargo-handling system is fitted, which allows two men to load the Freighter in half an hour. Maximum take-off weight of the 747-200F varies, depending on the engines fitted, but is similar to other Series 200 aircraft. The enormous cost of a purpose-built freighter of 747 type can easily be justified when figures are published like those of a few years ago that showed that British Airways had

Loading cargo through the side door of a JAL (Japan Air Lines) Boeing Model 747-200F.

The nose loading door of a 747-200F is hinged below the flight deck.

increased its revenue on cargo operations by more than 25 per cent following the purchase of a single 747 Freighter.

Although not related to the above details on the 747 Freighter, it is interesting to note that NASA operates what is undoubtedly the strangest Model 747 used for freighting. This aircraft, an ex-American Airlines Model 747-123, has been modified to transport America's Space Shuttle Orbiter piggy-back between launches.

Airbus Industrie has not been slow in appreciating the market for convertible and freighter versions of its aircraft. As an initial step it made available the A300C4, a convertible version of the A300B4 that can be operated in all-passenger, all-cargo or mixed traffic forms. As a freighter the C4 has a normal maximum payload of 41 100 kg (90,610 lb). Various sized pallets or bulk cargoes can be accommodated, which can include 13 2.24- by 3.17-metre (7 feet 4 inches by 10 feet 5 inches) pallets. The passenger and freight combinations of the C4 in convertible form include 145 passen-

gers and six pallets of the size mentioned previously. The range of the A300C4 with maximum payload is estimated to be up to 4 635 km (2,170 miles). The loading and unloading of upper deck cargo is via a large upward-hinged door. The first C4 was put into service by Hapag-Lloyd of West Germany, a subsidiary of the Hapag-Lloyd AG shipping group, in 1980. Three are operated by Kuwait Airways and one by South African Airways.

Airbus Industrie has also designed a 'pure' freighter version of the A300, known as the F4. Although generally similar to the C4, it has the side cabin windows removed, and the interior fittings necessary for conversion to and from passenger configuration in the C4 are deleted. Twenty 2.24- by 3.17-metre pallets can be accommodated on the upper deck. The maximum payload of the F4 is stated to be 46 000 kg (101,410 lb). C-200 convertible and F-200 freighter versions are included in the Airbus A310 range, but the large cargo door is standard on all A310s. As the A310 is a smaller aircraft than the A300, its maximum payload in a freighter role is 39400 kg (86,860 lb).

On a smaller scale, British Aerospace offered its One-Eleven Series 475 with a convertible interior for passenger or cargo operations. Loading of freight is via a large cargo door. This version is now produced in Romania as the Rombac 1-11 Series 495. BAe currently offers a version of its HS 748 turboprop transport as the Civil Transport, which is a Series 2B with a large rear cargo door and a strengthened cabin floor for freighting.

Shorts of Belfast offers its SC.7 Skyvan in freighter form, capable of accommodating a payload of 2085 kg (4,600 lb), and the Sherpa. The latter is the freighter version of the Shorts 330-200. Although its payload is no greater than that of the 330-200 when used for carrying cargo (at 3400 kg; 7,500 lb), it has a Skyvan-type door under the upswept rear fuselage for straight-through loading.

As one of the Nomad N24A options, GAF (Government Aircraft Factories) of Australia offered a freighter version, known as the Cargomaster. Typically of many smaller aircraft, the Brazilian EMBRAER Bandeirante is offered in convertible form with up to a 1712-kg (3,774-lb) cargo

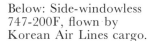

Left: Hapag-Lloyd Airbus A300C4 during loading operations.

Below: Side-windowless 747-200F, flown by Korean Air Lines cargo.

payload, and the company's latest aircraft, the Brasilia, is available in all-cargo form.

From Canada comes the de Havilland Canada DHC-7 Series 101, an all-cargo version of the Dash-7 with a payload of 5 130 kg (11,310 lb). Operators of this version include Gronlandsfly of Greenland. Another Canadian aircraft is the Canadair CL-215, which is a twin 2,100-hp Pratt & Whitney R-2800-CA3 radial-engined amphibian. This can be used for many tasks, but it is primarily used for firefighting and thereby carries 5 346 litres (1,176 Imperial gallons) of water (or chemicals) for airdropping. The tanks can be filled while the

aircraft is on the ground or the aircraft can scoop-up water while taxiing as a flying-boat. This latter tank-filling technique takes just ten seconds. As a cargo carrier, the CL-215 can accommodate a payload weighing up to 3 630 kg (8,000 lb), or 26 passengers can be carried. Its typical cruising speed is 291 km/h (181 mph) and its range with a 1 587 kg (3,500 lb) load is up to 2 094 km (1,300 miles). Another Canadian water-bomber is detailed in Chapter Three, known as the Avalon Canso.

The French Dassault-Breguet Mystère-Falcon 20 is basically a twin-turbofan executive jet. In 1972 the first flight was made of a Falcon 20 converted into a freighter for Pan American Business Jets. Features of the conversion included the substitution of the original door for a large cargo-loading door and a new cabin floor. Such was the success of the conversion that Federal Express subsequently began operating a fleet of 32 Mystère-Falcon 20DCs. All conversions are known under the name Falcon Cargo Jet, and the current production version of the Mystère-Falcon 20 (the Series F) is offered in this form. The payload is 3 000 kg (6,615 lb), at which the Falcon Cargo Jet can fly 2 250 km (1,400 miles). A quick-change convertible executive/cargo version of the Mystère-Falcon Series F is also available from Dassault-Breguet.

Bottom: Venezuelan Canadair CL-215.

Below: Tarom's BAe One-Eleven Series 475 cargo transport.

As detailed in the previous chapter, the Israeli IAI 101B Arava is available in cargo form, marketed in the United States under the name Cargo Commuterliner. Airspur, operating from Los Angeles, began flying the first of its 10 aircraft in early 1982. The cargo payload is more than 1 814 kg (4,000 lb).

Having produced the initial version of its F28 Fellowship twin-turbofan short-range airliner, Fokker offered a passenger/cargo convertible version designated F28 Mk 1000C. This was also available in all-cargo form. Seven Mk 1000Cs were produced and today five are operated by LADE (Lineas Aéreas del Estado), the Argentine state airline administered by the Argentine Air Force. This Air Force also flies two Mk 3000s with cargo doors, as does Garuda Indonesian Airways.

The Spanish CASA C-212 Aviocar has been available for commercial cargo carrying for some years, initially as an option of the C-212C (up to 2 000-kg; 4,410-lb load, including vehicles) and currently as an option of the Series 200 Aviocar, as detailed in Chapter Three. In the Soviet Union Yakovlev has produced a freighter version of its triple-turbofan Yak-40, which has a large cargo door for loading in the port side of the fuselage.

The final freighter to be mentioned in this chapter is, perhaps, one of the most interesting. In 1977 the President of Hawk Indus-

tries, a company specializing in oil- and water-drilling equipment and also fencing, decided that the company required an aircraft of special design to overcome transportation difficulties. Under the name Gaf-Hawk 125 (General aviation freighter HAWK), a prototype aircraft has been produced. It is a strut-braced high-wing freighter, with a single 1,173-shp Pratt & Whitney Aircraft of Canada PT6A-45R turboprop engine mounted in the nose of a mostly rectangular-section fuselage. Cargo can be loaded straight into the main cabin from trucks via a rear fuselage door. This prototype is estimated to have a maximum cruising speed of 282 km/h (175 mph) and a range of 1 668 km (1,036 miles) at maximum take-off weight. Of major importance to the company, it can operate to and from natural airstrips and can take off at full weight after a run of only 189 metres (620 feet).

Above: Hawk GafHawk 125, a specialist freighter designed by and for the use of Hawk Industries. Ten GafHawks have also been ordered by other operators, eight for use in Alaska.

Top: One of Federal Express's 32 Dassault-Breguet Mystère-Falcon 20DCs.

6 The Flying Farmers

Agricultural aviation is one aspect of general aviation, a term encompassing all types of civil flying other than commercial air transport for reward. It is true, therefore, that some of the aircraft detailed in the final chapter (and privately owned and flown aircraft) also come under the term general aviation. An agricultural aircraft is an aeroplane or helicopter employed to spray or dust crops, top dress or seed, control pests or help in the management of livestock over large areas. But it is *not* used to transport animals.

The use of aircraft for agriculture is nothing new but the scale of present-day operations all over the world is staggering. Many see agricultural aviation as a major tool in the quest to feed the starving people of the world, whether by increasing crops or controlling pests that ruin crops. As the majority of agricultural aircraft are not owned by the farmers themselves but are either hired to fulfil a particular task or are state-owned, agricultural aviation has become very big business. As a result there is a surprisingly large number of different aircraft on the market, ranging from the

purpose-designed single seaters to versions of transport aircraft and even agricultural microlights. Typical of the latter is the U.S. Mitchell Falcon, which has a maximum take-off weight of only 318 kg (700 lb) while carrying 53 litres (14 U.S. gallons) of liquid for spraying. In most cases during this chapter a chemical payload in kg/lb is given. This represents the maximum weight of chemicals, whether liquid or dry, that can be carried in the aircrafts' hopper/tanks.

The use of aircraft for agriculture is not cheap; a fairly large area needs to be worked to make the expense reasonable. But results can be dramatic, partly because of the even spread of chemical/seed released from the low-flying aircraft. For example, in 1980 China decided to use Y-5s to sow rice-paddy fields. The result was not only a quick and efficient operation but the crop was nearly doubled. The Y-5 is the Chinese version of the Soviet Antonov An-2. The U.S.S.R. itself, is a major user of agricultural aircraft, mostly An-2s. Before Poland became the main producer of the An-2, Soviet production lines produced a vast number of An-2S and later An-2M agricultural aircraft. The

An-2 agricultural biplane, with a sprayboom under the lower wings.

Polish PZL Mielec version is the An-2R, of which more than 5,500 have been produced, mostly for Soviet use. Each An-2R biplane has a tank in which 1 400 litres (308 Imperial gallons) of liquid chemicals are carried for spraying or dry powder or granulated chemicals for dusting.

Over the last decade or more the Antonov bureau has been engaged in the development of a turboprop-powered An-2, known as the An-3. Although a fairly straightforward modification, its priority has been low as it had been expected that the Polish M-15 would represent a modern and major improvement over the An-2. However, as detailed later, the M-15 has not been the success originally hoped for and this pushed

An-3 development to the forefront. In most respects the An-3 is just an An-2 fitted with a 940-shp Glushenkov TVD-10B turboprop engine, although other changes include the use of a much larger chemical tank. The sprayboom is carried under the lower wings.

As mentioned previously, the PZL Mielec M-15 Belphegor has not lived up to expectations. Nevertheless, it represents the first attempt to introduce turbofan power to this class of aircraft, the 1 500-kg (3,307-lb)st Ivchenko AI-25 turbofan engine being sandwiched between the upper biplane wing and the fuselage. Design of the M-15 began in the early 1970s as a next-generation aircraft to the An-2. Its development was initiated by agreement between

The PZL Mielec M-15 Belphegor is the world's only purpose-built agricultural aircraft with a turbofan engine. This one is flown by Aeroflot in the Soviet Union.

Left: PZL-104 Wilga 35R agricultural aircraft, carrying 270 kg (595 lb) of chemicals. It is especially useful for operating over small fields, due to its steep rate of climb and descent and tight turns.

133

Above: PZL-106AT
Turbo-Kruk.

Right: PZL-106B Kruk.

PZL Mielec M-18
Dromader.

Poland and the U.S.S.R., with the latter nation alone requiring several thousand aircraft. If successful, the M-15 could have been in widespread use throughout the eastern European countries. Its future use must now be uncertain.

The prototype M-15 made its maiden flight in 1973 and by the end of the decade the M-15 was being delivered from the Polish factory. However, despite a maximum take-off weight only a little heavier than that of the An-2 and a chemical tank capacity increased by 850 kg (1,874 lb) to 2 200 kg (4,850 lb), it has proved to be less economical in operation than expected. The result of this is that M-15 production ended in 1981 after delivery of just 120. Nevertheless, the M-15 remains a remarkable design for an agricultural aircraft. Chemicals are carried in two hoppers, positioned one each side of the fuselage between the wings, and are released from pipes in the lower wings. Twin tailbooms support the tail unit. The normal operating speed of the M-15 is 160 to 175 km/h (99 to 109 mph) and it can normally apply up to 25 litres (5½ Imperial gallons) of liquid chemical per second over a swath width of 40 metres (131 feet).

Apart from agricultural versions of the PZL-104 Wilga general-purpose light air-craft, all other agricultural aircraft of Polish manufacture are of the purpose-designed single-seat type, the most typical configuration outside the U.S.S.R. The PZL-106 Kruk first flew in 1973 and it is being manufactured in radial and PT6A or PZL-10 turboprop-engined forms. It is typical of many agricultural aircraft in having a high-mounted pilot's cockpit affording excellent vision. Because of the dangers associated with low-level flying and of striking unseen cables, it has a roll-over steel-tube structure and other cockpit safety features plus a steel cable cutter forward of the windscreen, again typical of most types. The PZL-106B version is powered by a 592-hp PZL-3S seven-cylinder radial engine. It can carry more than 1 000 kg (2,205 lb) of chemicals and can give a swath width of 35 metres (115 feet).

The Wilga and Kruk are products of the Okecie factory but at Mielec, home of the M-15, the PZL M-18A Dromader is produced. This succeeded the earlier production M-18, the prototype of which had first flown in 1976. It is an aircraft of similar layout to the Kruk but is slightly longer, has a much greater wing span and maximum take-off weight, and is powered by a 1,000-hp PZL Kalisz ASz-62IR radial engine. It can carry 50 per cent more chemicals than the Kruk. A version of the Dromader with a reduced wing span, a 600-hp PZL-3SR radial engine and a chemical capacity of 900 kg (1,984 lb), flew for the first time in 1982 as the M-21 Dromader Mini. Also being developed are ASz-62IR radial and PT6A/PZL-10 turboprop versions of the Dromader with chemical payloads of 1 800 to 2 300 kg (3,970 to 5,070 lb) and 2 100 kg (4,630 lb) respectively, known as the M-24 Dromader Super and Dromader Super Turbo. Reports have also been made of a possible Dromader Mikro version, powered by a small piston engine and with a capacity of only 500 kg (1,102 lb). This aircraft was being considered in 1982.

Aero Boero 150 Ag.

The South American way

South America is the home of many agricultural aircraft. The Argentine company Aero Boero has been producing light aircraft for many years. From the three-seat AB 95 lightplane, first flown in 1959, was developed an agricultural version known as the AB 95A Fumigador. From the follow-on AB 115 three-seat light aircraft were developed the AB 150 and AB 180, both of which have agricultural variants. The AB 150 Ag is a strut-braced high-wing cabin lightplane, powered by a 150-hp Avco Lycoming O-320-A2B piston engine. It can carry 270 litres ($59\frac{1}{2}$ Imperial gallons) of liquid chemicals. The AB 180 Ag is similar but is powered by an Avco Lycoming O-360-A1A engine. As for the AB 150 Ag, the chemicals are carried in an underfuselage pod. A biplane version is known as the AB 180 SP, the lower wings only carrying about 330 litres ($72\frac{1}{2}$ Imperial gallons) of liquid chemicals.

Aero Boero has also recently completed development of a specialized agricultural aircraft as the AB 260 Ag. It is powered by a 260-hp Avco Lycoming O-540-H2B5D piston engine, can carry 500 litres (110 Imperial gallons) of chemicals inside its new-style fuselage, and has strut-braced low-mounted wings. Accommodation is provided for two. Also in Argentina, Chincul, the Piper Aircraft Corporation's local distributor, is producing the Piper Pawnee

Right: Chincul two-seat conversion of the Piper Pawnee, with a very small chemical hopper.

Left: EMBRAER EMB-201A Ipanema.

D and a modified two-seat version for training pilots in spraying techniques and for glider towing. Compared to the Piper-built Pawnee, the chemical hopper of the two-seater is very small.

In 1970 EMBRAER of Brazil flew the prototype of a purpose-designed single-seat agricultural aircraft known as the EMB-200. Production of the EMB-200 Ipanema and early versions of the EMB-201 series was considerable and manufacture of the current EMB-201A has brought the total number of Ipanemas built to well over 400. The EMB-201A is a small aircraft, powered by a 300-hp Avco Lycoming IO-540-K1J5D piston engine. It can carry up to 750 kg (1,653 lb) of liquid or dry chemicals, using the normal dusting system, spray-booms or atomizers, the latter giving a very fine spray.

Colombia became an agricultural aircraft producer when Agricopteros Ltda began production of the Scamp B in the late 1970s, using kits of parts supplied by the U.S. company Aerosport. The Scamp was designed as a small open-cockpit light bi-plane by Aerosport, which offers plans and kits of parts to amateur constructors wishing to build their own aircraft. This home-built version, known as the Scamp A, is very popular and well over 800 sets of plans have been sold. Conversion of the Scamp into an agricultural aircraft was undertaken in Colombia, and since that time Aerosport has produced kits of the Scamp B for delivery to Agricopteros. Aerosport now also offers the Scamp B kit in the U.S.A. The Scamp B is slightly larger than the Scamp A, with a wing span and length of 5.94 metres (19 feet 6 inches) and 4.37 metres (14 feet 4 inches) respectively. It is powered by a 100-hp Revmaster 2,100 cc engine, which is a modification of the Volkswagen motorcar engine for aircraft use. Its chemical tank capacity is just 60 litres (13¼ Imperial gallons), probably making this aircraft the smallest – not only in size but also in chemical capacity – production agricultural aircraft of non-microlight type in the world.

This EMB-201A shows that low-level flying ability is a vital skill for an agricultural pilot.

AAMSA A9B-M Quail using an underfuselage dry spreader system.

To the North

In Mexico, the company Fabrica de Aviones Anahuac SA produced a small number of purpose-designed single-seat agricultural aircraft from 1970, known as Tauro 300s and Tauro 350s. The Tauro 350 is powered by a 350-hp Jacobs R-755-SM turbocharged radial engine and can carry a chemical payload of 800 kg (1,764 lb). Another Mexican type is the AAMSA A9B Quail. This, however, is not an original design but is based on the Rockwell International Aero Commander Quail Commander, one of two agricultural aircraft of Rockwell design taken over by AAMSA in the early 1970s. The other was the Sparrow Commander. More than 120 have been built, mostly of the original A9B type but also of the current A9B-M version with a 300-hp Avco Lycoming IO-540-K1A5 piston engine. The maximum chemical payload of this single-seater is 725 kg (1,600 lb).

Of the world's purpose-designed agricultural aircraft, the greatest number of different types have originated in the U.S.A. Perhaps the most prominent designer of American agricultural aircraft is Leland Snow. It was back in 1958 that his Snow S-2 single-seat aircraft was first delivered to customers and over the next seven years more than 260 were completed. Engine power for these ranged from 220 hp to 600 hp.

In 1965 Rockwell purchased the Snow Aeronautical Corporation and the company's Aero Commander division began its own production of the 600 S-2D Snow Commander. This was subsequently renamed Ag Commander S-2D, and was followed in 1968 by the Rockwell Thrush Commander-600 derivative with a 600-hp Pratt & Whitney R-1340-AN-1 radial engine. A more powerful version was later introduced as the Thrush Commander-800, powered by an 800-hp Wright R-1300-1B radial engine. Both were offered by Rockwell International's General Aviation Division with chemical payloads of 1 487 kg (3,280 lb).

In 1977 the Ayres Corporation purchased from Rockwell International all rights in the Thrush Commanders and

Above: Ayres Thrush
S2R-R1340.

Left: A9B-M Quail fitted
with spraying
equipment.

Right: Ayres Turbo-Thrush S2R-T34.

Marsh S2R-T Turbo-Thrush, a turboprop-engined conversion of the Rockwell Thrush Commander.

currently offers to customers four versions based on these. The Thrush S2R-R1340 is the basic version with a 600-hp R-1340 engine. It can carry 1 514 litres (400 U.S. gallons) of liquid chemicals or a large volume of dry chemicals, and is offered in single- and two-seat forms. A version with a similarly rated Pezetel PZL-3S radial engine (similar to that used on the Polish Dromader Mini) is designated Pezetel Thrush S2R-R3S. Far more power is offered with the Bull Thrush S2R-R1820, powered by a 1,200-hp Wright R-1820 radial engine and with a larger chemical hopper with a liquid capacity of 1 930 litres (510 U.S. gallons). This aircraft is said to be the most powerful agricultural aircraft in production in the world. The last version is the Turbo-Thrush S2R, which itself has three sub-variants with Pratt & Whitney Aircraft of Canada PT6A turboprop engines of 500 to 750 shp. The chemical payload of the Turbo-Thrush S2R versions is greatly increased, with a maximum liquid chemical capacity of 1 893 litres (500 U.S. gallons).

In order to improve upon the capabilities of the standard radial-engined Rockwell Thrush Commanders already in use, the

Marsh Aviation Company developed the Marsh S2R-T Turbo Thrush. This is a conversion with a Garrett TPE331-1-101 turboprop engine, derated to 600 shp for normal operation. Because of the light weight of this engine, the chemical payload is increased, allowing for either 1 514 or 1 893 litres (400 or 500 U.S. gallons) of liquids or a large volume of dry chemicals. Performance is also improved. About 70 of these aircraft are in use. Marsh also offers a turboprop-powered conversion of the G-164 Super Ag-Cat C, using the same Garrett engine as offered in the Turbo Thrush. This is known as the Marsh G-164 C-T Turbo Cat and a small number have been produced. Details of the Ag-Cat series follow.

Another company involved in modification of the Thrush Commander is Serv-Aero Engineering Incorporated. This company produces conversion kits to replace the original R-1340 or R-1300 engines with a 1,200-hp Wright R-1820-71 radial, driving a slow-turning propeller. Advantages offered by the conversion are numerous and include lower operating costs and noise reduction, but the original idea behind the conversion was to offer a replacement engine for the long-since-discontinued R-1340. The conversion is known simply as the Thrush Commander/R-1820. Serv-Aero also modifies the Ayres Thrush, by adding a streamlined fairing to the rear of the pilot's cockpit and using a new tailwheel leg that puts less strain on the fuselage structure when the aircraft is on the ground.

Leland Snow is currently President of Air Tractor Incorporated, which markets a series of agricultural aircraft designed in the 1970s. The Air Tractor AT-301 and AT-301A are highly successful purpose-designed single seaters, differing only in the size of the chemical tanks carried. Power for both aircraft is provided by the 600-hp Pratt & Whitney R-1340 radial engine, and

Marsh G-164 C-T Turbo Cat, a turboprop-engined conversion of the Grumman Super Ag-Cat C.

well over 500 have been ordered. Turbo-prop versions of the Air Tractor are designated AT-302 and AT-302A, each with a 600-shp Avco Lycoming LTP 101-600A1A engine, and the AT-400 Turbo Air Tractor with a 680-shp Pratt & Whitney Aircraft of Canada PT6A-15AG engine. Production of the turboprop versions has been fairly small. The AT-301A has a hopper for 1325 litres (350 U.S. gallons) of chemicals as standard but the largest capacity versions are the AT-302A and AT-400 with 1514-litre (400 U.S. gallon) hoppers.

Perhaps not unexpectedly, of the thousands of purpose-designed agricultural aircraft that have been built in the U.S.A., the two major producers have been Cessna and Piper. In 1965 Cessna produced its Agwagon single-seat agricultural aircraft, which became available with either a 230-hp or 300-hp engine. In 1971 the company launched three new agricultural aircraft based on the Agwagon. The first was the Ag Pickup, with a 230-hp Continental O-470-R piston engine and a 757-litre (200 U.S. gallon) hopper. Production of this low-powered model ended in 1976 after the construction of 53. The second was the new Ag Wagon with a 300-hp Continental IO-520-D engine, but this, too, went out of production in 1981. Of the three new aircraft, only the Ag Truck remains in

Above and right: Cessna
Ag Truck.

production, powered by the same engine as fitted to the Ag Wagon but with a larger hopper of 1 060 litres (280 U.S. gallons) capacity. Production of the Ag Wagon/ Agwagon and Ag Truck has totalled about 3,500 aircraft. The most powerful agricultural aircraft from Cessna is currently the Ag Husky, a new model introduced in 1979. Based on the Ag Truck, it is powered by a 310-hp Continental TSIO-520-T turbocharged engine. Production of this model has exceeded 340 aircraft.

In 1982 the Piper Aircraft Corporation ended production of its PA-25-235 Pawnee D and had by then also sold the rights to its PA-36 Brave to WTA Incorporated. These moves effectively ended a quarter of a century tradition for Piper, as no new agricultural aircraft bear the Piper name. However the break is not total, as Piper manufactures the Brave for WTA to market as the WTA New Brave.

The Piper PA-25 Pawnee dates back to 1957, when the prototype first flew. Two years later it became available to customers as the PA-25-150, a safe and economical agricultural aircraft powered by a 150 hp-

Avco Lycoming O-320 engine. Like the previously described aircraft from Cessna, the Pawnee type was designed with strut-braced low-mounted wings. The low power of the engine meant that the maximum weight of chemicals that could be carried was 363 kg (800 lb). In 1962 a version with a 235-hp O-540-B2B5 engine and a 50 per cent greater payload was introduced, followed in turn by the Pawnee B in 1965, with a larger hopper (same payload) and improved dispersal gear, and the Pawnee C in 1967. The latter had various airframe refinements and was also offered with a 260-hp O-540-E engine. The year 1973 saw the introduction of what was to become the final Pawnee version. The Pawnee D was offered with the Pawnee C's engine choices and fuel tanks in the wings instead of in the fuselage. Including those being produced in Argentina, production of the Pawnee since 1959 has totalled many thousands.

Details of a more powerful version of the Pawnee were first announced in 1972 and this aircraft went into production initially as the PA-36 Pawnee Brave. Apart from airframe refinements, among them cantilever

Cessna Ag Wagon.

wings (no bracing struts) and a more angular tail unit, the hopper capacity was increased. The initial Pawnee Brave 285 version was installed with a 285-hp Teledyne Continental Tiara 6-285-C piston engine. The Pawnee Brave 300 followed in 1977 with a 300-hp Avco Lycoming IO-540-K1G5 engine, and in the following year Piper introduced the Brave 375. This was produced with the most powerful engine, a 375-hp Avco Lycoming IO-720-D1CD, and had, as standard, the 862-kg (1,900-lb) capacity hopper that was an option for previous Pawnee Braves. At the same time the Pawnee Brave 285 was dropped and the Pawnee Brave 300 became the Brave 300.

In the early 1980s WTA Incorporated purchased the rights of the Brave agricultural aircraft and today this company offers the PA-36 New Brave 375 and the New Brave 400. The latter is a new model with a 400-hp Avco Lycoming IO-720-D1C engine but is otherwise similar to the Brave 375. Both are manufactured by Piper under contract.

Eagle Aircraft of Idaho has developed and is marketing a single-seat agricultural biplane as the Eagle 300. It is offered to customers with a 300-hp Avco Lycoming IO-540-M1B5D piston engine and the first were delivered in 1980. The wing span is unusually large, at 16.76 metres (55 feet), allowing for a 15.5-metre (51-foot) spray-

Ag Husky with spray-boom clearly shown.

Above: Cessna Ag Husky, the most powerful Cessna agricultural aircraft.

Left: Many thousands of Piper agricultural aircraft in the Pawnee/Brave series were built, this aircraft being among the last under the Piper name.

Above: Eagle Aircraft
Eagle 300.

Right: Schweizer Ag-Cat
600 B-Plus.

boom that forms the trailing-edges of the lower wings.

Back in May 1957 Grumman flew the prototype of a single-seat agricultural biplane which it named the G-164 Ag-Cat. Actual manufacture of the Ag-Cat in several versions, with engines ranging from 220-hp to the 600-hp Pratt & Whitney R-1340 radial on the Super Ag-Cat C/600 and a PT6A turboprop on the Turbo Ag-Cat D, was undertaken by the Schweizer Aircraft Corporation, which built nearly 2,500. The last of these were built by Schweizer for the Gulfstream American Corporation, the organization which took over from the former Grumman American

Aviation Corporation. However, within a short time of the formation of Gulfstream American, production of the Ag-Cat was ended by Schweizer. In 1981 Schweizer acquired the rights to the Ag-Cat and by the autumn of the same year was again delivering production examples. The current versions are the Ag-Cat 600 B-Plus, with an R-1340 radial engine and a hopper with a capacity of 1 514 litres (400 U.S. gallons), and the Ag-Cat 450 B-Plus with a 450-hp Pratt & Whitney R-985 radial engine. The former is the main version. They have now been joined by the Turbo Ag-Cat, available as the G-164B Turbine and the greater-capacity G-164D Turbine.

The Schweizer Turbo Ag-Cat.

149

Mid-Continent Aircraft Corporation of Missouri is offering a conversion of the Grumman Super Ag-Cat C, known as the Mid-Continent King Cat. This retains the 1 893-litre (500-U.S. gallon) hopper of the Super Ag-Cat C/600, which has a maximum chemical capacity of 1 814 kg (4,000 lb), but introduces changes including a 1,200-hp Wright R-1820-202A radial engine. The company also offers a kit to operators wishing to make their own conversion. Mid-Continent is also a distributor of Schweizer agricultural aircraft and engages in agricultural operations.

During the 1960s the Weatherly Aviation Company produced agricultural aircraft by conversion of the Fairchild M-62, and then went on to develop a larger agricultural aircraft, known as the Weatherly Model 201. Production of the Model 201 ended in 1979 after more than 100 had been built

and delivered. To take over from the Model 201C, Weatherly developed the new Model 620. Two versions are offered by the company. The first is the basic Model 620 with a 450-hp Pratt & Whitney R-985 radial engine and a 1 268-litre (335-U.S. gallon) hopper. The second is the Model 620TP with a 500-hp Pratt & Whitney Aircraft of Canada PT6A-11AG turboprop engine and a slightly larger capacity hopper.

Apart from the purpose-designed agricultural aircraft already detailed, light cabin aeroplanes and helicopters have been adapted in the U.S.A. for agricultural roles. Typical of the light cabin aircraft is the Bellanca Model 8GCBC Scout, which can be fitted with a 340-litre (90-U.S. gallon) underfuselage chemical tank and spraybooms. Helicopters are detailed at the beginning of the next chapter.

Weatherly Model 620.

Left: The Mid-Continent Aircraft Corporation's conversion of the Grumman Super Ag-Cat C is known as the King Cat.

Below: Weatherly Model 620TP.

A worldwide industry

The majority of agricultural aircraft produced have come from the U.S.S.R., U.S.A. and Poland. But, because of the worldwide operation of agricultural aircraft to improve the production of crops, aircraft of diverse types have appeared from manufacturers in several other countries, some of which have already been mentioned.

High on any list of unusual looking aircraft must be the Transavia PL-12 Airtruk (and derivatives) from Australia. Yet these are highly practical and successful agricultural aircraft. The prototype Airtruk flew for the first time in 1965. Intended originally for seeding and spreading dry fertilizer only, a liquid spraying conversion was subsequently produced. Well over 100 Airtruks are in use in eight countries. In design the Airtruk is a strut-braced sesquiplane, with twin rear booms and twin tail units that are not interconnected. The design of the tail unit allows a vehicle to drive up to the rear of the bulky fuselage pod to deliver chemicals or other loads directly into the hopper. Power for the standard PL-12 is provided by a 300-hp Continental IO-520-D piston engine. Two passengers can be carried in the fuselage for ferrying. A total of 819 litres (180 Imperial gallons) of liquid chemicals can be carried and a swath of 27.5 metres (90 feet) is possible. An even greater swath is made by the Airtruk when applying dry chemicals or seed.

The Transavia Skyfarmer T-300 appeared in 1978 as a development of the Airtruk with a similarly rated IO-540 engine. More recently the Skyfarmer T-300A has been produced incorporating refinements to the cockpit and airframe, aimed partly at improving the pilot's environment and making the aircraft even easier to operate. Also from Australia comes

Facing page: Transavia Skyfarmer.

Above: Loading a Transavia PL-12 Airtruk.

Right: The uniquely-configured Transavia Airtruk, which provides the pilot with an excellent forward and downward view from a position close to the aircraft's nose.

Aerospace FU-24-954 using a Micronair system.

the Wallaroo 605, a Garrett AiResearch TPE 331 turboprop-powered conversion of the de Havilland Canada DHC-2 for agricultural work.

In New Zealand agricultural versions of the piston-engined FU-24 lightplane and the similar turboprop-powered Cresco agricultural aircraft were built until 1982 by New Zealand Aerospace Industries. The FU-24 had first flown in prototype form in 1954 as a top-dressing aeroplane for agricultural work in New Zealand. The prototype and early production aircraft were the products of Fletcher Aviation in the U.S.A.,

but in the 1960s Air Parts (N.Z.) Limited took over the rights to the FU-24 and produced it until the firm became part of Aerospace in 1973. The Cresco 600 is powered by a 600-shp Avco Lycoming LTP 101-600A-1A turboprop engine and has a hopper to the rear of the cockpit with a 1 929-kg (4,254-lb) payload capacity.

In China the Harbin Y-11 (detailed previously) has been employed for top-dressing and pest control with a hopper of 900-kg (1,984-lb) payload capacity. For a decade from about the mid-1960s, Let Národní Podnik in Czechoslovakia produced the Z-37 and Z-37A Cmelák purpose-designed two-seat (pilot plus mechanic or loader for ferrying) agricultural aircraft. The Z-37A, the standard version from 1971 until the end of production, is powered by a 315-hp M 462 RF radial engine and has a hopper with a 600-kg (1,323-lb) payload capacity. About 600 were built for delivery to operators in 10 countries. In 1981 Let flew the prototype of a turboprop-powered version known as the XZ-37T Turbo-Cmelák, fitted with a 691-shp Walter M 601 B engine.

Hindustan Aeronautics Limited (HAL) in India designed an agricultural aircraft called the HA-31 Basant, which made its maiden flight in 1969. This did not come up

One of the production HAL HA-31 Mk II Basants (Springs).

Romanian ICA IAR-827A.

to expectations and so in 1972 the Basant Mk II was evolved. This was a new aircraft, with the Mk I's 250-hp Rolls-Royce Continental engine superseded by a 400-hp Avco Lycoming IO-720-Cl B piston engine. The hopper capacity for the 20 pre-production and 39 full production Mk IIs is 605 to 907 kg (1,333 to 2,000 lb). Although the Basant Mk II is no longer produced, a turboprop-powered version has been considered for development.

In the early 1980s production began in Romania of the ICA IAR-827A, a cantilever low-wing agricultural aircraft with a maximum hopper capacity of 1 000 kg (2,205 lb). It is unusual because it has side-by-side seats in the cockpit for a pilot and mechanic/loader. Power is provided by a 600-hp PZL-3S radial engine. A turboprop-powered version has been flown by fitting a 680-shp Pratt & Whitney Aircraft of Canada PT6A-15AG engine in an IAR-827A prototype. This appeared in 1981 under the new designation IAR-827TP.

In Switzerland Pilatus offers agricultural versions of the PC-6 Turbo-Porter and approximately 40 had been delivered to operators in five countries at the time of

Right: Turkey's KIBM
Mavi Isik-G.

Above: Pilatus PC-6/B1-
H2 Turbo-Porter fitted
with four Micronair
ultra-low-volume
spraying units.

Right: NDN 6
Fieldmaster spreading
fertilizer.

writing. Its chemical payload is 950 kg (2,093 lb). In Turkey the KIBM Mavi Isik-B and Mavi Isik-G have been developed as single-seat, strut-braced, low-wing agricultural aircraft. The former has a 210-hp Continental IO-360-D piston engine and the refined Mavi Isik-G has either a 260-hp Avco Lycoming O-540-G1A5 or a 235-hp O-540-B2B5 piston engine.

In the United Kingdom both companies involved with agricultural aviation are based on the Isle of Wight. Pilatus Britten-Norman offers crop-spraying equipment as an option for its Islander and NDN Aircraft Limited has developed an agricultural aircraft known as the NDN 6 Fieldmaster. (The location of both aircraft companies is not surprising as N.D. Norman, co-founder of Britten-Norman, formed NDN Aircraft.) The Fieldmaster represents an advanced design for a single-seat agricultural aircraft, because the hopper that carries the chemicals also forms the centre section of the fuselage itself. The forward fuselage and 750-shp Pratt & Whitney Aircraft of Canada PT6A-34AG turboprop engine, the rear fuselage and tail unit, and the strut-braced wings, are all attached to the hopper/centre fuselage. First flown in December 1981, the Fieldmaster is now in production. It is reported to have a swath width of 23 metres (75 feet).

In Yugoslavia UTVA has been producing light aircraft for many years. In 1965 the company flew the prototype of its UTVA-65 Privrednik, a single-seat strut-braced agricultural aircraft. The initial production version was the Privrednik-GO, with a 295-hp Avco Lycoming GO-480-G1A6 engine and a hopper with a 600-kg (1,323-lb) chemical payload. This was later joined by the Privrednik-IO, with an IO-540-K1A5 engine and refinements to help it break into new markets. The final version was the Super Privrednik-350, offered with a 350-hp IGO-540-A1C piston engine and a chemical payload of 660 kg (1,455 lb). Production ended some years ago.

Above: NDN 6 Fieldmaster spraying water.

Top: The advanced NDN 6 Fieldmaster, with its chemical hopper forming a section of the fuselage.

7 Travelling the Executive Way

The purchase of aircraft by companies to transport executives and other personnel between factories or places of business really 'took off' in the late 1920s and early 1930s, especially in the United States. Typical of the aircraft then flown was the Boeing Model 40X, owned and operated by the Associated Oil Company, with its tandem open cockpits and a small passenger cabin for two passengers in the forward fuselage between the biplane wings. Nowadays it is not unusual for companies to have very expensive jets.

Helicopters are also widely flown as company aircraft but they also perform important roles in commercial and agricultural aviation. The first commercial helicopter to receive a Type-Approval Certificate was the Bell Model 47, in 1946, and this model remained in production until the 1970s. Produced in many versions both in the U.S.A. and abroad, it has been widely operated as an agricultural aircraft. Many other small helicopters have also been employed in agricultural roles. These include Aérospatiale Alouettes, the Lama and AS

Bell Model 47 operating in an agricultural spraying role.

Left: Aérospatiale SA 315B Lama.

Below: PZL Swidnik Mi-2 Bazant.

Above: Soviet Kamov Ka-26 operated by Asahi Helicopter KK.

Right: Piston-engined Hiller UH-12E carrying a Simplex Model 3300 system comprising two glassfibre chemical tanks and folding spraybooms.

160

350 Ecureuil from France (the latter with a 735-litre; 161-Imperial gallon chemical tank); the Polish-produced PZL Swidnik Mi-2 Bazant, with a hopper on each side of its fuselage for a maximum chemical payload of 750 kg (1,650 lb); the Soviet Kamov Ka-26, with interchangeable loads carried under the contra-rotating rotors that can include a hopper with a payload of 900 kg (1,985 lb); the U.S. Hiller Aviation FH-1100A Pegasus and UH-12 (the latter with either a single or twin tanks for up to 530 litres; 140 U.S. gallons of chemicals); and the Hughes Model 300C. Also in the U.S.A., the Texas Helicopter Corporation has produced high-performance agricultural and utility helicopters based on the Bell Model 47 and military derivatives. Two single-seat helicopters are known as the M74 Wasp and M74A Wasp and the first tandem two-seater is the M79S Wasp II. Each of these is powered by a piston engine of Avco Lycoming TVO-435 type. A

Hiller's larger five-seat FH-1100 is turboshaft-powered and can be used for many purposes, including agricultural work.

Hughes Model 300C with a spraying system.

Texas Helicopter M79S Wasp II.

Facing page: The light two/three-seat Hughes Model 300C is a helicopter for pleasure as well as business and has many commercial uses.

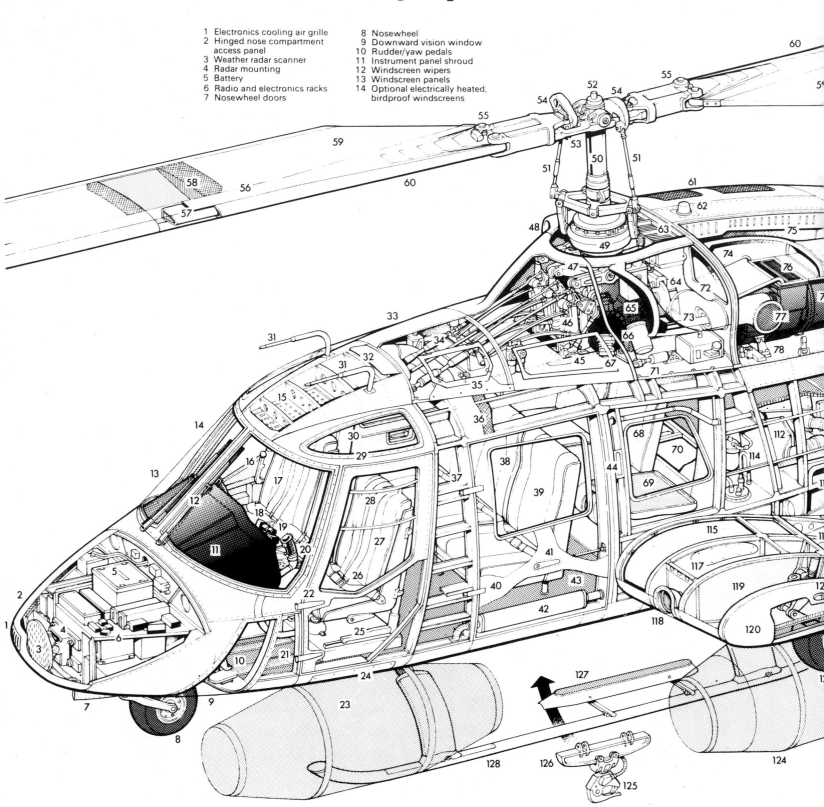

Plate VII
Bell 222

cutaway drawing key

1 Electronics cooling air grille
2 Hinged nose compartment
   access panel
3 Weather radar scanner
4 Radar mounting
5 Battery
6 Radio and electronics racks
7 Nosewheel doors

8 Nosewheel
9 Downward vision window
10 Rudder/yaw pedals
11 Instrument panel shroud
12 Windscreen wipers
13 Windscreen panels
14 Optional electrically heated,
    birdproof windscreens

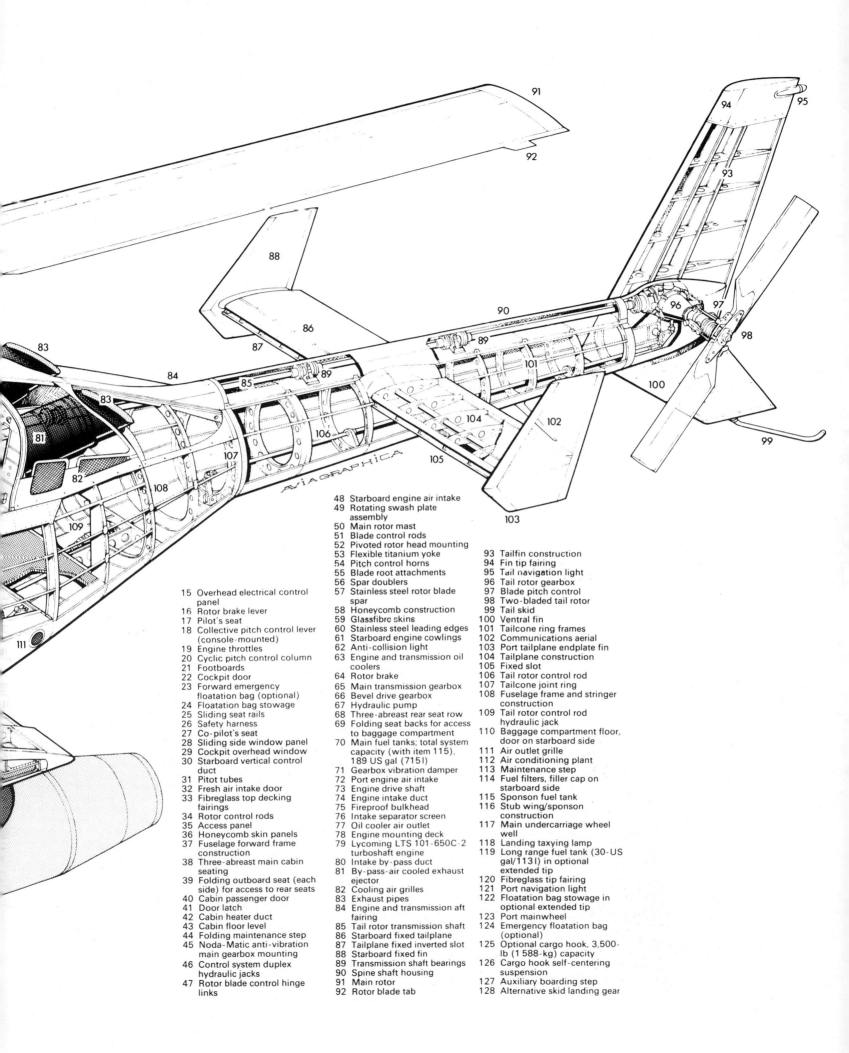

48 Starboard engine air intake
49 Rotating swash plate assembly
50 Main rotor mast
51 Blade control rods
52 Pivoted rotor head mounting
53 Flexible titanium yoke
54 Pitch control horns
55 Blade root attachments
56 Spar doublers
57 Stainless steel rotor blade spar
58 Honeycomb construction
59 Glassfibre skins
60 Stainless steel leading edges
61 Starboard engine cowlings
62 Anti-collision light
63 Engine and transmission oil coolers
64 Rotor brake
65 Main transmission gearbox
66 Bevel drive gearbox
67 Hydraulic pump
68 Three-abreast rear seat row
69 Folding seat backs for access to baggage compartment
70 Main fuel tanks; total system capacity (with item 115), 189 US gal (715l)
71 Gearbox vibration damper
72 Port engine air intake
73 Engine drive shaft
74 Engine intake duct
75 Fireproof bulkhead
76 Intake separator screen
77 Oil cooler air outlet
78 Engine mounting deck
79 Lycoming LTS 101-650C-2 turboshaft engine
80 Intake by-pass duct
81 By-pass-air cooled exhaust ejector
82 Cooling air grilles
83 Exhaust pipes
84 Engine and transmission aft fairing
85 Tail rotor transmission shaft
86 Starboard fixed tailplane
87 Tailplane fixed inverted slot
88 Starboard fixed fin
89 Transmission shaft bearings
90 Spine shaft housing
91 Main rotor
92 Rotor blade tab

15 Overhead electrical control panel
16 Rotor brake lever
17 Pilot's seat
18 Collective pitch control lever (console-mounted)
19 Engine throttles
20 Cyclic pitch control column
21 Footboards
22 Cockpit door
23 Forward emergency floatation bag (optional)
24 Floatation bag stowage
25 Sliding seat rails
26 Safety harness
27 Co-pilot's seat
28 Sliding side window panel
29 Cockpit overhead window
30 Starboard vertical control duct
31 Pitot tubes
32 Fresh air intake door
33 Fibreglass top decking fairings
34 Rotor control rods
35 Access panel
36 Honeycomb skin panels
37 Fuselage forward frame construction
38 Three-abreast main cabin seating
39 Folding outboard seat (each side) for access to rear seats
40 Cabin passenger door
41 Door latch
42 Cabin heater duct
43 Cabin floor level
44 Folding maintenance step
45 Noda-Matic anti-vibration main gearbox mounting
46 Control system duplex hydraulic jacks
47 Rotor blade control hinge links

93 Tailfin construction
94 Fin tip fairing
95 Tail navigation light
96 Tail rotor gearbox
97 Blade pitch control
98 Two-bladed tail rotor
99 Tail skid
100 Ventral fin
101 Tailcone ring frames
102 Communications aerial
103 Port tailplane endplate fin
104 Tailplane construction
105 Fixed slot
106 Tail rotor control rod
107 Tailcone joint ring
108 Fuselage frame and stringer construction
109 Tail rotor control rod hydraulic jack
110 Baggage compartment floor, door on starboard side
111 Air outlet grille
112 Air conditioning plant
113 Maintenance step
114 Fuel filters, filler cap on starboard side
115 Sponson fuel tank
116 Stub wing/sponson construction
117 Main undercarriage wheel well
118 Landing taxying lamp
119 Long range fuel tank (30-US gal/113l) in optional extended tip
120 Fibreglass tip fairing
121 Port navigation light
122 Floatation bag stowage in optional extended tip
123 Port mainwheel
124 Emergency floatation bag (optional)
125 Optional cargo hook, 3,500-lb (1 588-kg) capacity
126 Cargo hook self-centering suspension
127 Auxiliary boarding step
128 Alternative skid landing gear

Right: Continental
Copters Incorporated
also produced specialist
agricultural helicopters
based on the Bell Model
47. One such aircraft
type was the El Tomcat
Mk V-A.

Below: Aérospatiale AS
350D Astar.

Aérospatiale AS 355
Twinstar.

two-seater with an Allison 250-C20B turboshaft engine is known as the M79T Jet Wasp II.

Helicopters used as commercial and executive/business transports are numerous and several of these are illustrated. Among the most popular are the following: the six-seat Aérospatiale AS 350 Ecureuil from France and its Astar North American-market companion; the larger 10- to 14-seat Aérospatiale AS 355 Ecureuil 2 and North American-market Twinstar; West Germany's five-seat MBB BO 105; and the Italian Agusta A109A four- to six-passenger helicopter with a retractable undercarriage. U.S. types include the five-seat Bell Model 206B JetRanger series and the larger four- to seven-seat Model 206L LongRanger series, the Bell Model 222 six- to 10-seat helicopter with a retractable undercarriage, the three-seat Enstrom Models F-28 and 280, the five-seat Hughes Model 500 series, and the 12-passenger Sikorsky S-76 with a retractable undercarriage. More than 4,500 JetRangers and LongRangers have been delivered to civil operators alone, indicating the importance of these helicopters and their acceptance into worldwide service.

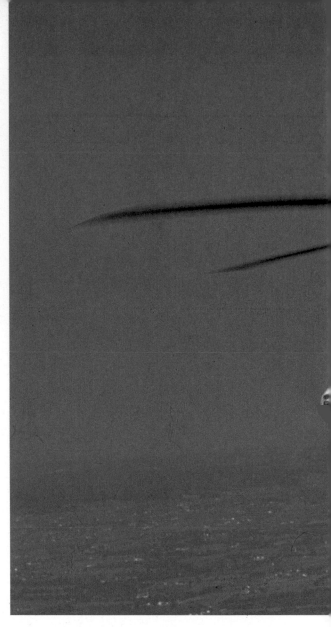

Above: MBB BO 105D supplied to the British Trinity House service and capable of night operations to offshore rigs.

Right: The MBB BO 105CBS is a slightly longer version of the standard BO105CB to accommodate five or six persons. This example has a nose radar, making it particularly suitable for offshore work.

Above: Agusta A 109A with a retractable undercarriage.

Left: Italian-built Agusta-Bell Model 206L-1 LongRanger II.

Right: Enstrom Model F-28.

Below: Hughes Model 500D.

The latest Model 206B JetRanger III has a maximum cruising speed of 216 km/h (134 mph) and a range while carrying the maximum payload of 608 km (378 miles).

Large helicopters perform many commercial tasks in passenger and non-passenger forms. Helicopters are often used as short-range airliners. Their ability to take off vertically makes them ideal for passenger services into and from city and commercial centres, or for carrying passengers, goods or perhaps stretchers to and from outlying but populated areas. But foremost in the minds of the public must be those serving offshore-oil platforms. Typical of helicopters used for serving offshore platforms are the Aéro-spatiale SA 330 Puma and AS 332 Super Puma. These Anglo-French helicopters are among the aircraft flown by Bristow Helicopters, a U.K. operator with wide-ranging activities. Bristow's 35 19-passenger AS 332L Super Pumas are known as Tigers. Each is powered by two 1,535-shp Turboméca Makila IA turboshaft engines, which bestow a maximum cruising speed of 280 km/h (173 mph).

One of Boeing Vertol's helicopters is the Model 234 Commercial Chinook, a 44-passenger, mixed traffic or cargo helicopter

Sikorsky S-76 Mark II, a twin-turboshaft commercial and corporate all-weather helicopter.

powered by two 4,075-shp Avco Lycoming AL 5512 turboshaft engines that drive two large rotors. Its maximum cruising speed is 269 km/h (167 mph). It can carry a massive 12 700 kg (28,000-lb) load that hangs below the helicopter from an external cargo hook in Utility form. Internally carried loads are lighter. Boeing Vertol also originated the 107 Model II, which is produced in Japan as the Kawasaki KV107II and KV107IIA. Typical of the series, which has been produced for military and commercial use, is the KV107II-2 25-passenger airliner. It is powered by two 1,250-shp General Electric CT58-110-1 or Ishikawajima-

The first customer for the Boeing Vertol Model 234 Commercial Chinook was British Airways Helicopters, which ordered several of the 234 LR long-range models.

Right: Bell Model 206B JetRanger III.

Above: Aérospatiale SA 330J Puma in Bristow Helicopters livery flies close to an offshore rig.

Left: Tyrolean Airways became the first operator of the AS 332C Super Puma.

Sikorsky S-61Ns operating from Aberdeen.

Harima CT58-IHI-110-1 turboshaft engines, which allow a cruising speed of 241 km/h (150 mph). Like the Commercial Chinook, the KV107II has twin rotors and a rear loading ramp. The operator with the largest number of KV107II-2s is Columbia Helicopters Incorporated.

Another widely operated commercial helicopter is the Sikorsky S-61 in 'L' non-amphibious and 'N' amphibious versions. Both helicopter airliners are powered by two 1,500-shp General Electric CT58-140-1 or CT58-140-2 turboshaft engines, giving

the S-61N an average cruising speed of 222 km/h (138 mph). Its range is 796 km (495 miles) with fuel reserves. Accommodation is provided for up to 30 passengers in the S-61L and 28 in the S-61N. One of the latest helicopter airliners is the 17- to 19-passenger British Westland 30, which can, like the others, perform many other tasks.

No commercially operated helicopter used for freighting, logging, construction work or the many other non-passenger roles suited to helicopters, is more unusual looking than the Sikorsky S-64 Skycrane.

Above: Sikorsky S-64 Skycrane carrying timber.

Left: One of Columbia Helicopters' Kawasaki KV107II-2s, which has been used for logging support.

Overleaf: Westland 30 twin-turboshaft helicopter, operated by British Airways Helicopters.

Above: The Model 214ST is just one of a range of Bell helicopters for commercial use. It is powered by two turboshaft engines, has a normal cruising speed of 256 km/h (159 mph), and can accommodate 18 passengers or cargo.

Right: The Soviet Mil Mi-26 is the world's largest helicopter.

This impressive helicopter was designed as a heavy flying crane, capable of lifting a 9 072-kg (20,000-lb) slung load, cargo or vehicles on a platform, or cargo/stretchers/passengers inside a detachable pod which can be fixed under the fuselage. The civil version was produced as the S-64E. Power is provided by two 4,500-shp Pratt & Whitney JFTD12-4A turboshaft engines. An unusual feature of the crew accommodation is that the third member has an aft-facing seat with flying controls, so that he can position the helicopter and view loading/unloading of cargo simultaneously.

The Soviet Union has its own flying-crane helicopter known as the Mil Mi-10K, but it is somewhat different in appearance. Other Soviet helicopters in service with Aeroflot and other airlines include the world's largest helicopter. This is the huge Mil Mi-26, known to NATO by the name *Halo* and operated in civil and military forms. Capable of carrying a 20 000-kg (44,090-lb) load internally or externally, its two 11,400-shp Lotarev D-136 turboshaft engines power an eight-blade main rotor

Mil Mi-8T general utility helicopter in Aeroflot colours.

The Kamov Ka-26, previously illustrated in agricultural form, is seen here with a six-passenger pod fitted.

Right: Prototype Lear Fan Model 2100 with a rear-mounted pusher propeller.

Below: Cessna Conquest II pressurized transport.

Above: Smaller than the Longhorn 55 are the turbojet-powered Gates Learjet 25D (upper) and turbofan-powered Learjet 35A.

Left: Gates Learjet Longhorn 55, an executive aircraft capable of carrying six to 10 passengers and with advanced-design wings and winglets.

179

with a diameter of 32 metres (105 feet). Other important Soviet helicopters include the large Mil Mi-6 with two 5,500-shp Soloviev D-25V turboshaft engines and accommodation for up to 90 passengers, 41 stretchers or the equivalent cargo, and the smaller Mil Mi-8 with two 1,700-shp Isotov TV2-117A turboshaft engines. In civil form, the latter is offered in 28- to 32-passenger Mi-8, Mi-8T utility and 11-passenger Mi-8 Salon de luxe versions. A new uprated version of the Mi-8 is the Mi-17, first seen in public at the 1981 Paris Air Show.

Business aeroplanes come in all shapes and sizes, with piston, turboprop, turbo-shaft and turbofan engines. They can be of traditional type, as typified by the very successful twin-turboprop four- to 10-passenger Cessna Conquest II, or something very different. A good example of an unusually configured business aircraft is the U.S. Lear Fan Model 2100. Accommodating six or eight passengers, its two turbo-shaft engines drive a pusher propeller mounted at the rear of the fuselage behind the Y-shaped tail unit. Among the twin turbofan executive aircraft can be counted the Gates Learjet Longhorn 55, just one of a series of Learjets built over the years, which features a wide-bodied fuselage for the six to 10 passengers and advanced-design wings

The eight/12-passenger triple-engined Dassault-Breguet Mystère-Falcon 50 (foreground) is joined by the eight/14-passenger Mystère-Falcon 20 (centre) and the four/seven-passenger Mystère-Falcon 10.

Above: Nineteen passengers are carried in the pressurized Gulfstream Aerospace Gulfstream III executive transport.

Left: BAe HS 125 Series 600 modified into the Series 700 prototype by the substitution of Rolls-Royce Bristol Viper 601 turbojets for Garrett TFE731 turbofans.

181

Above: The Italian company Partenavia produces the Victor, a twin piston-engined or twin-turboprop six- or seven-seat light aircraft. This is a P.68C-TC Victor, with turbocharged Avco Lycoming TO-360 engines.

Left: Originating in the 1950s, versions of the Rockwell Sabreliner business jet include the Sabreliner 75A with accommodation for six/10 passengers.

Facing page: Gulfstream Aerospace Corporation's Commander Division produces four twin-turboprop business aircraft. The Jetprop 900 was made available in 1982 and accommodated seven to 11 passengers.

Right: From Israel comes the twin-turbofan IAI Westwind I, accommodating up to 10 passengers.

Below: The Mitsubishi Diamond I is a seven-passenger pressurized twin-turbofan business aircraft, first flown in 1978.

Right: One version of the U.S.-built Mitsubishi MU-2 is the Solitaire, a six/seven-passenger pressurized twin-turboprop business aircraft.

From the Westwind I IAI has developed the Westwind 2, featuring new wings with winglets and other changes to improve range and economy.

with winglets. The French Dassault-Breguet Mystère-Falcon 50 has three turbofan engines and is one aircraft in the successful Mystère-Falcon range. British Aerospace contributes the popular HS 125, the current eight- to 14-passenger Series 700 having a maximum cruising speed of 808 km/h (502 mph).

Generally speaking, business/executive aircraft are privately owned by companies or individuals and are not operated commercially for hire or reward. They are, therefore, included in the term general aviation. Several of these aircraft can be seen in the accompanying illustrations but no further details will be given here as they are not part of commercial aviation in its true sense. But their importance cannot be overstated, as they provide one of the most time efficient ways of transporting executives/staff from one point of business to another as required. They might not be termed commercial aircraft but they are nevertheless looked upon by the companies that own them as important aids in today's fast-moving multi-national business world.

Plate VIII

Mitsubishi Diamond I

cutaway drawing key

1 Radome
2 Weather radar scanner
3 Radar tracking mechanism
4 Pitot tubes
5 Nosewheel housing
6 Retractable landing/taxiing lamp, port and starboard
7 Nose compartment access doors
8 Radio and electronic equipment bay
9 Gyro platform
10 Nose undercarriage leg strut
11 Forward retracting nosewheel
12 Nosewheel leg door
13 Undercarriage emergency lowering compressed air bottle
14 Cabin pressurisation valves
15 Front pressure bulkhead
16 Cockpit warm air ducting
17 Rudder pedals
18 Windscreen de-misting air duct
19 Instrument panel
20 Instrument panel shroud
21 Windscreen wipers
22 Curved windscreen panels
23 Cockpit roof framing
24 Fire extinguisher
25 Co-pilot's seat
26 Centre control pedestal
27 Control column handwheel
28 Cockpit floor level
29 Pilot's seat
30 Side window panel
31 Safety harness
32 Cockpit bulkhead
33 Forward baggage hold
34 VHF aerial
35 Two-seat settee

36 Galley
37 Bar unit
38 Entry door
39 Door latch
40 Folding boarding steps

41 Cabin floor level
42 Rearward facing passenger seats
43 Emergency exit window
44 Folding table

45 Starboard wing integral fuel tank; total fuel capacity 551 Imp gal (2 505 l)
46 Wing fence
47 Leading edge de-icing air duct
48 Fuel filler cap
49 Fuel system piping
50 Starboard navigation and strobe lights
51 Static dischargers
52 Roll trim aileron
53 Single-slotted Fowler-type flap
54 Flap guide rail
55 Flap control linkage
56 Two-segment primary roll control spoilers, also act as airbrakes/lift dumpers
57 Spoiler hinge links

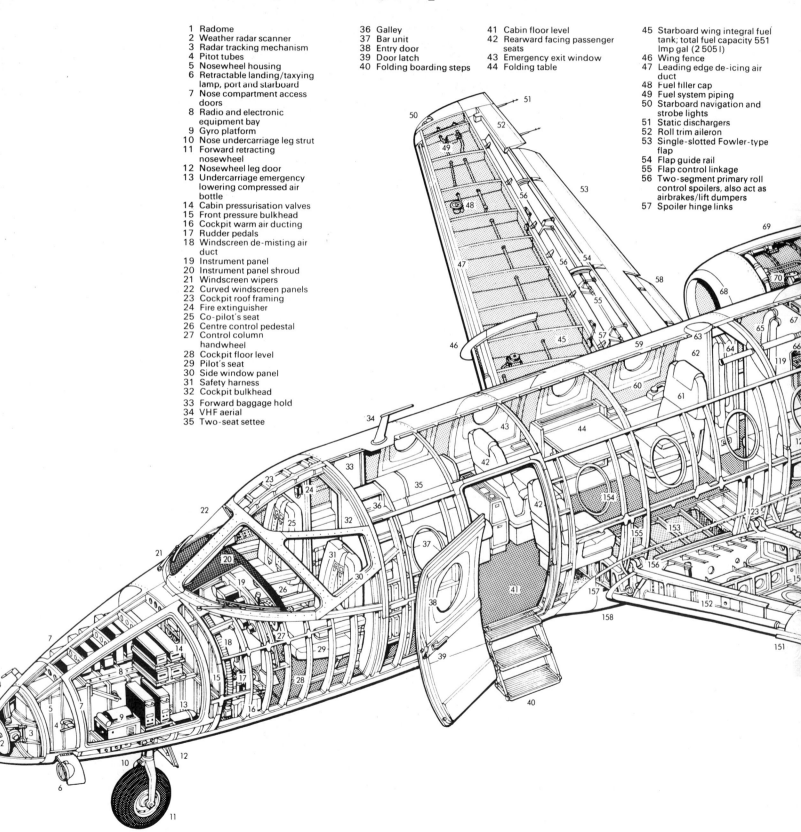

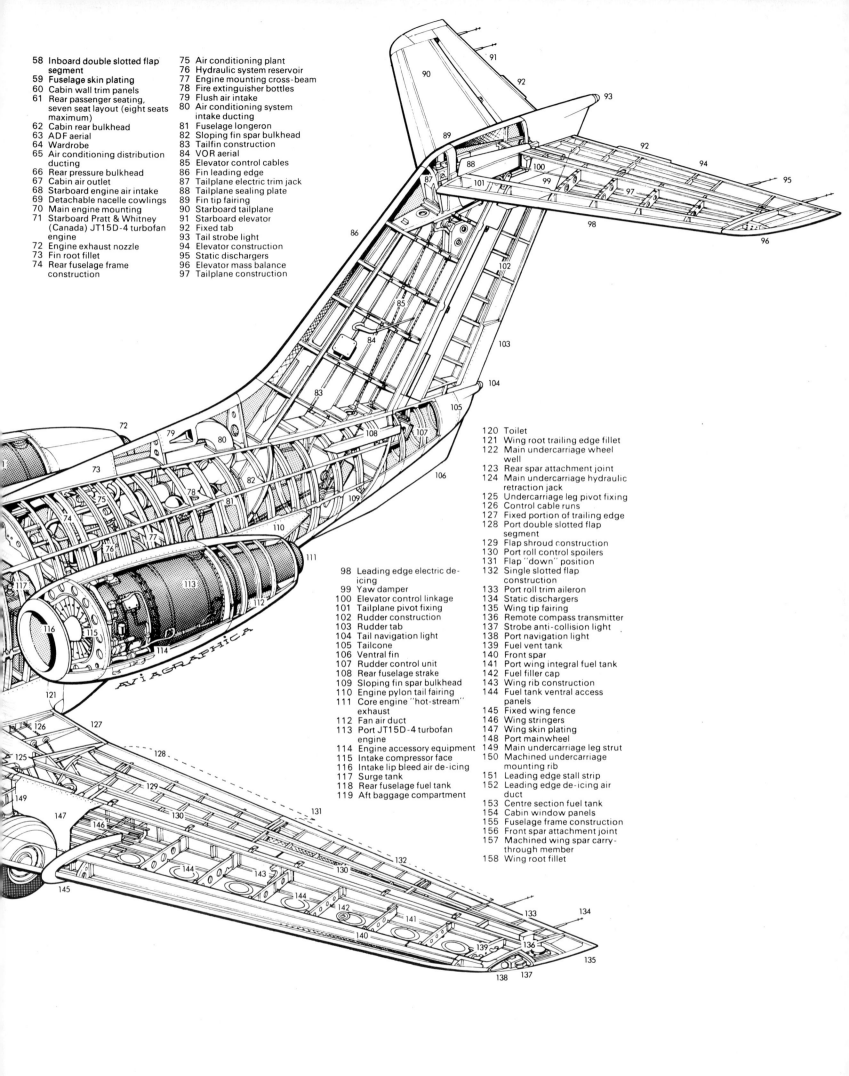

58 Inboard double slotted flap segment
59 Fuselage skin plating
60 Cabin wall trim panels
61 Rear passenger seating, seven seat layout (eight seats maximum)
62 Cabin rear bulkhead
63 ADF aerial
64 Wardrobe
65 Air conditioning distribution ducting
66 Rear pressure bulkhead
67 Cabin air outlet
68 Starboard engine air intake
69 Detachable nacelle cowlings
70 Main engine mounting
71 Starboard Pratt & Whitney (Canada) JT15D-4 turbofan engine
72 Engine exhaust nozzle
73 Fin root fillet
74 Rear fuselage frame construction

75 Air conditioning plant
76 Hydraulic system reservoir
77 Engine mounting cross-beam
78 Fire extinguisher bottles
79 Flush air intake
80 Air conditioning system intake ducting
81 Fuselage longeron
82 Sloping fin spar bulkhead
83 Tailfin construction
84 VOR aerial
85 Elevator control cables
86 Fin leading edge
87 Tailplane electric trim jack
88 Tailplane sealing plate
89 Fin tip fairing
90 Starboard tailplane
91 Starboard elevator
92 Fixed tab
93 Tail strobe light
94 Elevator construction
95 Static dischargers
96 Elevator mass balance
97 Tailplane construction

98 Leading edge electric de-icing
99 Yaw damper
100 Elevator control linkage
101 Tailplane pivot fixing
102 Rudder construction
103 Rudder tab
104 Tail navigation light
105 Tailcone
106 Ventral fin
107 Rudder control unit
108 Rear fuselage strake
109 Sloping fin spar bulkhead
110 Engine pylon tail fairing
111 Core engine "hot-stream" exhaust
112 Fan air duct
113 Port JT15D-4 turbofan engine
114 Engine accessory equipment
115 Intake compressor face
116 Intake lip bleed air de-icing
117 Surge tank
118 Rear fuselage fuel tank
119 Aft baggage compartment

120 Toilet
121 Wing root trailing edge fillet
122 Main undercarriage wheel well
123 Rear spar attachment joint
124 Main undercarriage hydraulic retraction jack
125 Undercarriage leg pivot fixing
126 Control cable runs
127 Fixed portion of trailing edge
128 Port double slotted flap segment
129 Flap shroud construction
130 Port roll control spoilers
131 Flap "down" position
132 Single slotted flap construction
133 Port roll trim aileron
134 Static dischargers
135 Wing tip fairing
136 Remote compass transmitter
137 Strobe anti-collision light
138 Port navigation light
139 Fuel vent tank
140 Front spar
141 Port wing integral fuel tank
142 Fuel filler cap
143 Wing rib construction
144 Fuel tank ventral access panels
145 Fixed wing fence
146 Wing stringers
147 Wing skin plating
148 Port mainwheel
149 Main undercarriage leg strut
150 Machined undercarriage mounting rib
151 Leading edge stall strip
152 Leading edge de-icing air duct
153 Centre section fuel tank
154 Cabin window panels
155 Fuselage frame construction
156 Front spar attachment joint
157 Machined wing spar carry-through member
158 Wing root fillet

Above: The Beechcraft King Air F90 is a twin-turboprop business aircraft, accommodating up to eight passengers. Deliveries to customers began in 1979.

Right: Cessna's high-speed business jet is the Citation III, a six/10-passenger twin-turbofan transport with a maximum cruising speed of 874 km/h (543 mph).

Left: Fairchild Swearingen Merlin IVA, a 12/15-passenger business version of the Metro II.

Above: The Piper Saratoga SP is basically a piston-engined Saratoga with a retractable undercarriage. Available with Custom and Executive option avionics and equipment packages, it accommodates six or seven.

Left: Lockheed produced a business jet as the JetStar/JetStar II, which first flew in 1957 and was finally taken out of production in 1979. Seating up to 10 passengers, the JetStar has turbojets and the JetStar II turbofans.

187

Abbreviations

AAMSA	(Mexico) Aeronautica Agricola Mexicana SA	LADE	(Argentina) Lineas Aéreas del Estado
AIDC	(Taiwan) Aero Industry Development Center	LOT	(Poland) Polskie Linie Lotnicze-LOT
ATP	Advanced Turboprop (British Aerospace)	LTU	(West Germany) Luftransport-Unternehmen
BAC	British Aircraft Corporation	MBB	(West Germany) Messerschmitt-Bölkow-Blohm
BAe	British Aerospace		
BEA	British European Airways	NASA	National Aeronautics and Space Administration
BOAC	British Overseas Airways Corporation		
BUA	British United Airways	NATO	North Atlantic Treaty Organization
CAAC	Civil Aviation Administration of China	QC	Quick Change
CASA	(Spain) Construcciones Aeronáuticas SA		
CSA	(Czechoslovakia) Československé Aerolinie	R.A.F.	Royal Air Force
		SAS	(Denmark, Norway, Sweden) Scandinavian Airlines System
ehp	equivalent horsepower	shp	shaft horsepower
EMBRAER	(Brazil) Empresa Brasileira de Aeronáutica SA	SNECMA	(France) Société Nationale d'Etude et de Construction de Moteurs d'Aviation
eshp	equivalent shaft horsepower	SP	Special Performance
		SR	Short Range
		st	static thrust
FFCC	Forward Facing Crew Cockpit	STOL	Short Take-Off and Landing
GAF	(Australia) Government Aircraft Factories	TAT	(France) Touraine Air Transport
		TEA	(Belgium) Trans European Airways
HAL	(India) Hindustan Aeronautics Limited	TMA	(Lebanon) Trans-Mediterranean Airways
hp	horsepower	TWA	(U.S.A.) Trans World Airlines
IAI	Israel Aircraft Industries	U.S.A.A.F.	United States Army Air Force
IATA	International Air Transport Association	USAC	United States Aircraft Corporation
ICAO	International Civil Aviation Organization	U.S.A.F.	United States Air Force
IPEC	(Australia) Interstate Parcel Express Company-IPEC Aviation	UTA	(France) Union de Transports Aériens
KLM	(The Netherlands) Koninklijke Luchtvaart Maatschappij NV	VFW-Fokker	(West Germany) Vereinigte Flugtechnische Werke-Fokker

Index

189

192